A STABLE EXTERNAL CURRENCY FOR EUROPE

Also by Jacques Riboud

EXPANSION ECONOMIQUE
DEVELOPPEMENT URBAIN: RECHERCHE D'UN PRINCIPE
LIBERALISME ET FINANCEMENT
LA VRAIE NATURE DE LA MONNAIE
UNE MONNAIE POUR L'EUROPE: L'EUROSTABLE
LA MECANIQUE DES MONNAIES, D'AUJOURD'HUI ET DE DEMAIN
LA MONNAIE DANS SES ARTIFICES
CONTROVERSE SUR LA BANQUE ET LA MONNAIE
MONNAIE EUROPEENNE: DE L'UTOPIQUE AU REALISABLE
THE MECHANICS OF MONEY
THE CASE FOR A NEW ECU

A Stable External Currency for Europe

Jacques Riboud

Translated by Stephen Harrison

Foreword by Sir Alan Walters

St. Martin's Press   New York

First published in the United States of America in 1991

Printed in Great Britain

ISBN 0–312–05363–0

Library of Congress Cataloging-in-Publication Data
Riboud, Jacques.
A stable external currency for Europe/Jacques Riboud:
translated by Stephen Harrison: foreword by Sir Alan Walters.
p.   cm.
Translated from the French.
Includes index.
ISBN 0–312–05363–0
1. Money—European Economic Community countries.   2. European
currency unit.   3. Monetary policy—European Economic Community
countries.   I. Title.
HG220.E86R53   1991
332.4′566′094—dc20   90–45829
                                                                          CIP

HG
220
. E86
R53
1991

Contents

List of Figures and Tables

Foreword

Money is not the root of all evil. It is a marvellous development of Man's ingenuity, God's gift to suffering humanity. We can all see what happens when money is debauched: the wheels of business slow down, or even stop altogether as barter takes over. Alas, both in the 1980s and today the state of barter is associated with despair and is often accompanied by the breakdown in social order. Examples are abundant in Latin America, in Eastern Europe and in the Soviet Union. Since the breakdown of the Gold Standard in the 1930s, many governments have thoroughly debauched their currencies – Germany in 1945 and Hungary in 1946 – and even the old Western democracies have continuously eroded both the value of, and the people's confidence in, the currency. Indeed, in Britain 98 per cent of the rise in prices since the Middle Ages has occurred in the last half-century. In our Western democracy, inflation in peacetime is not an inherited defect of the system: it is a modern disease.

Such inflation has robbed (or taxed) the public for the benefit of their rulers. But is has also destroyed the unit of account in which we write contracts and conduct business. The trouble is compounded by the fact that the rate of inflation varies considerably from month to month. This uncertainty and risk inhibits trade and business planning. Today we are often forced to calculate in terms of 'constant dollars' or 'constant francs', but such practices would have seemed quite outlandish to anyone in the nineteenth century. In those days currencies could be trusted to maintain a near-enough constant real value: a stable unit of account.

Is there any hope that governments will be induced to pursue monetary policies that will restore stability to the value of money? Some, perhaps. The way the Bundesbank and the National Bank of Switzerland have defended the value of the Deutschemark and the Swiss franc are admired and, in part, emulated. But the same was true in the 1950s of the Federal Reserve Board of the United States, and that was followed by the sad disappointments of the great inflation of the 1960s and 1970s. It would be unwise to rely entirely on the reputation of central bankers or governments. One should seek to set the example of a constant unit of account that is independent of politicians, bureaucrats, governments or central bankers.

This is the noble task to which Jacques Riboud has devoted his

prodigious energies. The reform of monetary systems and the con-
struction of new monetary constitutions are topics that have attracted
many pure theorists, dreamy idealists, Jacobin Utopians and, alas,
many cantankerous cranks. Mr. Riboud will have no truck with such
pipe dreams. His approach emerges from his wide and deep knowledge of the reality of financial markets, their infinite variety and
their important functions. Mr. Riboud, in a literal sense, knows
precisely what he is talking about. He proposes that the private sector
itself should set up a currency that has, by its very constitution, a
constant real value. With consummate political astuteness, however,
Jacques Riboud does not prescribe any reform of national currencies;
he proposes no vainglorious attack on the state bastions of monetary
sovereignty. What he suggests in this book is that the various
private-sector participants in the Euromarkets should together issue
financial assets defined in terms of a constant real value. In that way
people could eliminate the risks of varying and uncertain inflation
rates.

　　Mr. Riboud's proposal is that the constant-value money should be
used for *external* transactions only. There would thus be no threat to
any government's monopoly of the supply of domestic money. So,
the author contends, governments ought to promote the external
market for a currency with constant real value. No government
subsidy is needed, and neither is any central bank required to provide
additional lender-of-last-resort facilities. Without the blessing of one
or two governments, however, the author believes that his constant-
value payment currency is unlikely to take root.

　　But what if the new Riboud currency does come to pass? I suspect
that if it does it will soon be in such great demand that it will become
the normal vehicle for external transactions. And it will also create a
popular pressure for access to the constant-value currency for domestic transactions (indeed, governments may be worried about just a
contingency). Could this then be the beginning of a return to the
stability of the nineteenth century? Those, of course, are idle speculations, but the author of this book has proposed an eminently
practical and politically plausible first step on this grand highway to
monetary reform. To reformers, I say: read Riboud.

ALAN WALTERS

Introduction

Before setting out my proposals, before attempting to prove and convince, I think it would be useful if I shared with my readers some of my thoughts on the great adventure that is the movement towards European unification. It seems to me that they may help to cast a useful light on the specifically monetary discussions that follow.

European union is the great project of our times. For the first time in 2000 years of history the inhabitants of the continent of Europe find themselves caught up in a powerful movement of opinion – in the case of some people, a passion – towards understanding and union. At long last the futility and the murderous absurdity of fratricidal struggles between peoples who share the same cultural heritage and are part of the same civilisation has been admitted. On all sides there is a coming-together, a convergence of opinion, a calling for unification.

Feelings are not enough however: economic and political choices have to be made, and that is when the divergences start to appear.

These divergences deserve to be analysed, and before that classi-fied, because they can be found in all the questions raised, particularly in the monetary ones. If we simplify things (perhaps excessively), we can distinguish two tendencies as regards the approach that should be adopted. First there is the approach recommended by the 'idealists'. Their thesis can be summarised in these terms: 'Let's plunge in head first and let us not shrink from the commitments that we must enter into. Once they have been entered into, appropriate Community regulations and mechanisms will have to be devised. An excessively cautious and carefully thought-out approach will reveal the existence of too many obstacles and will thus lead to nothing.'

In the opposite camp, the pragmatists point out that excessively ambitious and even purposely vague and incompletely defined projects will not succeed in achieving a consensus on the part of the national governments. 'Even if they do succeed, they will not be put into practice. By aiming too high, by jumping the gun, by wanting to go too fast, we risk either mistakes or disappointments. The precious momentum towards a unified Europe that has been built up may perhaps slacken, and the risk is all the greater as we must expect that other promises which have been made for 1992, such as the abolition of customs barriers within the Community, will not be kept. And on

1

top of that, there is the danger that agreements between states which have been entered into too hastily will not be willingly renegotiated by those who benefit from them, in spite of the evidence of experience.'

Over and above these general considerations, there are others that are peculiar to monetary questions: a European Central Bank and a common European currency are the topics of the moment for the French government. But there is no chance of obtaining a consensus on this matter in the short space of time available, even if only for outside consumption, much less a consensus that will open the door to the practical achievement of these goals. The British government is openly hostile and the German government has no interest in promoting such ideas at a time when the Deutschemark is about to accede to the privileged position of European currency *par excellence*. That is why, if a European currency is to be introduced, an approach must be found which can be put into effect without the prior agreement of the national governments.

Whilst it is true that a European Central Bank and a common Community currency would be the crowning achievement in the work of European unification, it is equally true that we should not abstain from all other activity while we wait for something that is still a long way off. It is preferable to adopt a gradual approach whereby individual achievements are put together piecemeal.

The sort of European monetary union that is aimed at calls for an approach which eschews the familiar, well-worn road. The comparisons that have been made with the organisation of the Federal Reserve System in the United States are deceptive. There is no previous 'model' for such an enterprise, no past precedent. It is a question of creating something completely new, and in a field (that of monetary matters) which has not been adequately explored.

There can be no innovation without risks, without the need for experiment and gradual adjustment. There can be no innovation that does not include, for those who accept the risk, the right to be wrong and the right to correct mistakes. An undertaking of this kind is not within the reach of several governments acting in concert, or even of the Commission of the European Communities. Commitments would have to be entered into in respect of a 'system' which, in the light of experience, would confer benefits on some but would involve disadvantages for others, inequalities of advantage which it would be difficult, if not impossible, to go back on. The Community's monetary compensation amounts, the imbalance within the European

Monetary System (EMS) and many other disparities are proof of the lack of flexibility in intergovernment agreements.

The commitments which the governments would be expected to enter into must come after the innovation, not before it. What we must look for is a gradual but rapid way of achieving our aims which, at the beginning, does not require the formal consent of several sovereign states.

It was with these considerations in mind that a proposal which may be summarised in the following terms was conceived: a consortium of Eurobanks would be set up with the 'unofficial' blessing (the 'benevolent neutrality') of a particular government and with no attempt to reach agreement with any other governments on this initiative. The aim of this consortium would be to promote the conversion of the private ECU from a mere unit of account, which is what it is at present, into a genuine transaction currency for international financial relations. To that end the consortium would create a sort of interbank office, which would be the embryo (or the model) for the central institution which the Community would need at a later stage in order to issue and manage its own currency.

The private transaction ECU, once created by the consortium, would be reserved for extraterritorial financial transactions, just like the dollar in its capacity as non-national payment currency between traders in two different states. It would not circulate as a payment currency within any one state. Its territory would be the real or virtual monetary space that lies between the frontiers of states. In this same territory the Euromarket has grown up.

The creation of an extraterritorial currency unit, for use in a territory which lacks one of its own, will generate seigniorage. The prospect of the profits that will flow from that seigniorage ought to be enough to persuade a group of Eurobanks to come together to form the consortium.

Once the consortium has been set up and the interbank office created, we may expect that the commercial experience of 'selling' the private ECU will lead to the following observation: the ECU as it is at present defined is a mediocre currency which is less desirable than several of the major currencies in use at the moment in international financial circuits. The ECU is more severely affected than the Deutschmark by that universal malady, loss of purchasing power, which afflicts all national currencies. In addition, it also suffers from defects which are intrinsic to its composite nature.

A European currency will only have a chance of rivalling other well established currencies if it is better than they are and if it has a characteristic which confers prestige upon it and distinguishes it from all the others. That objective can be attained provided that full advantage is taken of the special property that is peculiar to a composite extraterritorial currency unit. That property is the ability to escape the law of the market and the comparison between consumption and final production which dictates the level of prices. Thanks to this special property, it is possible to define an extraterritorial composite currency unit in such a way that it can retain its purchasing power; something that no other currency, not even gold, has ever been able to boast.

This composite extraterritorial unit, christened the 'Eurostable' (or ES for short), would be introduced into circulation in the international financial circuits by the consortium, in parallel with the present private ECU, for which it could be seen as a possible substitute.

Up to this point, the experiment will have been under the control of private Eurobanks, supervised on an unofficial (or official) basis by the central bank of one of the member states. A time will arrive when reliable lessons will have been learnt from the experiment. Along with the incentive effect of a successful experiment of this kind, these lessons ought to be enough for the European Community to create, under the authority of the Commission, a sort of central institution, which could be seen as the embryo of a future central bank.

This central institution would issue and manage the Community's currency within the extraterritorial area defined above. It would be forbidden by the terms of the legal instrument setting it up to grant any kind of credit to a state or state-owned company. It would enjoy some but not all of the powers normally granted to a central bank within a state for the purpose of enabling the government to exercise its national sovereignty.

Payments effected within each member state of the Community system would be made exclusively in national currency. The exchange rates between the various national currencies would be fixed and the fluctuation margins which are permitted within the EMS would not apply to the ES.

This ES would be the European Community's external currency. Financial transactions between member states and with non-member states would be carried out in ES. The exchange rates of the national currencies into the ES would be calculated each day using the formula for the composition of the ES. Since exchange rates between the constituent currencies would be fixed, their ES parities would vary in parallel without being affected by market rates, either from one currency to another or in relation to the ES.

The central banks of the member states would manage their currencies themselves and would leave the question of regulating the exchange rates of the ES into foreign currencies to the Community's Central Institution. This Central Institution would be the exchange bureau for conversions of national currencies, ES and foreign currencies. The respective monetary positions of the member states would be measured in terms of the Central Institution's holdings of national currencies (in the case of deficit states) and its ES liabilities (surplus states). Persistent disparities which are considered to be too large would call for adjustments, from time to time, of the mutual exchange rates of the national currencies of the member states. These adjustments would be carried out on the basis of 'targeted creeping rates'. The rates of exchange of the various component currencies into each other would vary linearly each day for a given period.

Stage 3, which has just been summarised, corresponds in the main to what the proponents of European monetary unification are aiming for. Stage 4, which will now be described, is intended to mark the crowning point of the process of European integration. At this point, questions start to arise which are more political in nature than monetary. They do not come within the purview of this study, which is meant to be technical and pragmatic above all else and is more concerned with ways of tackling the objective than with the desirability of the objective itself.

Nevertheless, it is right to say something (briefly) on how, once Stage 3 has been achieved, further progress can be made if that is what the peoples of the Community decide they want. The member states will have succeeded in 'harmonising' their economies and their currencies will be following parallel trends, as will the positions of their currencies in the books of the central Institution. At this point it may be considered that the time has come to supplement, or even replace, the member states' national currencies with a single payment currency which could share the name 'ECU' but which would have a different definition and meaning from the present-day ECU. The ECU would then no longer be a composite currency but an autonomous currency unit, on the model of the main world currencies that we know today. It would be the Community's internal payment currency, whilst the ES would be its external payment currency. Payments within the Community would be exclusively in ECU whilst payments to third parties would be made in ES.

A central body, the nature of which is still to be defined, would take over the Central Institution's responsibilities and part of those that previously devolved on the member state's central banks. It is easy to imagine, as has been suggested by Jacques de Larosière, the Managing Director of the IMF, that some sort of federal system (like the American one) might be created. At the head of the system, the central body would manage the Community's internal currency, the ECU, and also its external currency, the ES. It would be responsible for regulating conversions of ES into foreign currencies.

It must be added that the description given here of Stage 4 is intended to answer a query that is often posed. Personally, I am not convinced that we shall get any further than Stage 3; it therefore seems to me to be premature to express any very decisive opinions on Stage 4.

By Stage 3 the main objectives will have been achieved: the European Community would then have a currency of its own which would not be the currency of any single state and which would help to identify it in the eyes of the outside world. This currency would be better than any other and would have a much sought-after characteristic: permanence of value in real terms.

This currency would enhance the Community's prestige but would also constitute a precious instrument for the use of other economies, not just those of Europe but those of the whole world, offering the international monetary system a stable standard of reference and the reliable medium of exchange, reserve and intervention that it at present lacks.

Now that the main features of this project have been set out, it only remains to explain, prove and convince. That is no easy task. The general public and politicians are alike 'allergic' to discussion of monetary questions. One cannot expect them to take sides regarding a monetary proposal. The press and public opinion will give one a chance when certain economic questions are at issue, even when such subjects are considered to be the prerogative of the experts. One has no such chance with monetary topics.

For high-ranking administrators in official quarters, any kind of innovation constitutes a problem and raises cases of conscience. Their own responsibilities are at stake. The uncertainty of knowledge on monetary matters and the unpredictable side-effects (and even the principal effects) require them to observe a degree of prudence which can be paralysing.

As for the members of the banking profession, their ingeniousness and the wide variety of new financial instruments that they have devised might at first seem to augur well. In fact, however, experience shows that they are reluctant to organise openly and outside national boundaries something that they are nevertheless tending to indulge in more and more within those very same boundaries, namely, monetary creation.

The novelty of this project and its ambitious aims (which may seem too ambitious to some people) oblige us to deal with both theory and practice. In this book there are certain formulae which may put the reader off on account of their (apparent) abstraction; there are also accounting examples which may seem dull. Both are necessary.

There has never been a payment currency with a value, in terms of what it could buy, that did not vary. Such a notion seems contrary to the 'nature of things', an anomaly that elicits reactions of instinctive rejection and persistent bad temper. That is why this proposal needs to be backed up by solid theoretical arguments, which there is no hope of finding in the works of the 'standard authors' because it is a fact that the science of economics ignores this subject. Let no one be surprised therefore if I am obliged to refer in these pages to the precepts for monetary analysis set out in my two previous books, *The Mechanics of Money* and *The Case for a New ECU*, published in 1980 and 1989 respectively by Macmillan, London.

I must also add that the breadth of the questions raised and the need to make constant references to fundamental principles have obliged me to go beyond the limits of the question of a European currency and deal with the more general questions that arise in connection with the subject of money, its nature, the way it is created and the way it is managed.

The mathematical examples are just as necessary for the purpose of clarifying, provoking reactions and showing why and how something that only a short while ago seemed to belong to the realm of Utopia may be realised in practice; and also (which is more important) that it does not necessarily have to be undertaken by governments but may be brought about as a result of the initiative of private promoters, who would thereby acquire both prestige and profit.

Whether as regards the theory or the practical application of that theory, finally, readers must be warned that this project does not lend itself to a superficial examination: it is only by immersing themselves in it that they will come to subscribe to this proposal. This should be all the easier for my British readers as it is the big banks in the City of London that are the best qualified to create the consortium that would issue and manage the ES in its role as a constant, external

ECU, following the example of the ECU Banking Association, which issues and manages the nominal payment ECU at present. It was, indeed, City of London banks which created the Euromarket and which continue to control it, and the objective of the constant external ECU, precisely because it is exclusively external, is to be the payment currency of the Euromarket and to function as a third currency between the established national currencies, in parallel with the main world currencies.

An enterprise of this kind would provide the banks that were prepared to undertake it with prestige and profit. It would also constitute a precious contribution to progress towards European Monetary Union, one that the United Kingdom could justly boast of; it would combine an advance in the field of theory (the constitutional stability of an external currency) with a measure of practical effectiveness: as it would not require prior agreement on the part of national governments, the enterprise could be launched straight away: it would offer a solution to the problems that beset the movement towards European union, whether political (national sovereignty would not be threatened) or financial (it would offer competition for the Deutschemark), without, however, putting any obstacles in the way of progress towards the realisation of the Delors Plan. On the contrary, it would keep the door to a single currency open by preventing the Deutschemark from taking the prize as Europe's common currency, something which the European Community's ECU cannot aspire to because of its much greater vulnerability to inflation.

In short, a giant step forward, in terms of both monetary matters and European affairs, is within the grasp of the Eurobanks of the City of London.

Finally, a few words of explanation are called for regarding the layout of the chapters. In the French version of this book the sections headed COMMENT were incorporated into the text and were printed in Italics, so as to separate them from the main body of the text. As they mostly consist of clarifications, or further examples, of points already made in the main part of the chapter, in this translation they have been collected at the end of each chapter like notes, with an indication of the pages to which they refer. Readers who feel they have already grasped the points in question and have no need of further examples may safely omit them.

1 The Consortium and its Interbank Office: Seigniorage

Europe needs a currency of its own, one that is exclusively European and is not the currency of any state, but the present trend of events is unfortunately not in that direction. As things stand at the moment, the European currency *par excellence* is the national currency of Germany the Deutschemark. The general public, misled by the illusions that are propagated by the news media, is unaware of this fact. It thinks that Europe's own special currency is, or will be, the ECU. Such assumptions are sadly mistaken.

Elsewhere in the world, when the talk is of international monetary matters, financiers do not refer to a European monetary area, only to a Deutschemark zone. But it is not in the interest of any of the member states of the Community that one of their national currencies should become the single currency of the European Community. The Germans, concerned for the future – and well aware of the past – are convinced of this.

It is also not in the interest of Europe as a whole that one of the member states should achieve a position of economic dominance, which would soon become political as well; neither is it in the interest of the Community that a member state should, thanks to its currency, assume the role of leader and representative of Europe in the eyes of the outside world. If this were to happen then the goal of European unification, which has been the hope of several generations, would eventually fade and a great project and a great ambition would have failed.

The time is long past when it was still possible to be content with agreements in principle and promises full of vague allusions: 'If all the words that have been spoken in favour of European unification had been bricks', Valéry Giscard d'Estaing once said, 'then the edifice of a united Europe would have been erected long ago' (speech at the EURO 92 conference at Unesco, December 1987). No, we can no longer be content with words. Eighteen years ago there was general agreement on the Werner Plan for a common European currency. Georges Pompidou, President of France at the

9

time, appeared on television to pledge that such a currency would be created by 1980!

However much willpower (and even goodwill) governments are prepared to invest in the project, the complexity of the task and the effects of the commitments they are required to enter into are such as to postpone the achievement of that consensus which is supposedly necessary for any innovation further and further into the future.

Time is running out: facts are more powerful than the willpower of governments, and monetary facts more than most. The only currency that will earn the title of European currency will be the one that millions of private citizens and companies have chosen for their daily transactions. Such a currency cannot be imposed on people; the European currency will not be born by decree of the European Commission in Brussels.

Once the Deutschemark has established itself and been recognised as the most reliable and practical means of exchange for international financial transactions, no amount of declarations and injunctions in favour of the ECU, proclaiming that it may be, must be and will be the common currency of Europe, will have any effect. That is why we must look for a practical way of turning the ECU into a genuine currency, instead of a mere unit of account, and we must do so without any expectation of, or reliance on, any kind of consensus between governments; without trusting in intentions and promises; and without setting the prior condition of the 'harmonisation' of social, economic, financial and fiscal policies, which are certainly desirable goals but which have no hope of being achieved in the immediate future and, when they have been achieved, will, if we do nothing now, find the ground already occupied by a triumphant Deutschemark, which will be too strong to be ousted and too strong to accept the presence, even in a junior capacity, of any European currency operating in parallel with it.

Never before in history has a form of claim money that was not at the same time the national currency of a state been in current use as a reserve and transaction instrument for financial relations between states. Never has an artificial – and, what is more, a composite – currency been imposed on the world. The very novelty of a project of this kind is enough to reveal its difficulty and the need, if the difficulties are to be overcome, for full and complete pragmatism in approaching it, coupled with a determination not to mistake words for deeds, or desires for realities.

THE 'HIGH SEAS' OF FINANCE

It is a pragmatic rule for any new enterprise that the market sector selected for its launch should be the one where it will meet with the fewest obstacles. In this case, there is no point in selecting the territory of a national state, where there will be competition from a national currency, for the launch of the private ECU. It must not be offered for use in transactions within a state, in parallel with the national currency. To attempt that would be the surest way of thwarting the development of the private ECU as a transaction currency.

The territory that the ECU must attempt to occupy is to be found outside the borders of states. It is a brand new monetary space which is unfettered by the constraints that hamper free movement within a national territory. This space does exist: it consists of the real or virtual space that is to be found between the frontiers of states through which international financial dealings pass. That is where a national currency finds, in a common pool, the intermediary (the dollar, for example) through which it will be exchanged for the currency of another state. It is a kind of 'high seas' of finance, the territory of stateless capital, of 'non-resident' Euromarket deposits.

There is no central bank with responsibility for this territory and there is no currency that is peculiar to it. It is 'occupied' by various national currencies, which are now admitted to be unsuitable for the task of providing a proper foundation for an international monetary system. This is the chance that is offered to a private transaction ECU. This is the territory which this new European currency is most suited to serve, being, as it is, similarly non-national, rather than circulating in parallel with national currencies on their own ground and competing with them.

The reality of this Euromarket territory is sometimes not fully perceived. All that is needed, in order to be convinced that it does indeed exist, is a moment's consideration of how financial transactions between states are conducted. Such consideration will reveal that, almost every time, a third currency intervenes between any two national currencies. Importers in Brazil do not exchange cruzados directly for the currency of their suppliers in order to pay them: they use a third currency. For a long time that third currency was the pound sterling, but sterling was succeeded by the US dollar and today this role is being performed more and more by the Deutschemark. This is exactly the role that the private ECU should also seek to perform during its early days, and no other.

Having thus defined the limits within which the private ECU would operate, we must now look at the conditions of use that will have to apply on the territory assigned to it (which it shares with the Euro-market currencies). The first observation is that the body which is needed to enable a new unit of this kind to circulate may be set up by private initiative, with the prodding (where appropriate) of government.

It is normally possible, for most human institutions, to arrive without too much difficulty at a precise definition of the respective roles of the government and the private sector, distinguishing the one from the other. As regards monetary and banking institutions, the line of demarcation is blurred. Even if it is considered to be a private institution, a bank is not private in the same way as other commercial and industrial establishments. It is always more or less under the tutelage of the state, if only because it enjoys the privilege of creating money.

However, this is only true within states. The territory defined above, being outside national boundaries, is not subject to the authority of any government. Financial institutions which operate there enjoy considerable independence and freedom of initiative. It is with this in mind that Stages 1 and 2 of this project have been presented. It requires, for its realisation, an initiative by Eurobanks, which are considered to be private – or rather non-public sector – institutions.

It must be admitted, however, that in spite of the prospect of considerable profit from such a venture, it is doubtful that private institutions will be prepared to take the initiative in this field on their own, if only because of what is at stake and the responsibilities involved. That is why they must be 'prodded' into taking the initiative, with the explicit or implicit support of a government or governments. It may be supposed that a government which is prepared to do the prodding will not want to act officially, out of concern for its international responsibilities or because it fears what other governments may think. In that case it would operate through the agency of some large financial establishment which would insure the risks involved in return for a premium, such as the ECGD in Britain and the Federal Deposit Insurance Corporation (FDIC) in the United States. Economic history offers many examples of this kind of arrangement.

This is the point of view from which the creation of the consortium and its interbank office has been envisaged. They would be the agents – and the beneficiaries – of a policy of national interest and they would be assured of the more than benevolent neutrality of the government. Negotiating the nature and terms of this 'benevolence' will be up to the financial establishments which agree to set up the consortium, or apply to join it.

THE BASIS OF MONETARY ANALYSIS: THE 'TRANSACTION FUNCTION'

The primary task of the consortium will be to achieve the transmutation of the private ECU from a unit of account, which is what it is at present, into a payment currency. In other words, to endow the private ECU with the jealously sought after quality of being a genuine currency, for which purpose it must acquire the 'transaction function' for international transactions.

Before going any further, we must stop and reflect for a moment on the significance of the notion of 'transaction', the role it plays in the economy and the distinctions that must be made between units of money that have this transaction function and those that do not. This will be a convenient moment to pause before penetrating the fog of uncertainty that is cast over everything by the unhelpful contemporary passion for amalgamating all categories and continually broadening the definition of what is money, confusing the various 'Ms' that are enumerated by statistics, mixing cash resources up with savings, the mobile with the inert, the mobilisable with the frozen, and thus, in the end, putting what can be used to make a payment in the same sack as what cannot, on the pretext that in both cases claims on institutions are concerned – and reserves for the 'creditor'.

Transaction is the fundamental phenomenon on which the working of the economy depends. It determines exchanges of goods and services and transfers from one economic agent to another. Amongst these multifarious types of exchange, we must single out conversions of final production (when the process of adding value is completed) into immediate or deferred consumption on the grounds of their role in the working of the economy. Money is the instrument of these conversions. In physics, we would say that there is a change of state.

Value is added, moving from one thing to another as the transactions take place, up until the moment when there is a final conversion, the final operation which fixes the exchange value of the unit of money in question. We need to have a clear idea of this very special mechanism. It will be discussed again later, when we come to look at the Eurostable and its peculiar property of being able to escape the law of the market, which is what decides the exchange value of a currency.

Meanwhile, let us simply admit that, if it is to become a genuine currency, the ECU must be used to make payments. At present it is no more than a unit of account because it is not used in payments: it is only used for counting. In order to make a payment, a claim or right to money denominated in ECU must in practice be converted into a national currency.

A unit of money, which is a claim on an institution, only becomes a fully-fledged payment money when the claim is denominated in the unit in question and is kept in that form for a certain time after the payment has been made, without being converted into a unit of some other denomination.

There are many units of account; there are very few which have the transaction function on an international scale. The kilowatt-hour, the cost of travelling a kilometre by rail, underground tickets and *Louis d'or* all have been, or are still being, used as units of account. That is the stage the ECU has reached today: whenever an ECU claim is used to make a payment it is first converted into a national currency at the ruling exchange rate. Turning the ECU into a transaction instrument is quite a different matter. No one has ever succeeded in, or even attempted, setting up an 'artificial' payment currency with comparable rights to those that are enjoyed by national currencies.

An 'ECU system' that put claims denominated in ECU into circulation could not function without some central body to centralise, equalise and distribute claims and responsibilities and which, in spite of being private, would carry out on behalf of the member banks of the consortium some of the functions that are assigned to a central bank within a state.

Once a currency no longer has any intrinsic value – that is, once it is no longer anything more than a claim on an institution – the only guarantee of its value is to be found in the quality and the reliability of the institution on which it constitutes a claim. That is why the payment circuits in a national monetary system lead up to the central bank which, because it is ultimately an arm of the government, can alone offer an absolute guarantee.

This absolute guarantee is no longer, these days, the promise to hand over a quantity of precious metal to the bearer of a claim. It is nothing more than the commitment to hand over to that bearer another claim, on another institution, which may be located abroad, in the case of foreign exchange. Only by basing themselves on a central body (an interbank office) can the member Eurobanks of our consortium, and with them the banks of the whole world, hope to be able to open credits and accept deposits denominated in ECU and, in so doing, create and circulate money that will have the transaction function. They will be able to do that because such a central office will make it possible for them to refinance themselves in ECUs and thus offer guaranteed convertibility into foreign currency.

What counts is the volume of transactions that are effected. This volume, over a given period of time, is the product of the mass of units of payment and the average number of times that each one of them carries out a transaction (the velocity of circulation, a fraction of which is the income velocity; on average five transactions a year, see p. 200). An asset held in a time deposit that is mobilised and a transaction unit that is exchanged for another (such as a sight deposit that is exchanged for a bank note) have no part in the economic function of transaction. An asset held in a term account (such as a NOW account in the USA), however, *may* be used to make a payment. Payments made in this way occur only occasionally and their effect is also negligible, since the frequency may be ten months, whereas the average transaction frequency is six days.

Statistics cannot make rigorous distinctions between units of money merely on the basis of the use that is made of them. Nevertheless, if we wish to analyse monetary mechanisms correctly we must still match up each supply of goods or services with a movement of a sum of equal value, and one only. For this purpose, we must be careful not to get carried away by the confusion of different categories of money (money and near-money) that is the intellectual fashion in monetary economics at present.

If this rule is not obeyed there is a risk that the significance of the relationship between the mass of units of payment, the velocity of circulation, the rate of production in volume terms and the price level (the relationship on which interpretation of monetary regulation is based: see p. 187) will be distorted and our new currency will not achieve the status that we seek for it and which is its due.

A NEED THAT HAS AT LAST BEEN RECOGNISED AND WHICH HAS CREATED AN EXCEPTIONAL OPPORTUNITY

There is an exceptional opportunity waiting to be seized: never have circumstances been more favourable to the creation of a new currency unit for international transactions. Such a unit, once created, would be followed by other units of money produced by groupings of states for the purpose of facilitating their trade (monetary zones).

Never has the time been more ripe: the decadence of the US dollar as an international monetary standard is now proved and accepted. At long last the disorders and abuses resulting from a standard which more than doubled its value in five years (from 1979 to 1984) in terms of other currencies, and then lost almost 50 per cent of its value in terms of those same currencies during the following three years as a direct result of how it was being managed, have been admitted. At long last, too, the inability of a *numéraire* to function as a reserve instrument when it has lost at least 90 per cent of its purchasing power over 50 years has also been acknowledged. People will not be slow to express their astonishment that it took so long, and so many unfortunate experiences, before the need was recognised for a transaction currency to be used in trade between states which is not the currency of any one state, and is thus not subject to the vicissitudes of any national monetary policy.

The private ECU is the first manifestation of this evolution in our way of thinking. One objective, which is as much political as economic, overrides all others: namely the need to transmute the private ECU into an extranational transaction currency in the full sense of the term.

An ever-expanding monetary space is opening for this new currency. It offers to a group of banks that are prepared to collaborate an exceptional opportunity to introduce this transaction unit and pocket not just the credit distribution margin, as Eurobanks do with the dollar, but also the seigniorage which flows from the creation and management of a currency.

In addition to these favourable economic factors, there is another; namely, the prodigious progress that has been achieved in the means of communication and transmission for banking operations. Their effect is to abolish the sense of distance in the monetary universe; they make it possible to extend to the entire planet forms of monetary and banking management which only yesterday no one thought could ever transcend the frontiers of the state.

The creation of a transaction currency or, more precisely, the creation of a mass of units of payment of a new kind for one or more sectors of the world which at present are without one and which are ready for such a new unit, may be a source of considerable profit. The fact that no one has yet seized the initiative in this field, which is without precedent in economic history, can only be explained in terms of the prevailing confusion as to certain aspects of the way the monetary mechanisms work. That is why it is necessary to say a few words now about how they do work, at the risk of telling readers what they already know.

First, a reminder: transaction money, real money, the money that is used to make payments, is issued for the most part today, in all countries, by the banking system: that is, by an agglomeration of commercial banks. Only a fraction is now issued by the central bank under the control of the government. The authorities have relinquished – some would say that they have been deprived of – their almost regal power of issuing money. In France in 1985, for example, nine-tenths of all the transaction money that was put into circulation that year (M1) came from the banking system, through the mechanism of the granting of loans and purchases of foreign currencies. One-tenth only was created by the Bank of France. The way that these two forms of money, bank money and central bank money, are put into circulation, created, managed, and so on is the result of an ingenious mechanism, which is itself the product of experience and which reconciles the authority and the responsibility of state officials with the initiative of the banking sector in the distribution of credit. The mechanism which this project has set out to propose has been inspired by national systems of this kind.

It is intended for the use of a consortium of Eurobanks which would issue and manage private transaction ECUs to be used in international financial transactions. It would make it possible for these banks to collect the seigniorage on the new payment money created by them, in addition to the credit distribution margin (otherwise known as the 'spread'). That is what is new about this proposal and it constitutes a source of additional profit for the member banks of the consortium.

THE CENTRAL BANK'S SEIGNIORAGE ON ITS BANK NOTES

Whereas the notion of a spread is a familiar one, however, seigniorage is less familiar and needs to be explained. The simplest form of seigniorage arises when a bank note is issued by the bank of issue. The notes are put into circulation by a bank at the moment a depositor mobilises the assets held in his current account. In order to obtain the notes, the bank in question purchases them from the central bank and pays for them in foreign currency or in bills. Its account in central bank money is then credited with the corresponding amount. This gives the bank access to the bank notes that it needs to fund withdrawals at its branch counters.

In order to analyse the operation, we must go back to the origin of the bank deposit which the bank's customer has just mobilised. This deposit resulted from a loan by another member bank of the banking system to a borrower. It was created by simultaneously entering (a) the sum lent (minus interest yet to accrue) on the liabilities side of the bank's balance sheet (and crediting the corresponding sum to the borrower's account) and (b) entering the bank's claim on the assets side of its balance sheet. In order to obtain the notes, the bank sells an asset on the money market or submits a bill for rediscount. The central bank purchases or rediscounts the bill at a price that is calculated on a particular yield rate (for example, its intervention rate or rediscount rate). It thus deducts from the capital the interest yet to accrue at this rate.

The commercial bank keeps the difference between the interest it receives from the borrower and what it pays to the central bank. This is the credit distribution margin. It is actually made up of the difference between the price paid to the commercial bank by the central bank (for the bill) and the sum paid to the borrower by the commercial bank, less any interest still to accrue to maturity (the gross margin). If the asset sold to the central bank was foreign currency the seigniorage is equal to the proceeds of investing it on the money markets in Treasury bonds.

The counterpart of assets consisting of notes lasts only as long as the life of the bill; it thus needs to be renewed until the notes are destroyed (a glance at Figure 1.1 will clarify the mechanism that has just been described).

The operation is then completed at maturity when the customer pays the bank back and the bank pays the central bank back. If this reimbursement is in bank notes they are used (figuratively) by the bank in order to pay back what it owes the central bank. They are then 'destroyed'. If, as is usually the case, the customer pays back what is owed by cheque or bank transfer, a new source of central bank money of the kind described above must take the place of the central bank money paid back at maturity by the bank to the central bank.

For their part, the bearers of the bank notes (which are central bank money, and therefore represent a claim on the bank of issue) that have been put into circulation receive no interest, whereas the central bank receives the full value of the interest on the assets it received in exchange for the bank notes that it put into circulation. The reason for, and justification of, the non-payment of interest to the holders of bank notes (even supposing payment of interest to be a practical proposition) is that the essence of transaction money is that it should circulate. It consequently never stays in one place for very long before being re-used and moving on.

This observation on the velocity of circulation is of fundamental importance if we are to grasp what follows, because the aim of the system of monetary organisation proposed here is precisely the use of the private ECU in transactions, with the resulting velocity of circulation (which present-day means of communication make possible). The actual use of the private ECU in transactions will have the corollary of a rate of interest on deposits which will fall as the ECU's velocity of circulation increases. In other words, the more successful the conversion of the ECU into a transaction currency the lower the rate paid on deposits (and, correspondingly, the higher the seigniorage).

Before going on to bank money, let us complete our discussion of bank notes. Once holders of bank notes no longer have short-term use of them they become savers. They entrust the notes to an establishment of one kind or another which makes use of them in their place. The notes are thus recycled. There is no creation of any new payment money, only non-monetary intermediation. This form of intermediation has no effect on the seigniorage, which continues to accrue to the central bank. The bank notes handed in by savers at their banks are passed on to borrowers. The same note can be lent and re-lent several times and thus can act as the foundation for several credit distribution margins, whereas seigniorage is a once-and-for-all occurrence.

The expression 'seigniorage' originated in the power enjoyed by an

	Zero time (A)	1st day (A)	5th day (A)	6th day (B)	15th day (B)
Reserves	100	100 100	100 100 −100	100 +100	100 −100
Customers		C+100	+100(1)100	100(1) −100	+100(2)	100(2) −100

	16th day (C)	30th day (C)	40th day (A)	50th day (D)	100th day (D)
Reserves	+100	100 −100	0 +100	100 +100	100 −100
Customers		+100(3)	100(3)100 −100 −100	+100(1) −100	+100(4)	100(4) −100

Zero time: Bank (A): situation

1st day: credit of 100 by (A) to (1)

5th and 6th days: transfer by (1) to (2)'s account at (B)

15th and 16th days: transfer by (2) to (3)'s account at (C)

30th day: withdrawal of deposit by (3)

40th day: loan repaid to (A) by (1)

50th day: time deposit by (4)

100th day: withdrawal by (4)

INTEREST RATE/DAY: on loans: Ic. On R reserves and on E borrowings: MM
Demand deposits: no interest (transaction function)
Time deposits: It

CALCULATION OF INTEREST

Seigniorage		Credit distribution margin	Total	
A	5 MM	40(Ic − MM)	40(Ic − 35 MM)	40 Ic
B	10 MM		10 MM	
C	15 MM		15 MM	
D			50(MM − It)	

Figure 1.1 Seigniorage and the credit distribution margin

Note

No account is taken of banks' rules regarding crediting to accounts and calculation of days of value.

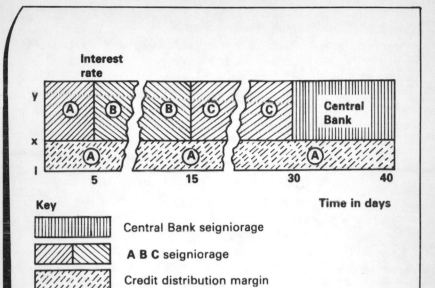

Key

Central Bank seigniorage

A B C seigniorage

Credit distribution margin

ly: Interest rate on loan lc
xy: MM rate (money market or LIBOR)

Gross margin: A: 40 lx + 5 xy
B: 10 xy
C: 15 xy

Notes

Seigniorage is the difference between the return on an asset (taken at the MM rate) and the interest paid by the bank on any corresponding deposits.

It accrues to the bank to which the deposit has been transferred in payment, after being created by the granting of a loan (100 created by A and transferred to B on the 5th day).

The credit distribution margin is the difference between the interest paid by the borrower at the lc rate and the return on the asset from which the seigniorage is deducted; in other words, the credit distribution margin here amounts to (lc − MM). It accrues to the bank that made the loan (A) until the moment of reimbursement (40th day).

institution (like the *seigneur* of times past) of being able to acquire a productive asset (approximately at the MM rate) in exchange for payment money, which the institution in question issues at minimal expense to itself since such a form of money consists of a claim on the institution on which no interest is payable and which has an indeterminate maturity. The banking system enjoys such power, which is also a privilege. The stock of non-interest-bearing payment money included in M1 amounted to 950 000 million francs in 1985 and 1 010 000 million francs in 1986, figures that bear eloquent witness to the extent of this privilege.

THE BANKING SYSTEM'S SEIGNIORAGE ON ITS OWN MONEY

The two components of credit, which were revealed in connection with central bank money, are faithfully transposed to bank money with one difference: whereas the credit distribution margin continues to be kept by the institution that made the loan, the seigniorage, in contrast, accrues to the commercial bank where the unit of bank money that has been created is deposited, rather than to the central bank.

It passes from one bank to another as one transaction succeeds another. What therefore happens is that the banking system as a whole takes the place in this respect of the central bank.

In order to demonstrate this breakdown into credit distribution margin and seigniorage in the case of bank money, we must take the operation from the beginning, at the moment the bank, Bank A, makes a loan of 100 to its customer at an interest rate of, say, 11 per cent. The profit margin for the bank, as it is usually described by bankers, is the difference between this rate of 11 per cent and the 'cost of money', as calculated at the MM rate. In other words, it is the spread. In fact, once the borrower's account has been credited he will make use of these resources in order to pay a creditor by drawing a cheque on Bank A. This cheque may then be deposited at another bank, Bank B, as a result of which this latter bank becomes the creditor of Bank A and asks for payment in central bank money (through the clearing) within a very short period. This payment of B by A results in the transfer from A to B of 100 units of central bank money which A either withdraws from its reserves at the central bank (and which is therefore no longer available to it for use on the money market) or obtains by selling assets on the money market (or at the central bank rediscount window), which were earning interest at, let us say, the MM rate of 8 per cent. In both cases this involves a 'cost' for Bank A equal to the MM rate of interest. Bankers are thus justified in claiming that their profit margin is the difference between what they receive from their borrowers at 11 per cent and the cost of their resources: that is, $11 - 8 = 3$ per cent.

This margin is only the credit distribution margin, however. It does not include another more important source of profit, seigniorage, which is represented by the ratio of the price of funds to the MM rate, on the 100 transferred by A to B. Whereas A retains its distribution margin ($11 - 8 = 3$) on the loan it has granted until the moment the borrower pays back the loan, B receives the seigniorage at the rate of 8 per cent on the asset transferred to it by A. The seigniorage thus remains with B until another bank, Bank C, to which a deposit has been transferred, receives it in turn, followed by Bank D and so on until the unit of money is finally destroyed (by being used to repay a loan, pay for foreign currency or withdrawn in cash).

Bank A, for its part, continues to receive the interest paid by its customer on the loan of 100 it granted him. A has lost the benefit of the reserves it transferred to B but it benefits, in its turn, from the MM rate paid on the reserves transferred by X, as a result of a transfer order in favour of A by one of X's customers. The seigniorage is lost by the bank that created the unit of money in question but it stays with the member banks of the banking system as a whole.

The daily clearing of mutual claims and the money market, on which banks buy and sell claims in return for central bank money, are the mechanisms which make it possible for a group of banks operating together within a banking 'system' to function to all intents and purposes like a single bank.

SEIGNIORAGE AND THE CREDIT DISTRIBUTION MARGIN IN THE EUROMARKET

In order to establish who has the benefit of the seigniorage in the Eurodollar market, and show how our consortium could take the place of the beneficiary, we need to take our analysis further and look at the clearing process, which is one of the essential elements in monetary creation.

These days, in all countries, payment money consists of claims on institutions, whether central banks or commercial banks grouped together in a banking system. A payment usually sets in motion several other transfers from account to account. Suppose someone draws a cheque on his savings bank. The payee receives from the savings bank a cheque drawn on a commercial bank where the savings bank has an account. He then withdraws the sum in cash. The *final* movement of units of money is the handing over to the payee of a bundle of bank notes, which are a claim on the central bank. These notes have the payment function.

In order to establish where the transaction takes place – and which instrument is responsible for completing the operation – we must look for the final movement of units of money, because it is only at this stage that the payer's debt is extinguished and the payee receives what is owed to him, thus validating the payment (see the section headed 'Comment' at the end of the chapter).

The institution in question, whether a central bank or a commercial bank, is only revealed at the clearing stage. That is why, in the matter that concerns us here, we need to consider the mechanism of the clearing house in order to understand what is going on. A payment in the Euromarket (which could therefore also be made in ECU) causes movements of claims on banks which are often located on both sides of the Atlantic and sometimes even the Pacific. We need to know which ones and, more specifically, which of them is responsible for the final movement. Understanding the clearing process will at the same time explain how it is that banking systems have come to take the place of the central banks as principal issuers of payment money.

Multilateral clearing, either directly or in tiers, has the effect of making it possible for any bank whatsoever to settle its debts in respect of other banks (A, B and C, for example) using the claims that it has on yet other banks (X, Y and Z, say), even though X, Y and Z only have claims on banks other than A, B and C. What is more, all of this can be accomplished in a matter of hours, even though the banks in question may be many hundreds (and in the United States, thousands) in number and have no direct relations with each other.

Central bank money, which is transferred each day between the various member banks at the end of the day's clearing, for the purpose of settling outstanding balances, constitutes the heart of the mechanism which has thus made it possible for ordinary commercial banks gradually to replace the money that is issued by the central bank with their own transaction money. The core of central bank money required for the clearing to work is very small (1 per cent of the quantity of bank money) as a result of the fact that the clearing session's total of negative balances (debits) is equal to the total of positive balances (credits). The clearing mechanism brings together the pluses and the minuses in one common ledger whilst, on the money market, banks with a positive balance are able to negotiate their surpluses in exchange for productive assets which will produce seigniorage for them.

The effect of the clearing is to allocate to or withdraw from each bank those assets that need to accompany the movements of deposits as and when transactions occur and thus to redistribute the seigniorage, and to do so each day and without exception.

The fact that it was some time before anyone realised that the issue of payment money had gradually passed from the central bank to the banking system had serious consequences. This oversight is largely responsible for the errors of money management that have been committed in the past. The great deflation of the 1930s and the great inflation of the 1970s were two of the consequences (see p. 203).

In the preceding pages we have only been discussing non-interest-bearing bank deposits (M1, demand deposits or payment money), in respect of which the banks receive the seigniorage in full. But the tendency now is to pay interest on demand deposits, thus proportionately reducing the net seigniorage.

Although the project proposed in these pages is intended for the Euromarkets and not for a national banking system, it is not out of place to refer to a national system for the purpose of bringing out the relative importance, for the banks, of their credit distribution margin and of the seigniorage (and the reduction in the seigniorage that results from paying interest on demand deposits). The following figures concern the French banking system in 1986 (source: Conseil National du Crédit).

Total bank payment money (M1, minus bank notes and Post Office Giro deposits) amounted to 1010 thousand million francs. Reserves at the central banks amounted to 8000 million francs. The average MM rate (overnight) may be taken to be 7.8 per cent. Total earnings from seigniorage (on M1) during the year were therefore $(1010 - 8) \times 7.80 = 78\ 000$ million francs.

The credit distribution margin, at an average rate of 11 per cent, on payment money (M1 demand deposits) amounted to $1010\ (11 - 7.80) = 32\ 320$ million francs.

The credit distribution margin on so-called 'stable' deposits covered 1.438 thousand million francs, on which interest was paid at an average rate of 5.50 per cent, giving a margin of $(11 - 5.50) \times 1438 = 79\,090$ million francs.

The overall gross credit margin was therefore 189 000 million francs, of which 78 000 million was accounted for by seigniorage and 111 000 million by the credit distribution margin.

Before looking at the international sector, let us consider the velocity of circulation. This variable does have a direct effect on the cut in the seigniorage (taken at the MM rate) that results when interest is paid on demand deposits. On the domestic market in France the average time spent in a given account by non-interest-bearing deposits (demand deposits) amounts to three days for company accounts, 19 days for family business accounts and 34 days for private customer accounts. The period during which interest-bearing deposits remain in a savings account is ten months. In the case of short-term SICAVs (a form of unit trust), the period is four months and three weeks.

The present trend is for the holders of deposits to look for some form of return on any period, however short, during which a deposit is immobile; account will be taken of this trend in calculating the seigniorage on a private transaction ECU.

There is one precept for monetary analysis which states that if we wish to interpret transactions correctly we must take our analysis as far as the clearing process. This precept is itself nothing more than a special case of another precept, which is more general and of fundamental importance for a correct understanding of how monetary mechanisms work. That precept is that a right to money should not be confused with the thing to which it gives a right, and is not necessarily identical in nature to that thing. If we confuse them we shall risk finding two things where in reality there is only one.

THE NEW YORK CLEARING HOUSE

We can move from consideration of the national sector to the extranational and international sector by replacing the financial institutions in the national sector by Eurobanks (a Eurobank being a bank that operates in a currency other than the currency of the country in which it is domiciled). The resources of Eurodollar banks, for example, are obtained from deposits or loans in US dollars: that is, in claims on the US banking system (see Figure 1.2). Euromarket transactions in dollars give rise to several movements of funds from account to account. The final movement is carried out at the New York Clearing House, amongst American banks, in US dollars issued by the American banking system, the seigniorage on which remains with the American banks.

The fact that these Eurobanks are scattered around the globe, the different time zones in which they are located and other causes, such as the way banking rules and practices differ from one country to another, have the result of limiting the extent to which Eurobanks can clear their mutual claims to only a small part of the total sums. They mainly function as non-monetary intermediaries. Eurobank A carries out a transfer order in dollars in favour of Eurobank B by transferring the sum in question from the American bank at which it has an account to the account held by B at another American bank, both of them being domiciled in the United States.

Eurobanks operate in dollars as non-monetary intermediaries (also called non-banks). That means that they operate using dollars that have been created not by them but by the United States banking system. They only receive the credit distribution margin (or spread): namely, the difference between the interest income they receive from their loans and the interest they are obliged to pay to their lenders or depositors. This margin is often less than 1 per cent.

As far as the US banks (such as the Chase) are concerned, there is no difference between the dollars that their customers abroad (including Eurobanks) make use of and those that are deposited and transferred by their domestic customers (with one difference: non-resident deposits are not subject to any reserve requirements).

The seigniorage on the deposits that non-residents and Eurobanks manipulate within the United States is kept by the US banks. Demand deposits of this kind in US banks receive interest, at best, for the actual period they remain in the account (calculated on an overnight basis). Average interest paid during the year, bearing in mind the very high rate of turnover, is unlikely to exceed one-half of LIBOR (the international MM). If LIBOR stands at 7 per cent, the seigniorage accruing to the American banking system amounts to half of 7 per cent (that is, 3.5 per cent).

Seigniorage on Eurodollars is a source of considerable profit for American banks. There is now a clearly expressed desire to introduce a private ECU as a payment currency, and this offers a group of European banks the opportunity to recover a source of seigniorage

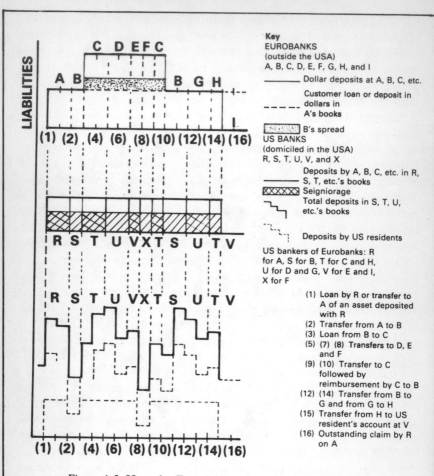

Figure 1.2 How the Eurodollar banking system functions

Notes

A 'Eurodollar' is nothing more than a right to a US dollar. A right to something should not be confused with the thing itself. All payments in Eurodollars are ultimately made in US dollars. These dollars are created by the US banking system, which keeps the seigniorage on them.

The 'value' of the dollar depends solely on the way it is managed domestically. The Federal Reserve Bank takes no account of Eurodollars when selecting its monetary targets.

which can no longer justifiably continue to be transferred to American banks.

The Euromarket grew up as a result of private initiative. Central banks and governments had no part in its creation. But the use of the dollar, or any national currency, as the currency of those markets deprives those banks of a proportion of the profit to which their initiative rightly entitles them.

The mechanism proposed in the following chapter makes it possible for a consortium of Eurobanks to put an autonomous currency into circulation which would not be the currency of any nation, so that they would retain the seigniorage resulting from the creation of all payment money. At the same time, however, this mechanism will also be capable of functioning with a currency of distinctly higher quality than the ECU. This question of quality is of vital importance for any new product which is about to be launched on a market where its use cannot be rendered obligatory. For this reason it is necessary to state without further delay that the private ECU is only seen here as a stage on the road to a payment currency that will be 'better than all the others' (see Chapter 6).

COMMENTS

Comment on page 15. It is pointless to attempt to convert the ECU from the unit of account that it is at present into a payment money without having a clear understanding of what a transaction is, the mechanism by which it works and the property that a given unit of money may or may not have of effecting a transaction. It is illusory to try to introduce a new transaction currency so long as the role performed by the concept of transaction in the economy has not been recognised.

Goods and services change hands thanks to transactions. Within the territory of a state, transaction is the mechanism by which production takes place, by successive additions of value, up until the moment of destruction through final consumption.

Any commodity or service may be the subject of a transaction. A silver-plated teapot which is exchanged for 30 kilos of potatoes contributes its exchange value, say £60, to the total transaction volume. No account is taken of this because the teapot is not intended to be a medium of exchange. It has no transaction function.

Barter of this kind is the exception rather than the rule and has a negligible effect on the volume of transactions. A bond or a Treasury Bill may also be used to pay for a service, and their value *should* be included in the total volume of transactions, but cases of this kind are also exceptional.

Comment on page 19. Let us suppose, for example, that the commercial bank discounts for its customer a bill worth 100 at a rate of 12 per cent. It credits the customer's account with a sum which it calculates by deducting the interest yet to accrue until maturity (three months) from the face value (100). At a rate of 12 per cent, this amounts to $100 - \frac{12}{4} = 97$. The bill is then rediscounted by the central bank which, in turn, deducts interest yet to accrue at the rediscount rate, say 8 per cent. The commercial bank receives $100 - \frac{8}{4} = 98$. Ultimately, it keeps the difference between 98 and 97 (that is, 1 per cent). That is the credit distribution margin. The central bank receives interest (2 per cent) at the rediscount rate; that is the seigniorage (which arises when the customer pays back the principal of 100 to the bank, which in turn transfers it to the central bank). The gross margin is the sum of the seigniorage and the distribution margin (2 + 1 per cent).

Comment on page 24. A cheque for 100 is drawn on Bank A and deposited at Bank B. A cheque for 120 is then drawn on B and deposited with A. The clearing causes two mutual obligations of 100 to cancel out, leaving a balance of 20, which is settled by a transfer of central bank money from B to A. The final transactions were carried out to the extent of 200 in claims on Banks A and B and 20 in claims on the central bank.

As a result of cheques deposited or transfers received, A owes 110 to B, B owes 113 to C and C owes 105 to A. At the end of the clearing, A's and B's central bank accounts are debited, respectively, with 5 and 3, whilst C's is credited with 8. The final movements resulting from the transactions were carried out to the extent of 105, 110 and 105 (that is, 320) by claims on a commercial bank and 5 + 3 + 8 = 16 in claims on the central bank.

Comment on page 26. The size of these figures should not be misunderstood: it would be wrong to see in them evidence of excessive profits for the banks. Economic growth depends on enterprise and risk-taking in the use of capital. Those risks are largely taken by the banks and it is they who absorb the cost of any failures. Any reduction in their profits would have the effect of encouraging the banks to be more cautious, which would be sterile and would have a negative effect on economic expansion.

Comment on page 26. In the interest of a thoroughgoing analysis, we must never lose sight of the need to look for the last of the movements of money that are set off by a given transaction: for example, when payment is made by a cheque on a savings bank. The bank pays by drawing a cheque on its own account at a bank which, itself, settles its debt, after the clearing, by a claim on the central bank or by a claim on another bank of the banking system.

The actual transaction must be located in the final debit and credit operations, and nowhere else. If the search is confined to the first movement of a unit of money no account can be taken of institutions whose debts are ultimately exchanged by the effect of the transaction, whereas it is these institutions (and their debts) that constitute the pivot of the mechanism set in motion and the very essence of a system of claim money.

This rule of analysis makes it possible to define and distinguish – without confusing them – the monetary roles of money and near-money, dollars and Eurodollars, monetary intermediaries and non-monetary intermediaries, 'transformation' and *ex nihilo* creation of money.

Comment on page 27. A visit to the New York Clearing House gives a concrete representation of this mechanism as applied to the Euro-market. At the same time it shows how the various interest rates paid by borrowers to Eurobanks are calculated.

In the basement, transfer orders to US banks deriving from Euro-banks overseas throughout the world are entered into computers and cleared. On the first floor, in parallel with this, payment orders and cheques issued within the territory of the United States, denominated in US currency and drawn on US banks, are similarly cleared. At the end of each day's session, at four in the afternoon, the balances of the two clearing operations are combined. From these figures, the net balances are calculated for each US member bank of the Clearing House, giving the sums in Federal Reserve Funds (the central bank money held by each bank in its account with the Federal Reserve) that each bank needs to transfer or can expect to receive in order to clear the outstanding positive and negative balances of the day's clearing session.

During the visit to the Clearing House described in my book *The*

Case for a New ECU (published by Macmillan, London 1989), the day's accounting for the Chase Manhattan Bank ended in a negative balance of 1300 million dollars on its domestic operations and a positive balance of 1200 million dollars on its international operations, giving a final negative balance of 100 million dollars.

The visit in question took place ten years ago and more, and the figures quoted were those of a single bank. Today the total quantity of US dollars transferred from debtor to creditor and centralised in the basement of the New York Clearing House may be in excess of 400 000 million dollars in a single day!

Comment on page 27. This coefficient of one-half is only approximate. It corresponds to a cut in the overall seigniorage of one-half as a result of the payment of interest on demand deposits. In fact, the banks pay interest on non-resident deposits at a higher rate. But the velocity of circulation of these deposits (more than one movement per day, on average), the time zone differences and the fact that the payment orders are scattered round the globe have the effect of delaying the calculation of the interest due on these demand deposits by a period that is greater than the time they are actually immobilised in an account, so that the coefficient ought certainly to be less than one-half. The seigniorage accruing to the member banks of our consortium will be greater since interest on deposits will be paid in ECUs issued by the consortium.

2 The Consortium and its Interbank Office: A Currency to be 'Sold'

The territory within which the new currency will circulate has been defined: it is the vast area, virtual or real, that is to be found between states. This area has no currency of its own, nor has it a central bank. Within this same area there is also the Euromarket. Virgin territory of this kind offers exceptional opportunities. The aim now is to imagine the kind of banking and monetary organisation that must be created for this new market so as to be able to put them to use in optimum conditions. The system proposed in these pages was inspired by the national systems to be found in all countries, the value of which has been proved by experience. What characterises these systems is the combination of a body (the central bank) which is under the explicit or implicit control of the government and a group of commercial banks. In order for this system to work, there is an instrument: the central bank money issued by the central bank in the form of claims on itself. This system makes it possible for the banks that are located within a national territory (13 500 in the United States) to create payment money in claims on themselves and to put it into circulation among the public, whilst at the same time remaining within the limits of a minimum of solidarity and discipline.

In our system, by very reason of the nature of the territory to which it will apply, there is no government or central bank. The role of the central bank will be played by a kind of interbank office, set up by the member Eurobanks of the consortium. This consortium, together with its interbank office, will comprise the system.

The consortium will be headed by a committee which will be responsible for ensuring that the member banks obey the rules of operation of the system as well as the rules governing the commitments entered into by the banks as a consequence of the operation of the mechanism that will be briefly described in the following pages, starting with the interbank office.

A KEY BANKING INSTITUTION THAT IS NOT A CENTRAL BANK

This office will carry out the work of a central bank without being one. Its tasks will be both commercial and administrative. Responsibility for running it could be handed over to certain member banks or, preferably, to a private management company. The central money issued by the office (in private ECUs) will be reserved exclusively for the consortium's interbank transactions: no central ECU will reach the hands of the public. This 'central ECU' will function like a kind of counter, such as is used in board games, and it will make it possible for the banks to effect numerous mutually binding operations whilst leaving them total freedom as regards their individual initiatives.

The central office will have interest-bearing reserves in foreign currencies (dollars, yen or Deutschmarks) which the consortium will obtain by borrowing on the market or from the member banks' treasury departments.

The central office will then issue, in the form of claims on itself, a number of 'central ECU' which it will lend in equal shares to the various member banks. These shares will be the banks' 'quotas'. Each member bank, in turn, will then issue bank ECUs, again in the form of claims on itself, which it will put into circulation by making loans or purchasing foreign exchange.

Customer transfers will be carried out in the usual way, from one bank to another. They will be accompanied by transfers of central ECUs to and from the accounts that each consortium member has in the office's books. Creditor or debtor balances on these accounts will bear interest at the interbank rates established by the Committee.

Each member bank will be able to obtain refinancing from the central office, in ECU or in foreign currencies, within the limits of its quota. The quotas may be increased with the agreement of the Committee. Each bank will be directly responsible for its operations and there shall be no obligation for the central office beyond the quotas that are agreed by the Committee.

From time to time the accounts will be cleared, and each bank will re-establish its starting quota in central ECU by purchasing or selling, in exchange for foreign currency, its deficit or surplus compared with its starting quota. If necessary, this mechanism may be completed by introducing credit expansion restrictions, or by fixing a minimum interest rate on customer borrowings, something that practical experience would reveal the need for (or not, as the case may be).

This mechanism would serve to equalise cash resources in foreign currency over time and among the banks; it would make it possible for each bank to maintain its ECU positions in constant balance; it would offset in the banks' mutual accounts the various movements of funds by their customers, as and when they occurred; and it would ensure strict distribution of the seigniorage accruing to each member bank on the bank ECUs deposited with it whilst at the same time leaving each institution with its credit distribution margin on the interest it receives from borrowers.

In addition, the mechanism would also constitute an instrument with which the commitments entered into by each bank with regard to each of the other banks (revealed by a debtor balance on the bank's account in central ECUs at the central office) could be constantly measured.

As can be seen, the system is based on the one that is used in the United States by certain Federal Reserve Banks whereby they record, for each bank for which they have responsibility, payments by their customers in bank money. They are thus in a position to make Federal funds immediately available to the banks within the limits of their credit balances.

Such a system ought to make it possible for a consortium of Eurobanks of the kind we are talking about here to issue the new currency, manage it efficiently, put it into circulation and thus garner the profit that derives from the creation of means of payment in the form of bank money without there being any need for corresponding non-interest-bearing reserves.

In Chapter 3, on p. 47, there are some examples using figures which show cases of the purchase of foreign currency and the granting of a loan by a member bank of the consortium, interbank transfers, time deposits, repayments, conversion of ECU into currency, clearing of mutual claims and refinancing at the central office in ECU or foreign currency. These examples show that the mechanism does work and is effective.

EPHEMERAL UNITS THAT NEED TO BE RENEWED

The mechanism proposed here and the results that may be expected from it may be summarised as follows. The bank payment ECU will be created by two simultaneous entries: one on the asset side of a member bank's balance sheet, representing its claim on the customer to whom it has made a loan or the quantity of foreign currency that it has purchased, and, on the liabilities side, the sum it has credited to the borrower's account or to the account of the seller of the foreign currency. There is no raw material, no commodity that the money could be claimed to 'represent', not even a case of the 'transformation' we hear so much about and which would be difficult to show starting from nothing.

The central office and its central ECU would provide the consortium, which would have become a 'system', with the same services as a central bank (and its central bank money) provides a national banking system with, whilst the bank ECUs created by the member banks would circulate by passing from account to account in their books. These ECUs would have the transaction function: in return for the movement of an ECU from (1)'s account at Bank A to (2)'s account at Bank B, a commodity or a service would pass from (2) to (1).

This same bank ECU is destroyed at the moment its holder uses it for the purpose of paying back a bank loan or purchasing foreign currency; it is 'reprieved' from death, or is 'revived', when it is invested in a time account or savings account and is thus divested of its transaction function.

As long as the payment ECU has not established itself, the life of each ECU that is created will be brief and the operations of creation and destruction (by a purchase of currency or a loan in the first case and by a conversion or reimbursement in the second) will be repeated over and over again, whilst the loans that give birth to new ECUs will continue to be short-term operations. As it moves from account to account, our typical ECU will, in fact, be very quickly refused, either by the payee or by his bank (if it is not a member bank of the consortium). The ECU deposit will then have to be converted into currency by the member bank from which the payment emanated. The private bank ECU will then be destroyed.

The foreign currencies needed by the consortium for the purpose of guaranteeing conversions will be obtained by purchase, in exchange for ECU, or by issues of ECU bonds, most probably by the Treasury departments of the member banks.

Building up a quantity of working capital in foreign currency would not involve any financial burden. The return on such funds must be such as to compensate for the cost of raising them. In any case, the working capital needed will be limited in quantity because of the short-term nature of the loans, a necessary condition that will be imposed on the banks as a result of the fact that the ECU created by these loans will be as yet short-lived.

The system outlined above is thus modelled on the Eurodollar system, of which it is in fact a transposition, the Federal Reserve being replaced by the central office and the US banking system by the member banks of the consortium. In addition, it also has the machinery of commercial coordination, which is indispensable for the launch of a brand-new currency unit, and it gives the banking system, which is the issuer of the payment ECUs, the benefit of seigniorage on them. The profit from this seigniorage is greater than can be earned from the credit distribution margin, or spread, that accrues to Eurobanks on a currency (the US dollar, for example) which they have not created.

A form of organisation of the kind set out above, though it is a necessary precondition, is not in itself enough for the purpose of launching a new currency. It could be enough for an existing, well established currency. Launching a new currency in a territory that does not have one of its own (the Euromarket, in other words) is quite another affair, even if the territory in question is ripe for such an innovation. What is called for is a full-blown commercial approach, not merely administrative machinery, and commercial promotion is something that does not usually come within the province of a central bank.

The problem that arises in the case of the ECU is one of *selling*. This is what should decide the way the enterprise is organised. Success will depend on the extent to which the private ECU has penetrated its market. If the ECU is to become a payment instrument it will have to circulate from payers to payees, and for that to happen four decisions will have to be taken whenever a transaction takes place: one by the payer, one by his bank, one by the payee and one by *his* bank. Each participant must agree, or better still, prefer, without any element of duress, to transact business in ECU rather than in dollars or Deutschmarks.

Once the transaction is completed, the ECU must remain on deposit for a few days, as any other currency would. It must then be used for another purchase and, once again, take part in a transaction between a debtor and a creditor, after which, once the creditor has been paid, it must be used once again to settle one of the creditor's debts.

This kind of result can only be achieved after a programme of intense commercial promotion, involving constant lobbying on the part of the various local branches of the member banks involved in the transactions. It will not be enough to encourage companies to publish price lists in ECU, or to issue proclamations to the effect that 'Europe at last has a currency of its own.' It will be necessary to persuade payees and their banks not just to accept payment in ECU but to *insist* on payment in ECU, after which it will be necessary to persuade the payee's creditors and their banks also to accept payment in ECU.

This sort of objective requires a publicity campaign in the various media, in parallel with the creation of a body of commercial promoters, or 'sellers', of ECU, who will back up the activities of the bank branches, which should, *a priori*, be well informed and motivated to seek out customers who are prepared to accept and use the private ECU.

Each transaction involves a payer and a payee. The one may be 10 000 miles away from the other and in a city, country or even continent that is different from the one in which the persons who were involved in the previous transaction were located, some days previously. This is where the central institution comes in, performing the essential and politically very delicate task of relating operations which have no direct link between them and which are scattered around the globe, whence the need for centralisation of information, which makes it possible to set in motion a series of operations which are very close in time but separated physically by thousands of miles. The best instrument for spreading the use of the ECU will be the branch network of the member banks, involving institutions of different nationalities but with offices in every major city.

CENTRAL ECUs, THE 'COUNTERS' OF THE SYSTEM

The central ECUs issued by the central office constitute the key to the mechanism. They make it possible for imbalances in the member banks' positions *vis-à-vis* the central office to be rectified easily and quickly, along with the redistribution of foreign currency between surplus and deficit banks. It makes full use of the remarkable resources that the clearing mechanism gives banks, in terms of the ability to create bank payment money with a minimum of reserves (see p. 44).

Each bank's initial working capital in central ECUs will be made up of claims on the central office, in return for a debt of the same amount, also in central ECUs. The banks' operations in bank ECUs, in whatever financial centre, anywhere in the world, will be processed by a money transmission service company (such as SWIFT) and the results communicated to the central office's computer. The latter will thus be able not only to record the changing positions of each member bank but also to coordinate the commercial promotion work that needs to be done.

In addition to the Euromarket spread, the consortium will also enjoy seigniorage which, allowing for the cost of paying interest on deposits, should amount (with LIBOR at 7 per cent) to the figure calculated above, namely 3.5 per cent (on the ECUs created *ex novo*). The additional benefit of seigniorage, on top of the credit distribution margin, will put the members of the consortium in an especially favourable position compared with banks that operate in Eurodollars, as the latter are obliged to forgo the seigniorage (which is retained by the American banking system) on the dollars that they lend. The consortium will be able to take advantage of this situation and offer more favourable conditions to ECU borrowers, which ought to help the penetration of the private ECU in the Euromarket whilst still leaving substantial profits for the consortium members.

A system of this kind, consisting of a consortium of banks and a central office, will have, as compared with the present Eurodollar and Eurocurrency system, the following advantages:

(a) it will combine within one organisation the activities of creating money (like the US banking system) and making loans (like Eurobanks located outside the territory of the USA);
(b) it will not require any non-interest-bearing reserves;
(c) there will be no need to purchase bank notes from a central bank in order to cope with withdrawals.

That said, this market will not be ignored for much longer. Initiatives will start to accumulate as people begin to realise that the decline of the dollar has left the field wide open to any new currency which will not be subject to the changing economic policies of a particular country, as the dollar is.

The theoretical bases of this project will become familiar. Until very recently, the concept of a non-national currency reserved for use exclusively in international financial transactions was little understood in the world of banking, just as the Euromarket was 20 years ago. That will no longer be the case in the future and the new possibilities that will be offered by the creation of an *ex nihilo* payment currency will make the old unit of account ECU obsolete.

That is why the profits that are to be made in this enterprise will go to those who are the first to fill this market gap and who succeed in imposing their personal prestige on the extranational payment ECU by issuing it as a claim on themselves, ahead of any rivals.

When one stops to look for the reasons for the delay in introducing a genuine extranational transaction currency one cannot but conclude that they have nothing to do with the risks involved, or even with the need to arrive at a consensus of Community member states, which is not needed in this case. What has been lacking is the will to create something new; the problem has been timidity in the face of a monetary innovation for which there are no precedents.

Perhaps, too, there has been some doubt as to the 'quality' of this new currency, a scepticism regarding the probability that a unit such as the ECU, which from the strictly monetary point of view is of mediocre quality, will be able to penetrate the international market, where its use cannot be rendered obligatory. This will be the theme of Chapter 6. Before that, though, we shall look at some simulation model examples, which will show the reader our proposed system 'in action'.

COMMENT

Comment on page 38. An exporter in Bangkok has agreed to be paid in ECU. He also needs to be persuaded to keep his payment for several days in that form (or to pass it on to another customer of the same bank who will keep it in ECU). After that, a supplier in Le Havre will need to be persuaded, in turn, to agree to be paid by *his* Bangkok customer in the same currency. First of all, therefore, promotion and persuasion work must be carried out in Bangkok, then in Le Havre, and probably, moreover, by a different bank from the one that was involved in Bangkok. That is the commercial and political problem the conversion of the ECU into a payment currency poses, whence the need for the central institution to perform a coordinating role which goes well beyond its purely monetary responsibilities.

3 The Central Interbank Office: A Simulation

A payment currency, if it is to be launched and stand a chance of 'working', needs a 'system'. Systems do not develop spontaneously; they must be organised. The private ECU will be no exception to this rule: it will not be able to work without a system of its own, which will also have to be private and will need to be designed in the light of the lessons that may be learnt from the models that we have before our eyes, which have been analysed at some length in the previous pages.

The form of monetary organisation described in the previous chapter will be subjected to 'simulations' of its working procedures in a series of examples, accompanied by accounting tables and diagrams, starting with the pivot of the whole enterprise, which is the central office. Before going on, let us pause to recall what happened in the autumn of 1929, after the Wall Street Crash, when confidence in the banking system was rapidly eroded and the result was a major crisis. It was not until 1933 that the Federal government, acting through a newly created semi-government agency known as the FDIC, provided state guarantees to holders of bank deposits, up to a maximum of $10 000. A similar organisation was set up to insure savings bank depositors. Since then, the guarantee ceilings have been regularly increased, and relatively recently, when the seventh largest bank in the USA – Continental Illinois – got into trouble, the ceilings were removed altogether. The decision to abolish the ceilings, and thus offer unlimited guarantees in respect of deposits, some of which amounted to millions of dollars, was taken overnight, thus showing how vital is the role of bank money in the economy and how important the confidence upon which the edifice of bank money is based. It also reveals the responsibility attaching to a central body (which could also be private) for turning a claim on a single bank into a claim on an entire 'system', the *sine qua non*, along with a clearing house, for any payment currency.

In the extranational banking sector with which this project is concerned there is no central bank and no banking system. If a currency unit operating within this territory is only used as a unit of account it is nothing more than an aid to making calculations: it does not require a system. On the other hand, if that same unit is to become a transaction unit such a system *is* needed, for the simple reason that the word 'transaction' implies movement, movement from one bank to another; for the holder of the unit, it is a change of debtor, whilst for the bank it is a change of creditor. From this, various mutual responsibilities flow, and with them the need to transpose to the international level that indispensable component of a national banking system that is usually known as the 'clearing house'.

Such a transposition has been attempted in the case of the ECU by the 'ECU Banking Association'. Its clearing house, which used to be known as the 'Mutual ECU Settlement Accounts' and is now called Clearing-ECU, operates under the supervision of the Bank for International Settlements (BIS). The money transfer system SWIFT provides the member banks with a network within which to carry out settlement transfers. Final balances are worked out each day at the beginning of the afternoon and the debtor and creditor banks then attempt to match themselves up in pairs, those with negative final balances borrowing the amounts of component currencies that they need from the banks with positive final balances until, at the following day's session, the situation is reversed and the borrowings thus contracted are repaid.

The creation of this ECU clearing house is a welcome initiative, but the most important factors in the equation – a central bank and its central bank money – are still missing because the BIS has no such role. All it does is supervise the accounting operations. This international ECU clearing house has opened the door to a private transaction ECU, but only by a few inches. It could be opened much wider (see p. 57 for a detailed description of the clearing house).

The simulation set out below in Figure 3.1 shows how this mechanism would work. The banking procedures are identical for both present and future ECUs and the Eurostable, and the letter E stands for both units. The simulation first deals with the composition of the interbank office and the member banks of the consortium. It shows how, using a brand new currency unit with unrivalled powers of attraction, a group of banks could undertake to create, *ex nihilo*, a mass of means of payment which would be a source of seigniorage and profit from loans.

Chapter 4 gives an example of how the unit would work in the hands of banks' customers, bringing out the promotional role played by the central office with a view to lengthening or renewing the lives of the units of money thus created. Chapter 5 explains the relations that the consortium would maintain with non-member banks as well as the services that the consortium could provide for these same non-member banks, offering them a source of refinancing.

These simulation exercises help to reveal the problems that are to be encountered and to take the full measure of the financial effort that is required to launch the project, an effort which is negligible when compared with the profits that the member banks stand to make.

A DAY IN THE LIFE OF THE CENTRAL OFFICE AND THREE MEMBER BANKS OF THE CONSORTIUM

The central ECUs or Eurostables (represented by E in the following paragraphs) are created as claims on itself by the central office and then immediately lent to the member banks A, B and C, the procedure being identical to what it would be between the member banks and central bank of a national monetary system.

Central office	A	B	C
300 ⎮ 300	100 ⎮ 100	100 ⎮ 100	100 ⎮ 100

One and the same sum thus represents central Es in both the central office's books and those of the banks, as an asset and a debt.

The central office obtains a reserve of foreign currency, by borrowing (100*d*), and this will be used to satisfy requests by holders of E deposits for conversion into currency. It must be expected that, initially, a number of operators and borrowers will prefer national currencies as means of payment and will ask for their loan or deposit in E to be converted into a national currency.

The member banks will carry out all the usual banking transactions in E, such as opening lines of credit, buying and selling national currencies, carrying out transfers from one bank to another on behalf of customers and refinancing non-member banks, and so on.

The bank Es will be created by the member banks in the form of claims on themselves. The deposits thus created will be payment money within the consortium: customer transfers will be initiated by transfers to the accounts in central Es that each member bank has with the central office. The example in Table 3.1 describes one day's business.

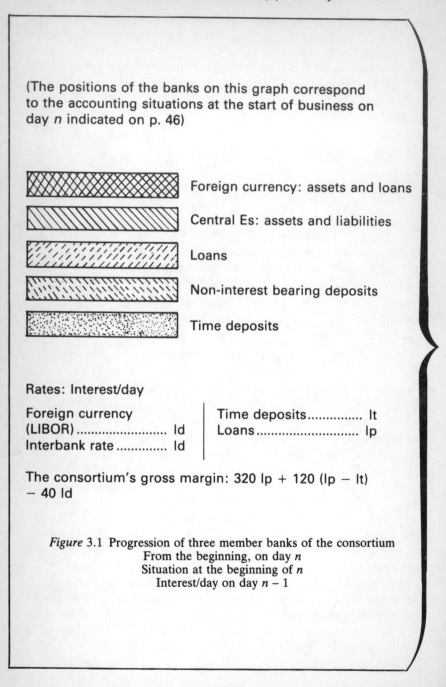

(The positions of the banks on this graph correspond to the accounting situations at the start of business on day *n* indicated on p. 46)

Foreign currency: assets and loans

Central Es: assets and liabilities

Loans

Non-interest bearing deposits

Time deposits

Rates: Interest/day

Foreign currency (LIBOR) .... Id
Interbank rate .... Id

Time deposits............... It
Loans............................ Ip

The consortium's gross margin: 320 Ip + 120 (Ip − It) − 40 Id

Figure 3.1 Progression of three member banks of the consortium
From the beginning, on day *n*
Situation at the beginning of *n*
Interest/day on day *n* − 1

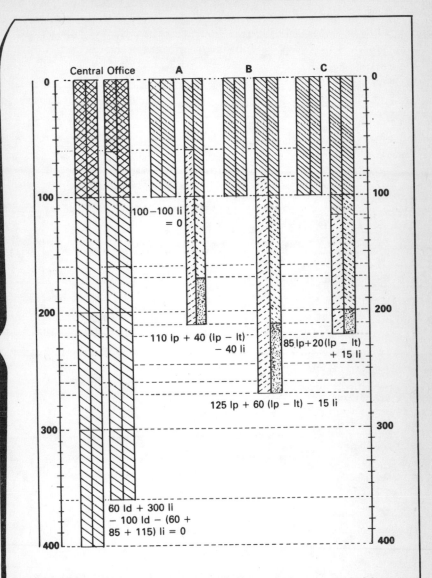

This diagram shows how the consortium would progress and how a stock of money (demand deposits) could be created at minimum cost to the banks.

Table 3.1 Schematic representation of one day's business involving the central office and three member banks of the consortium

Central office

E = ECU or ES

d = national currency ($1E = 1d$)

	National currency		*Central Es*	
Reserve	100	100 (borrowed)	Building of reserves (100 to A, 100 to B, 100 to C)	300	300
Total previous sales to A, B and C	− 40			
Balance of sales by and to A, B and C: 8 − 6 − 5 =	− 3		Counterpart of nat. curr. sold to A, B and C	− 40 −3
			Token entry: Balance of A, B and C's transfers − 5 + 4 + 1 = 0	
	57	100		300	257
		357	357		

Consortium

Customers		A		B		C
Situation:	150	110	185	170	105	120
Loans made	5	5	15	15		
Loans repaid	− 8				− 6	− 6
Movements in nat. curr.						
customers	+ 8d		− 6d	− 6E	+ 3d	− 8 + 3E
central off.	− 8d		+ 6d	− 8	+ 5d	
Transferred to customers of B		− 10 to customers of A		− 8 to customers of A		− 9
C		− 12 of C		− 5 of B		− 7
Received from		from customers		from customers		
customers of B		+ 8 of A		+ 10 of A		+ 12
C		+ 9 of C		+ 7 of B		+ 5
	147	110	200	183	99	110

Central Es

Situation	60	100	85	100	115	100
Counterpart of movements of nat. curr.	+ 8		– 6		– 5	
Transfer to						
B	– 10	to A + 8		to A – 9		
C	– 12	to C – 5		to B – 7		
Received from						
B	+ 8	from A + 10		from A + 12		
C	+ 9	from C + 7		from B + 5		
	63	100	83	100	111	100
	210	210	283	283	210	210

Notes

A: Granting of a loan of 5. Reimbursement of a loan of 6, in national currency, which A sells to the central office in return for central Es.

Received on behalf of customers: 17

22 transferred by credit and debit in central Es

B: Granting of a loan of 15. Sale to customers of 6 in national currency, which B obtains from the central office.

Received from A and C: 13

Transferred: 17

C: Reimbursement of a loan of 6 in E and destruction of 6E by C.

Conversion of 8E into national currency by customer

Deposit of 3 in national currency in return for E

Sale to C of 8 – 3 = 5 in national currency by the central office, which debits C's account in central E

Received 17 and transferred 16 for customers

Banks A, B and C have returned their E accounts to balance and no longer hold any national currency. (The banks' positions are as represented on page 45.)

At the start of the day's business, before the books are opened, outstanding credits in bank Es amount to 150, 185 and 105, respectively, for A, B and C, making a total of 440 bank Es, compared with E liabilities of 110, 170 and 120, making a total of 400. The difference of 40 E is accounted for by the national currency (d; $1d = 1E$) paid out to customers who have asked for conversion.

The member banks hold or rather pass on to the central office any national currency that they receive and they turn to it for any national currency needs that crop up in the course of daily business.

Now the day's operations are entered in the records. The traditional accounting methods have been replaced by a condensed procedure which saves space and is easier to follow (see p. 46).

A makes a loan of 5 and receives reimbursement in national currency of 8 from a borrower. It sells the currency to the central office and is credited with the corresponding amount in central Es. A then transfers 10 bank E to B on behalf of one customer and 12E to C on behalf of another one, its account at the central office being debited accordingly and the corresponding amounts being credited to B's and C's accounts in central Es. A receives 8 and 9 from B and C in the same way.

At the end of the day's business, credits to A's account amount to 147 whilst its E obligations come to 110. Its central E assets have increased from 60 to 63, as compared with the starting figure of 100; hence a final negative balance of 37.

B makes a loan of 15 and converts a deposit of 6E into national currency, which it obtains from the central office by a corresponding debit to its central E account. It receives 17 from A and C and transfers $8 + 5 = 13$ on behalf of its customers.

C receives reimbursement of a loan in E equal to 6. It also receives a deposit in national currency equal to $3d$ from a depositor whose E account it credits with 3E. It then converts 8E into national currency, whence a national currency shortfall of $8 - 3 = 5$, which it covers by purchase from the central office. At the end of the day its central E assets have fallen from 115 to 111.

When the books are closed, the central office's national currency reserves have increased to 57 whilst it has contracted borrowings amounting to 100, thus resulting in a deficit which is balanced out by the corresponding central E amount of 43 (representing a debt for the central office) which was debited to A, B and C's accounts.

Initially the member banks borrowed 300E from the office compared with a claim for the same amount on the office. At the end of the day, their debt of 300E towards the office has not changed but their joint claim has decreased to 257; hence the interest that they have to pay to the office at the interbank rate on 43E, which makes up for the latter's own interest charges on its national currency deficit (100 − 57 = 43).

Thanks to this mechanism, therefore, the gross credit distribution margin (interest received from borrowers) may be broken down into the distribution margin (which accrues to the lending institution) and the seigniorage, which is received by the bank where the money that has been created is deposited (for example, the 10 and 12 transferred by A and B to C). In the case of B, transfers for customers resulted in a positive balance of 10 + 7 − 8 − 5 = 4. This balance is to be found as a credit to B's account in central Es and thus receives interest at the interbank rate which is debited to the accounts of the other banks.

At the same time, its central E account is debited by 6E, the counterpart of the national currency purchased by B for the conversion of a deposit of 6E. This conversion has no effect on B's assets. The difference between the interest received by B and the interest which it pays to the central office at the interbank rate on the 6 central Es represents the credit distribution margin.

The central office receives interest, supposedly at the same rate, on its national currency assets and on the E counterpart of the national currency that it has sold. It is therefore able to balance its debtor and creditor accounts (creditor in the case of the 57 national currency balance and the 43E, and debtor in the case of the 100 of national currency which it has borrowed).

The example on pp. 46–7 shows how the central office is able to even out national currency requirements between the member banks, how it helps them to balance their positions in E, how (thanks to the mechanism of interest payments at the interbank rate) it distributes the distribution margin and seigniorage, and, finally, how it provides a source of constant information on each member's liabilities *vis-à-vis* the member banks of the consortium as a whole (40 and 15 respectively for A and B and a credit of 15 for C).

Unlike the situation in a national banking system, there are no leaks out of the system for conversions of deposits into bank notes and there is no loss of interest as a result of non-interest-bearing compulsory reserves. In addition, the mechanism also makes it possible for the central office to perform a commercial, coordinating role which is necessary if E deposits are to move from account to account and acquire the transaction function, which is the fundamental aim of this project (see examples in the following chapter).

4 The Consortium: A Simulation

The simulation that is the subject of this chapter deals with the 'commercial operations' carried out by the member banks in conjunction with the central office, such as purchases of national currency, loans, transfers from one bank to another, sales of national currency to the central office, conversions of E into national currency, deposit accounts, loan repayments and so on. A tabular representation of the transactions is given in Figure 4.1.

The object of the exercise is to show how customers would be found for the new currency throughout the world, and the role that would be played in this search by the member bank branches and the central office as the centralising body. Customer (1) of member bank A is asked by a supplier, (2), to settle his account in E. This supplier will have been approached beforehand by one of A's or B's branches. (1) obtains the sum in E that he needs to pay (2) by borrowing 40E from A and selling 60d to A, in return for which he receives, at the 1d = 1E exchange rate, 60E. If (2) is not a customer of one of the member banks, he opens an account in E or asks his bank to do it for him.

Customer (1) transfers 100E (bank Es) to (2)'s account at member bank B. (2) in turn uses the 100E to pay (3) at bank C. (3) was approached by the consortium's commercial department well before (2) was paid. The local branches of A, B and C had already enquired which of (2)'s creditors he would have to pay. Of those, the ones who seemed most likely to accept, or even prefer, payment in E have been approached by the commercial department and their willingness sounded out.

After the E created by A have remained on deposit with B for a short while, the operation is repeated until the E arrive in (4)'s account at member bank D, n days after being created by A and transferred to B. The journey is over because (4) soon makes use of the 100E which have been received on his behalf by D, converting 70 into national currency and putting 30 into a one-month deposit account.

The 100E will by then have effected three transactions, from A to B, from B to C and from C to D, in n days. The transaction velocity

50

was thus $\frac{n}{3}$ (the M1 velocity in France is 6–7 days for individuals and 3 days for companies).

One month after opening his 30E deposit account, (4) withdraws his asset and converts it into national currency. When his loan falls due for repayment (after two months), (1) repays A in national currency.

In order to draw up the profit and loss account for the operation we shall divide it into two stages, according to the two ways in which the 100E were issued: by a loan, first of all, of 40E, and then by the purchase of 60d from (1) by A, which were paid for with 60E.

Each time E were created *ex nihilo*, even if, as a counterpart, there is a claim of 40E on (1) or a quantity of national currency corresponding to the 60E. This is the traditional process of creation of bank money, by making a loan or purchasing foreign currency.

The operation comes to its completion when (1) repays the loan that A made to him in E using national currency (or, even better, when he repays A in E which he has obtained from a different source but which cannot be anything other than claims on the consortium). A then sells the national currency to the central office, which credits A's account and reconstitutes its national currency reserves.

A further 60E have been created by A as a result of the purchase of 60 in national currency from (1), paid for in Es. The representation in accounting terms is similar: A credits (1)'s account with 60E and transfers the 60d to the central office, which credits A's account and then simultaneously debits it by the same amount when (1) makes a transfer to (2)'s account at B. A does not receive any distribution margin. The seigniorage is represented by the return on the 60d and is distributed between B, C and D.

Once the sum of E has reached (4)'s account at D, some of it stays there because (4) has opened a one-month deposit account into which he pays 30E: these 30E then lose the transaction function.

The interest received by D as long as the E stand to its credit in the books of the central institution represents the seigniorage to the full amount up to the moment (4) opens his deposit account; this seigniorage is then reduced by the amount of the interest paid to (4) by D on the balance of his account.

The operation is completed and the E held on account with D are destroyed when the deposit account in (4)'s name is closed and the deposit paid out in national currency, after which A is repaid, also in national currency, by (1). The central office's national currency account would look like Table 4.1.

	A			**Central office** **Central *d* and E**		
Reserves in central ES	100	100	Reserves (A)		100	100
Borrowing and sale of *d* by customer (1)	+ 40 (claim) + 60*d*	40(1) 60(1)	Sale of *d* by A	60*d*	60	
			Transfer from A to (2)'s account at B			−100
Sale of *d* to central office	− 60*d* + 60E		Reserves (D)		100	100
Transfer to (2)'s account at B	−100	−100(1)	Transfer by debiting C			+100
Reimbursement by (1) in *d*	+ 40*d* − 40E (claim)		Sale of national currency to D		− 30*d*	− 30
Sale by A to central office	− 40*d* + 40E		Sale of national currency to D		− 70*d*	− 70
			Sale of national currency by A		− 40*d*	+ 40
	100	100			200	200

	D	
Reserves	100	100
Transfer to (4)'s account	+100	100(4)
Sale of national currency by central office to D	+ 30*d* − 30E	
Withdrawal of national currency by (4)		− 30E(4) − 30*d*
Term deposit by (4)		− 70 + 70
Sale of national currency by central office	− 70 + 70	
Closure of account	− 70*d*	− 70
	100	100

Notes

Customer (1) borrows 40E from A and sells it 60*d* in national currency, in return for 60E, after which (1) pays (2) by a transfer of 100.

(2) transfers 100*d* to (3)'s account at C, which transfers the sum to (4)'s account at D.

(4) withdraws 30E in national currency and places 70 in a *d* term deposit; subsequently the account is closed.

(1) repays the 40E borrowed from A in national currency.

Figure 4.1 The consortium's commercial operations

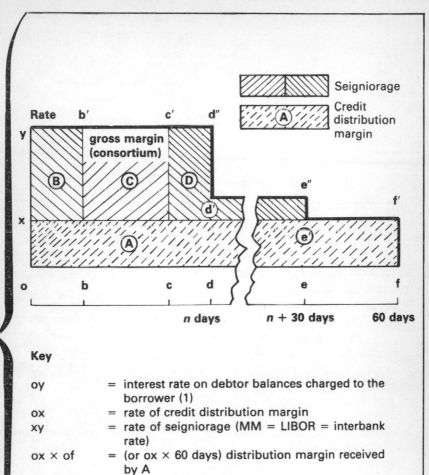

Key

oy	=	interest rate on debtor balances charged to the borrower (1)
ox	=	rate of credit distribution margin
xy	=	rate of seigniorage (MM = LIBOR = interbank rate)
ox × of	=	(or ox × 60 days) distribution margin received by A
xy × ob	=	seigniorage received by B
xy × bc	=	seigniorage received by C
xy × cd	=	seigniorage received by D
d″d′ × de	=	*prélèvement* on the return on assets for the conversion of 30E into national currency and creditor interest paid on 70E in a term account
e″e′ × ef	=	additional *prélèvement* on return on assets for the reimbursement of 70E term deposit
oyff′ polygon:		the consortium's gross margin.

Table 4.1 An example of the central office's national currency account

Time (in days)	Movement	Balance	
O	+ 60	+ 60	Purchase by A and transfer to the central office
n	− 70	− 10	Transfer by the central office to D to cover conversion by (4) of 70E deposit
n + 30	− 30	− 40	Transfer by the central office to D to cover the withdrawal by (4) of his deposit
60	+ 40	0	Reimbursement by (1) to A of 40E loans

Outflows of national currency from the central office's reserves could be reduced, or even eliminated, by reducing the maturities of loans or deposit accounts, but at the price of a reduction in the credit distribution margin.

As all attempts are made to limit n to the minimum (because the seigniorage is reduced by the amount that has to be paid in interest on stagnant deposits), the account is in overall deficit in terms of national currency. It would probably show a creditor balance in Eurostable after a certain time because customers would sell their national currency to the central office in order to acquire stable deposits. In that case, at all events, the interest burden for the central office on national currency borrowings would be compensated for by what banks A, B, C and D would pay to it at the interbank rate out of the interest received by them from their borrowing customers.

The example given above demonstrates the role that the central institution would play in circulating the Es from account to account, 'effecting transactions', and doing so rapidly, because increasing the circulation velocity is the only way for the bank at which the deposit is placed to reduce the proportion of the seigniorage that it loses as a result of having to pay interest on deposits.

The example also shows how, thanks to the centralisation of accounts and its equalising role, the central office is able to make up for the handicap that the short-lived nature of each creation of money represents, by facilitating the repetition of the sort of operation that was described above so as to create a mass of M1 money.

As was pointed out on p. 38, 'each transaction involves a payer and a payee. The one may be 10 000 miles away from the other and in a city, country or even continent that is different from the one in which the persons involved in the previous transactions, some days previously, were located. This is where the central office comes in, performing the essential task of relating operations which have no direct link between them and which are scattered around the globe'.

COMMENT

Comment on page 51. In order to see how interest paid on bank loans is distributed between seigniorage and the credit distribution margin, we must follow the progress of the 40 central E which were included in the 100 central E that were transferred to A, B, C and D and accompanied the 40 bank E created as a result of the loan by A to (1). The interest on creditor or debtor balances (at the interbank rate) on the accounts of A, B, C and D at the central office, which are established each day, has the effect of breaking down the interest received by A from its customer (1) into the seigniorage accruing to each bank at the interbank rate and the credit distribution margin which A retains on the 40E.

The 60*d* received by A from (1), in return for which A created 60E, also generated seigniorage at the interbank rate, and this is kept in its entirety by the bank provided that the corresponding deposits are not interest-bearing.

The seigniorage is represented by the interest earned when the central office invests the 60*d* which A received from (1) and which were transferred (this interest is supposedly paid at the same rate as the interbank rate). This interest income is distributed between A, B, C and D through the mechanism of the creditor or debtor interest on the balances of their central E accounts with the central office, which are established each day.

The net seigniorage is higher in proportion as the interest rate on the deposits corresponding to the 60E is low, which implies a high velocity of circulation. That, in turn, shows the importance of the role of accounting and commercial centralisation played by the central office, and the equal importance of the SWIFT money transmission network.

5 Banks Outside the Consortium: A Simulation

This simulation applies more particularly to the ES (stable ECU or Eurostable). It presupposes, in fact, that the consortium will gradually have replaced its old ECU customers with ES customers. It will retain the exclusive right to issue transaction ES for a long time, which will have an effect on its relations with outside banks. This is true of the following example.

By this stage the consortium and its central interbank office would constitute, to use the correct term, a 'monetary system' comparable to a national system, in which the central office would correspond to the central bank and the member banks would represent the commercial banks of a national system.

Outside the consortium there would be other banks which would have a similar role to Eurobanks in respect of the dollar. There would thus be a complete, 'world-wide' monetary and banking system for the ES, faithfully mirroring the system of domestic and external dollars.

There is a difference, however: the central money (central ES) issued by the central office is for the use of the member banks only. It would not circulate outside the consortium. The central office would not issue any bank notes, still the very symbol for many people of payment money. Nor would it make any loans, except to the member banks, and within strictly defined limits. It is the emanation of the member banks and the physical expression of their joint and several responsibility. That is why each member bank's liabilities towards the central office would be constantly determined.

When the point is reached where a central Community institution has been set up (Stage 3), this restriction on the institution's ability to make loans ought to dispel any fears of laxity. Excessively generous and imprudent loans, either to member states of the Community or to indigent Third World countries, would not be allowed. There is no reason why the role of issuer and manager of the central stock of money should be combined with that of lender to governments or large companies. In this system these two roles would be kept distinct. On the other hand, the central institution has one function that it does not share with conventional central banks: the specifically commercial function of coordinating the consortium and building up the customer base.

To continue this parallel with a national system, the member banks of the consortium in an ES system would make loans, issue bank money and clear their mutual claims, just as in a national system.

A LOOK AT AN ECU CLEARING ORGANISATION

Any discussion of the relations between the consortium and outside banks that use the ECU needs to look at the role of the MESA (the private ECU clearing house) separately, because of the role played by this institution in the development of the ECU as a transaction currency (see p. 42). For this purpose, we need to clarify some of the points that were made on p. 42 and complete them with an analysis of how it operates.

The clearing mechanism used for the private ECU differs from the mechanism used in a national banking system (see p. 205) in the sense that there is no central bank in the private ECU system, and therefore no central ECU, consisting of claims on a central bank, to be used as the settlement currency.

In order to 'relate' the private ECU clearing system to the sort that we are familiar with in national systems and at the same time grasp both the problems that it raises and the opportunities it offers the consortium, the best approach is to imagine that there is a 'centraliser' present in the system (a short-lived one, as we shall see).

A member bank of the MESA creates ECUs in the form of claims on itself in return for a purchase of national currency or a loan. The process of creation is identical to the one described on p. 43. At the same time, the bank sets up a reserve of ECU component currencies, just as a Eurobank does when, before crediting its customer's account, it borrows the US dollars (claims on banks in the United States) that it needs for the purpose. These dollars will then move from bank to bank in the United States, as the customer to whom the loan was granted disposes of the funds that have been made available to him.

The whole purpose of a clearing system, however, is to reduce transfers of component currencies, which would be the ECU equivalent of the movements of US dollars, to a minimum or to eliminate them altogether. For this purpose, before the start of the clearing session, the centraliser would redeem all the claims by issuing bank

ECUs in the form of claims on itself, which would be as imaginary as it is but which serve our purpose. The clearing would then be carried out as in a national system, these imaginary claims on the centraliser acting as the settlement currency.

At the end of the session there will be creditor banks and debtor banks (in imaginary central ECUs). This is the point at which the parallel with a national system breaks down, since the final balances cannot be settled, for lack of a settlement currency that is *not* imaginary. But the centraliser knows that the total of all the positive final balances is equal, down to the last cent, to the total of all the negative final balances. Before leaving the clearing session, there-fore, the centraliser addresses the representatives of the member banks in the following terms: 'I cannot settle my debts, but the amount owed to me by you jointly is exactly equal to what I owe to all of you together. Sort it out between you.' And that is what the banks proceed to do, pairing themselves off so that the debtor banks can credit the accounts that the creditor banks have in the books of the debtor banks.

It will by now be obvious that if clearing by the MESA is to be effective certain conditions need to be laid down: there must be mutual accounts between banks and balances which cancel out after a time; until that happens there must be provision for overnight inter-bank loans until the unbalanced accounts are settled at the next session; failing that, there must ultimately be settlement in compo-nent currencies. The system in fact works because the number of banks that are really active in the market is small (there are no more than 15), and their business is not excessively divergent.

A PARALLEL BETWEEN AN ES-BASED SYSTEM AND THE EURODOLLAR SYSTEM

Banks outside the consortium operating in ES are in the same position, *vis-à-vis* the member banks, as Eurodollar banks *vis-à-vis* the American banking system.

These external banks would obtain their ES funds in the form of bank ES (for a sale or loan) by making deposits or contracting loans, just as a Eurodollar bank obtains funds by making deposits or contracting loans in US dollars (claims on a bank domiciled in the United States).

A Eurodollar bank carries out a transfer order by instructing an

American bank at which it has an account to transfer the sum in question to an account at another American bank. In the same way, an external bank which receives a transfer order in ES makes a transfer from the consortium member bank at which it has an account to another member bank.

Just as there are Eurodollars – which are not payment dollars but 'rights' to payment dollars (claims on the American banking system) – so there will be 'Euro-ES', which will not be payment ES but rights to payment ES (the precept according to which a 'right' to money should not be confused with money itself is explained on p. 26).

In our system, 'final' payment ES are claims denominated in ES on a member bank of the consortium. This is the sense in which the ES consortium – which will be a private organisation – will be able to claim a privileged position even after the ES has been officially recognised as the Community currency and a central institution responsible for issuing central ES has been set up.

This examination of how the Eurodollar market, which is based in London and uses dollars deposited in banks located in the United States, actually works justifies an extrapolation respecting the ES. One *de facto* priority – the advantages that the consortium would offer outside banks, throughout the globe (for refinancing and conversion) – ought to help it to retain its prior rights on the ES and combine the profits earned from Euromarket activities by Eurodollar banks in London (the spread) with the profit that American banks make from monetary creation (seigniorage).

The number of external banks is very large. Transactions in ES, even if only occasional and limited to a few banks within a country, will very soon constitute a considerable volume. When that happens, the member banks of the consortium will enjoy all the benefits of the mechanism that has been created, especially the advantages of the clearing of mutual claims between banks. The visit to the New York Clearing House described on p. 31 gives some idea of this.

This discussion of how the consortium and outside banks will interact gives a good idea of the wealth of possibilities that this project offers for those who are prepared to take the initiative and launch it before anyone else does.

6 From the ECU to the ES

For anyone who proposes to launch a new product on the market, the quality of that product, in comparison with the products it will be competing with, is a matter of the first importance. This is a question that the promoters of the private ECU will also have to address.

The advantage of the ECU is that it is a composite currency and as such spreads the risk of currency depreciation, as well as the exchange risks. These risks, however, are not completely eliminated, and in the end, although it is superior to the weakest of its component currencies, the ECU is not as good as the strongest. More particularly, it comes far behind the Deutschemark in any quality ranking and the Deutschemark accounts for only a third of the ECU, the rest of the basket being made up of ten other currencies, of which the most recent is the peseta (the escudo has not yet been included).

Even if the ECU were as good as the Deutschemark, it would still not be any less subject than the Deutschemark itself to uncertainty of value in real terms over time, something from which no national currency is exempt. In addition to that, there is also a defect that is due to its very definition and which means that it will always be a mediocre reference and intervention unit: the risk of mathematical incongruence.

To define a currency in terms of its equivalence to the value of a weighted average of other currencies which themselves are defined by reference to that same average is acceptable for one specific purpose, namely calculating reciprocal exchange parities within a system such as the EMS. But a currency that aims to circulate and become a payment and reserve currency for trade between countries, and not merely the countries of the European Community, cannot be properly defined in such a way.

We need to aim higher and take advantage of the fact of having to create something new by creating the best thing possible: it is preferable to create something that is better than what one already has, even if that means starting from scratch. Money is used for making payments. It is also an instrument of measurement and it is perhaps the most important of all such instruments because it is the common denominator by which we measure value. Looked at from this point of view, the ECU does not represent any kind of progress: this observation and this reflection justify a recapitulation in these pages of the studies and proposals that have been made in the past in connection with the Eurostable.

How indeed when, for the first time in history, the undeniable need to create a new currency for use in transactions between nations that is not the national currency of any of them has at last been recognised; when a new kind of *numéraire* which is full of promise has been discovered in the form of a composite currency; when there is a call for a stable unit of value which will constitute a standard of measurement worthy of the name, one which will have a fixed value, independent of time and place; how, then, in these circumstances, can one help but go back to the remarkable property which is peculiar to a composite currency that is reserved for international transactions only, namely the fact that it can be defined in such a way as to retain its value in real terms?

The point is that if a given currency is used exclusively as a third currency between two national currencies it is protected from the effects of the relationship between consumption and final production, which is what decides the value of money as means of exchange. If that value is defined by the right kind of formula, the currency unit can acquire stability of value in terms of its purchasing power, something that no currency has ever really had before, much less in recent times, notwithstanding that such a property is the *sine qua non* for any currency that aims to carry out correctly the three functions that have been required of money at all epochs: standard of measurement, store of value and medium of exchange.

Although it is true that the time is not yet ripe for too radical an innovation and that the enterprise proposed in these pages must take as its basis the ECU as it has been defined by the European Community (so as to have the benefit of the progress that has already been achieved with the ECU used as a unit of account), it is equally true that the consortium must also observe the golden rule that applies to all manufacturers of new products. That rule is that they must aim to produce a better product than comparable ones already available on the market and they must be ready to launch it when the time is right. The ES justifies this kind of approach because the progress that will thereby have been achieved and the commercial 'attractiveness' of a currency unit with stable value are so great.

International trade needs a payment money which is less volatile and less encumbered with risk than the currencies at present available on the market. The existence of this need is the reason why traders and bankers have taken what was available, within easy reach, something that was definitely not the carefully-thought-out tool for a purpose which is quite different from the question of regulating reciprocal parities within a monetary system.

At the beginning of 1988, the French Finance Minister, Mr E. Balladur, said that he had asked his staff to devise for him a 'new-look' ECU. Later in the year, Dr K.O. Poehl, Governor of the Bundesbank and a dominant figure on the European monetary scene, spoke of his doubts regarding the ECU in an article in the *Frankfurter Allgemeine Zeitung* (27 June 1988):

The free movement of capital and unrestricted convertibility of European currencies, one into the other, are the essential preconditions for a single internal market. The other decisive criterion of monetary unity is the establishment of fixed and irreversible exchange rates. The Werner Plan of 1970 contained the following definition of monetary union, which is still valid today: monetary union presupposes, within the Community, eliminating exchange rate fluctuation margins, irrevocably fixed exchange rates and the complete liberation of capital flows . . .

Currencies must be accepted by the market. A parallel currency (the ECU) will not help us to avoid taking the essential political decisions that will have to be taken if a monetary union is to be created. It is not very realistic to think that a parallel currency can be imposed by the expression of an official preference for it over national currencies. The market decides whether a currency is acceptable in the light of interest rates and exchange rates. Attempts to sidestep the market by means of administrative measures will have scant success, as the recent history of the private and official ECUs has shown: they are losing their attraction now that restrictions on free movement of capital are being lifted, exchange controls and convertibility restrictions are being abolished and exchange rates are more stable.

Introducing the ECU as a parallel currency – or even just as a currency – raises difficulties, in particular because of the particular way that it is made up. A basket-based ECU, as a weighted average of national currencies, would not be likely to have enough of a 'crowding out' effect.

A parallel European currency ought to be of a level *at least* equal to the best of the national currencies. Failing that, the central banks of the Member States would be obliged to support it in the market with unlimited purchases so as to maintain its parity. An obligation to intervene in this way would have considerable monetary consequences; in the end, it would come down to constant creation of stronger currencies in order to pay for purchases of the European currency.

A strategy based on a parallel currency presupposes that such a currency would have the effect of 'crowding out' the other currencies available on the market. The necessary balanced replacement by the parallel currency of all the Community's national currencies (including the DM) will only happen if the parallel currency is able, bearing in mind exchange and interest rate developments, to compete as an investment currency with even the strongest Community currencies.

This quotation deserves to be read and re-read, and first and foremost by the promoters of any European currency.

The problem that is posed by the creation of a new currency unit is one of *selling*. Success depends on being able to penetrate one's market. The ECU is not different in this respect from many other goods that are offered on the market. The problem is not one of investment, manufacture or transport, but of attracting the customer's interest. Selling is the principal concern, and not just in the case of car manufacturers and washing powder producers. Politicians, writers and film producers also have to sell their wares, and so will the promoter of a parallel European currency.

This will also be, and must be, the concern of all those who desire the monetary unification of Europe, and a unification other than one that is centred on the Deutschemark, Germany and the Bundesbank.

As Dr Poehl reminds us, it is not possible to oblige people to use a payment currency, still less so outside their national frontiers, far from the reach of the monetary authorities. Against the wishes of many Germans, and certainly against Dr Poehl's, the European currency *will* be the Deutschemark if the Community does not make available to states, governments, importers, exporters and all those who buy, sell and make payments internationally a currency unit which has properties that no other currency has. Only on this condition will the Community currency have any chance of competing with the world's main currencies.

This is what will establish a stable *numéraire* which, thanks to its constant value, will achieve exceptional powers of market penetration because it will be immunised against that universal sickness of currencies which has reduced the value of the US dollar by 95 per cent in the space of 50 years, which has left the franc with only one-half of a thousandth of its value 75 years ago and has reduced the German currency to zero twice this century, in the space of 25 years.

IN ORDER TO UNDERSTAND A COMPOSITE CURRENCY: ADDING UP PURCHASING POWERS

The term 'ECU' has entered the language. The word has a familiar ring. On their economics and financial news pages, the newspapers publish the latest exchange rates of the ECU into other currencies. There are regular issues of bonds denominated in ECUs. Investors know that the ECU includes the Deutschemark in its definition and that knowledge reassures them. On the television, commentators speak easily of the ECU as the European currency, and politicians cite it as a proof that Europe is moving towards unification. One minister has said that one day there will be ECU notes in circulation.

In contrast to this, the expression 'composite currency' is less common. It is confined to the language of monetary experts, just like the IMF's SDR. People know that it is a new type of currency, a sort of aggregate; one that, like the SDR, brings together various components that are by their nature heterogeneous, different from each other.

However well accepted these terms are, though, they do not evoke a precise image in people's minds. Behind the words there is usually nothing more than a vague or even mistaken notion. The significance is not properly perceived, much less the substance.

The ES is, like the present ECU, a composite currency. Only when the ECU has been understood will the ES also be understood. How, in fact, can one transpose something that is vague? How can one define something on the basis of something else that is indeterminate? How can the transition from the ECU to the ES be effected when the ECU is not properly understood or, which is worse, when the image it conjures up is the mistaken one of a 'basket in which currencies are mixed up'?

Europe needs a currency which will be accepted as it is, because it is better than any other. The ES satisfies this requirement, but it will never be accepted until it is understood, and it will never be understood until it has first been stripped of its abstraction. Let us try to strip some away now.

A composite currency, U, is defined on the basis of quantities of component currencies A, B and C (three only in the interest of simplifying the demonstration, but it is equally true of any number of components). The value of U – its purchasing power – results from the sum of the purchasing powers of the quantities of A, B and C, represented here by m_A, m_B and m_C.

In order to calculate the value of U, we must add up the values of each of the quantities of the component currencies m_A, m_B and m_C. For this purpose, we must use a common denominator. The equivalence of what can be purchased by U on the one hand, and m_A, m_B and m_C on the other can only be established by using a common unit in which the purchases are paid for.

That common denominator may, for example, be a national currency, X. We can say that the quantity of X that one U can buy – that is, $t\dfrac{X}{U}$ (the rate of exchange of U into X) – is equal to the total of the sums of X that are obtained by converting each quantity of component currency into X.

The m_A quantity of X (the sum of X which m_A can buy) is $m_A \cdot t\dfrac{X}{A}$ ($t\dfrac{X}{A}$: rate of exchange of A into X, or the quantity of X for a unit of A).

The amount of X which m_B can buy is $m_B \cdot t\dfrac{X}{B}$ ($t\dfrac{X}{B}$: rate of exhange of B into X, or amount of X for one unit of B), and so on.

The amount of X which one U can buy – that is $t\dfrac{X}{U}$ (the rate of exchange of U into X) – is thus equal to the total of the amounts of X obtained by converting m_A, m_B and m_C into their equivalence in terms of X:

$$t\frac{X}{U} = m_A\, t\frac{X}{A} + m_B\, t\frac{X}{B} + m_C\, t\frac{X}{C}$$

It is also possible to take U as the common denominator. One unit of U is equal in value to the sum of the three fractions that make up U, each being equal to the expression in terms of U of m_A, m_B and m_C.

If $t\dfrac{U}{A}$ and $t\dfrac{U}{B}$ and $t\dfrac{U}{C}$ are the exchange rates of A into U (the amount of U that equals one A), B into U and C into U,

$$\text{One } U = 1 = m_A\, t\frac{U}{A} + m_B\, t\frac{U}{B} + m_C\, t\frac{U}{C} \qquad (6.1)$$

It is convenient to define U in terms of a component currency, A for example: the value of one U in terms of A (that is, $t\dfrac{A}{U}$) is equal to the sum of the values of m_A, m_B and m_C (the components of one U) in which m_B and m_C are converted into A using their exchange rates into A; that is, $t\dfrac{A}{B}$ and $t\dfrac{A}{C}$

$$t\frac{A}{U} = m_A + m_B\, t\frac{A}{B} + m_C\, t\frac{A}{C}$$

$$\text{or} \quad t\frac{B}{U} = m_A\, t\frac{B}{A} + m_B + m_C\, t\frac{B}{C} \tag{6.2}$$

The same formulae can be arrived at by starting from the definition of U in its role as an indicator, as the weighted average of a number of exchange rates. Let there be a national currency, X. The exchange rate of U into X is the weighted average of the market rates of exchange of U's component currencies, A, B and C, into X:

$$t\frac{X}{U} = m_A\, t\frac{X}{A} + m_B\, t\frac{X}{B} + m_C\, t\frac{X}{C} \tag{6.3}$$

If we multiply the two sides of the equation by $t\dfrac{U}{X}$ and replace $t\dfrac{X}{A} \cdot t\dfrac{U}{X}$ by its equivalent, $t\dfrac{U}{X}$ (doing the same thing with B and C), we come back to the basic formula for U. In this way we can establish the correspondence between U, the payment currency, and U, the position indicator on the exchange markets.

Before going any further, any readers who are not familiar with composite currencies should carry out some experiments with formulae (6.1) and (6.2): in (6.1), for example, $t\dfrac{U}{B}$ and $t\dfrac{U}{C}$ could be replaced by their equivalents, that is $t\dfrac{U}{A} \cdot t\dfrac{A}{B}$ and $t\dfrac{U}{A} \cdot t\dfrac{A}{C}$. On that basis, we then come back to formula (6.2).

In the case of the ECU, m_A, m_B and m_C are fixed in nominal terms. In terms of value (and it is in terms of value – that is, purchasing power – that a composite currency takes on its fullest significance), m_A, m_B and m_C vary in inverse proportion to the A, B and C price indices.

So far, the ECU has been looked at as a unit of account and even a payment unit, in the form of a weighted average of purchasing powers. In fact, though, the ECU was invented in order to provide an exchange market indicator; more precisely, it was invented for the purpose of constituting a weighted average of the exchange rates of its various component currencies into another currency (which may be any currency provided it is convertible on demand). If we write out the formula for the ECU as an indicator, we come back to the formula (6.3) that results from its definition as a weighted average of purchasing powers:

$$t \frac{X}{U} = m_A \, t \frac{X}{A} + m_B \, t \frac{X}{B} + m_C \, t \frac{X}{C}$$

If we multiply the two terms by $t \dfrac{U}{X}$, bearing in mind that $t \dfrac{X}{A} \cdot t \dfrac{U}{X} = t \dfrac{U}{A}$ and so forth we come back to the basic formula (6.1).

THE ECU AS A UNIT OF MEASUREMENT AND FOR RESERVES AND INTERVENTION

Composite currencies are so different from the currencies that we are used to, those that we use every day, that it will take some time for the merits and handicaps of such currencies to be fully perceived.

The main merit of a composite currency is that it is governed, as regards its value, from 'inside', as it were, instead of being governed from outside, by the market. But that is only true in special circumstances, which are not present in the case of the ECU (but which are taken full advantage of by the ES). The handicap derives from the fact that a composite currency is captive and that it depends on its component currencies, which restricts its use in the market and leads to certain measures (applied in the case of the ES) such as freezing the mutual exchange rates of the component currencies (abolition of the fluctuation margins).

The consequence of a formula in which the quantities of component currencies are fixed is that the ECU is only worth, as a weighted average, what the component currencies are worth. What they are worth is not always a great deal. In 1988 the Deutschemark experienced a rate of inflation which was very low (the lowest in Europe), somewhere around 1.2 per cent. Its weight in the ECU formula, though the largest of all the component currencies, was still only 33 per cent. The French franc and Sterling together account for more than that, and the franc experienced 2.5 per cent inflation and sterling 4.5 per cent, whilst the lira was exposed to inflation of 5 per cent (according to the European Investment Bank). It is doubtful whether the other component currencies, whether present or future (the escudo is not yet included), will improve the average.

The habit is now ingrained, and rightly so, of classifying currencies according to their resistance to inflation. By virtue of its constitution, the ECU will never be any higher than the third rung of the ladder, or even the fourth. That is a serious handicap for a new product which is about to be launched on the market. Can anyone imagine a computer or a motor-car awaiting its launch on the market when it was already known to the public to be less good than the competitors (see Figure 6.1)?

A PROBLEM OF CONGRUENCE

The ECU is a mediocre reserve instrument and it is just as deficient as a medium of exchange market intervention. The European Community's currency is not used just to define the parities of the national currencies among themselves: it is primarily used to regulate the currencies against each other and defend their parities on the foreign exchange market. In order to regulate the exchange rate of the franc in terms of the dollar, francs are sold or bought for dollars on the market in the light of the market situation. But it is not possible to regulate the rate of the franc in terms of the ECU by exchanging francs for ECUs. An intermediary currency has to be used. If the Deutschemark is up against its ceiling (+ 2.5 per cent above its parity) and the franc is at its floor, in terms of the parity fixed against the ECU, the Bundesbank will buy francs for Deutschemarks (and convert those francs back into Deutschemarks at the Bank of France some weeks later) whilst the French authorities purchase francs, which they pay for with dollars. The ECU, as such, is not involved: it observes. It is not the instrument by which the operation is carried out, but merely an indicator.

Using the ECU as an intervention instrument for regulating parities or carrying out arbitrage operations is in fact not compatible with the fact that the component currencies are traded separately and independently on the same markets. At any given moment, the value of the ECU in terms of currency A is not properly determined if (in parallel with the rate quoted for the ECU in terms of A) B and C are exchanged for A at rates which are incompatible with formula (6.1). This question of compatibility is all the more uncertain as the number of component currencies is at present 11, and will eventually be 12.

There thus arises a problem of congruence, in the mathematical sense of the term. The ECU formula, like that of any composite currency, links the component currencies to each other. A relationship of this kind results in a need for congruence (see Figure 6.2). The fluctuation of the component currencies on the exchange markets, by flouting this rule, introduces an element of incongruence into the formula which undermines the very significance of the ECU.

Let us go back to the example in Figure 6.1. A composite currency, U, is defined by three fixed quantities of currencies A, B and C. The weights of each of these currencies (the product of multiplying each quantity by its rate of exchange into U) are: $0.5 + 0.3 + 0.2 = 1$. On the exchange markets, the exchange rates of A and B into U are at their upper limit, or 'ceiling'; that is, they are 2.25 per cent above the agreed parities. The weights of A and B increase proportionately; that is, the combined weight of the two currencies increases by: $(0.5 + 0.3) \times 2.25$ per cent $= 0.018$. The need to remain within the limits of a total weight of 100 per cent (by definition) in the expression defining U means that the weight of C must logically fall in order to accommodate the rise in the weights of A and B, or, in other words, a reduction of $\dfrac{0.018}{0.2} = 9$ per cent. Since, however, the quantity of C is fixed this fall of 9 per cent can only be achieved through a change in the rate of exchange of C into U. The exchange rate would thus have to fall by 9 per cent, or four times the maximum permitted margin of 2.25 per cent.

If C were to stay within the margin $(-2.25$ per cent$)$ whilst A and B remained at their respective ceilings, the increase in C's weight would have repercussions on U of $(9 - 2.25) \times 0.2 = 1.35$ whereas the quantities of A, B and C should add up, as percentages of the whole, to 100 per cent; this leads to mathematical incongruence which could only be resolved by a modification of the quantities of the component currencies. The composition of U would then be altered, and indeterminately.

An intervention currency on the exchange markets has a role of arbitration. But it cannot arbitrate by aiming simultaneously at two incompatible targets: namely, congruence within the formula and the fluctuation margins. This constitutes a handicap for the ECU and it explains why national currencies are preferred for intervention and arbitrage purposes and why the intermediary currency most usually chosen is the dollar.

It is, however, hard to imagine a currency that cannot even be used

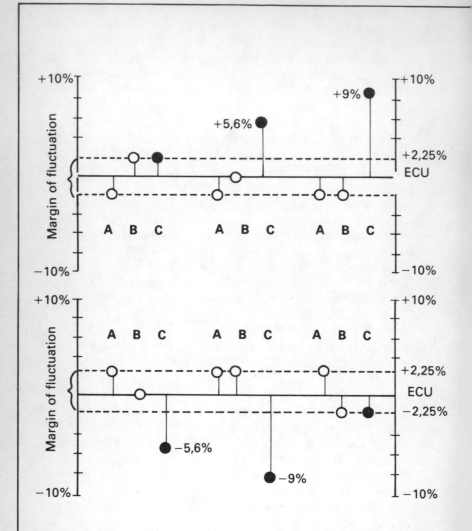

Figure 6.1 Constraints on the use of a composite currency: incongruence

Notes

The ECU, which was devised as an indicator for the component currencies of the EMS, is defined as a weighted average of the various exchange rates of these component currencies. The exchange parities of the component currencies are defined and chosen in relation to this average which also defines the ECU itself.

The amounts of the component currencies are fixed. The currencies are also bought and sold on the foreign exchange markets, and their exchange rates are not supposed to fluctuate by more than certain predetermined margins above and below the exchange parities (2.25 per cent). The ECU formula creates a form of interdependence between the exchange rates of the component currencies; hence the risk of incompatibility with the fluctuation margins.

Let us suppose there are three component currencies, A, B and C, which together define the composite currency, U, according to a formula similar (but simplified) to that of the ECU: the weights of A, B and C are $0.5 + 0.3 + 0.2 = 1$. Since the amounts of the component currencies are fixed, these weights vary in proportion to the upwards or downwards movements of the exchange rates *vis-à-vis* the parities. When they touch their fluctuation ceilings, A and B make U heavier by $(0.5 + 0.3) \times 2.25 = 1.8$ per cent. In order to counter this tendency for the value of U to increase, the exchange rate of C into U ought to fall by $1.8 : 0.2 = 9$ per cent, which is four times the permitted fluctuation margin. There is thus an incompatibility between the formula and the margins, which in the case of the ECU means that there is a risk of mathematical incongruence.

The ECU is a good indicator, by reference to which the exchange rates of the EMS currencies can be stabilised and regulated, but this definition and this role are not compatible with the aim of using the ECU as a standard of measurement, intervention currency and international means of exchange.

Composite currencies are 'formula currencies', which is something new. This very fact means that certain constraints, which we are not used to, must be abided by. At the same time, however, composite currencies also have remarkable special properties, thanks to which it is possible to define a neutral international currency which will carry out the functions mentioned above better than any other currency at present in use. These are the properties of a composite currency that are put to use in the ES.

as a medium for intervention on the exchange markets being accepted as the occupant of the privileged position of international payment currency.

As well as being vulnerable to changes in its value over time, the ECU is not even a useful instrument of measurement, for the simple reason that one cannot correctly measure the volume of the contents of something in terms of the thing that contains it, since the volume registered by the container is calibrated in terms of the volume of the contents. The ECU, through its 11 components, is open to the criticism that is always made of claim money: it is not strictly speaking anything more than a claim on another institution.

The only way to define the value of a unit of money is to look at what it can buy and, therefore, to take as one's standard of reference a standard sample of its purchasing power and then freeze it in time.

A PERTURBED AND PERTURBING PARITY ADJUSTMENT

Apart from the drawbacks mentioned above, there is also the very mechanism by which ECU parities are adjusted. In nine years there have been 11 such adjustments: the French franc has been devalued four times and the Deutschemark revalued six times. Such adjustments cannot be considered exceptional; they merely reflect what is called 'the changing economic environment'.

Each time such adjustments take place they are preceded by a distressing ritual that is unworthy of a great institution such as the European Community: first, ever more vehement denials that anything is afoot, increasing as the evil hour approaches, and then secret and hurried negotiations over a weekend, preferably one that is followed by a Bank Holiday Monday. At the same time as this is happening, speculators are engaged in one-way bets against which the central bank attempts to defend itself with expensive offers to purchase currency on the Euromarket.

Subsequently, as conditions continue to evolve, the new parities once again diverge from equilibrium and cause growing trade distortions until the moment when a further parity adjustment becomes inevitable. The disappearance in the foreseeable future of all the traditional means of defence open to a state, such as customs tariffs, subsidies and exchange controls, renders essential the choice of equitable exchange rates between the currencies of the Community such as will be judicious and able to follow changing conditions.

The ECU has been, and is still, a great enterprise in a field that is still relatively unexplored. Valéry Giscard d'Estaing and Helmut Schmidt rendered a great service to Europe and the cause of monetary order by helping to create this currency unit. They would be the first to admit that any innovation must be examined after a time, so that any lessons can be learnt from the project and improvements worked out. No mechanism, least of all a monetary mechanism, is exempt from this basic rule.

Europe wants a currency of its own. This is a great moment in its history. It is looking for something that will symbolise its unity and represent it in the eyes of the world, something that will also be an effective instrument for its economy. That is the subject of Chapter 7.

COMMENT

Comment on page 72. A sudden change in parities also has the disadvantage of perturbing the relative positions of the member state currencies, instead of stabilising them, which is the well known objective of the EMS. A 4 per cent rise in the parity of the Deutschemark, for example (not accompanied by the simultaneous devaluation of another component currency) has the effect of increasing the value of the ECU in proportion to the weight of the Deutschemark in the composition formula: that is, by about one-third of 4 per cent. If, after a rise of this kind, the Deutschemark/dollar exchange rate has not changed (and why should it since Deutschemark/dollar trade does not concern the ECU?), the ECU/dollar exchange rate ought to fall by 4 per cent. The exchange rates of the other component currencies would have to fall more in order to make up for the increase of the weight of the Deutschemark in the ECU: that is, in line with the ratio of their respective weights, 2 per cent, making a total of 4 + 2 = 6 per cent. Such a disturbance in the scale of rates cannot but upset the very thing that the EMS is intended to stabilise.

If it were based on the same data, a ruler would be elastic and would shrink in order to measure something that had grown bigger, whilst it would lengthen in the case of an object that had grown smaller.

7 A Currency that is Better than All the Others

An unprecedented opportunity exists to equip the fledgling European currency with an illustrious property, one that has long been sought after but never achieved.

Alone among systems of measurement, the one that most needs it, namely the monetary system, lacks a stable standard of reference which is independent of time and place, something which can be referred to in order to measure and compare, which can be used to define payment, reserve and intervention instruments.

Now, it *is* possible to give a composite currency stable value by taking advantage of the singular property which has already been alluded to and that is peculiar to a composite currency used only in international financial circuits (as a third currency); more precisely, to that vast monetary space, which may be considered virtual or real, that lies between the frontiers of nation states and which is occupied by the Euromarkets. The property in question is the ability to be freely exchanged whilst conserving its purchasing power. This is possible because in the extranational monetary space in which such a currency would change hands there is no final production or consumption.

For reasons that are unclear, this extremely promising concept meets with incredulity, a wall of incomprehension which closes the door to any kind of demonstration. This is perhaps because composite currencies are usually defined, and therefore seen, as 'baskets of currencies'. This way of looking at them is a source of many misunderstandings. It results in people thinking of transactions in such a currency unit as involving a basket – which ought rather to be a wallet – that actually contains the sums in national currency needed to make up a given quantity of the composite currency.

It is more rational – and closer to the truth – to define a composite currency in terms of its equivalence of value. A composite currency unit is one whose value – and therefore its purchasing power – is not determined by the laws of supply and demand on the market. Instead, it results from adding up a number of other values: that is, the individual purchasing powers of each of the quantities of national currency which are included in the formula that defines the unit. If we

74

approach it from the point of view of purchasing power we can grasp the notion of a composite currency and perceive the possibilities that it opens up, which are not the same as those pertaining to the conventional currencies with which we are familiar. And if we adopt this approach we also arrive at the notion of a constant purchasing power currency, such as our ES, a currency whose value has become invariable.

All that is needed to achieve this result is that each sum of component currency should be denominated in constant monetary units instead of nominal ones, which means that the sum of nominal currency should vary each day instead of being fixed. The variation coefficient may be obtained by adding to the index of 100 at time O (the point of origin) the value of the increase in the price index (as revealed by the statistics).

The figures published by the statistics offices of most countries are monthly figures. Several weeks go by between the moment the statistics are collected and the moment they are applied to a given amount of national currency. Two observations flow from this fact: the first concerns the transition from a monthly index to a daily one. The daily increase in the amount of each component currency which must be calculated needs to be continuous from one day to the next, without any of the abrupt changes that distinguish one monthly figure from another. For this purpose a daily growth coefficient for the price index must be devised by dividing the last known monthly increase by the number of days in the month. (see Figure 7.1).

The second observation concerns the time lag, due to the fact that the figure taken to calculate the extent to which the index should be modified relates to a period some weeks earlier than the one in which it is to be applied. The Comment section at the end of this chapter shows that the difference which exists between the figure that is applied and the figure that would result from an exact daily calculation is a second order magnitude which has a negligible effect on the accuracy of the calculations.

Let us take an example: the price index taken for one of the component currencies of the ECU – Sterling, say – stands at 127.00 on 30 April. The most recently recorded increase is 0.5. The daily increase in the index during May (a 31-day month) will thus be:

$$\frac{0.5}{31} = i = 0.0161$$

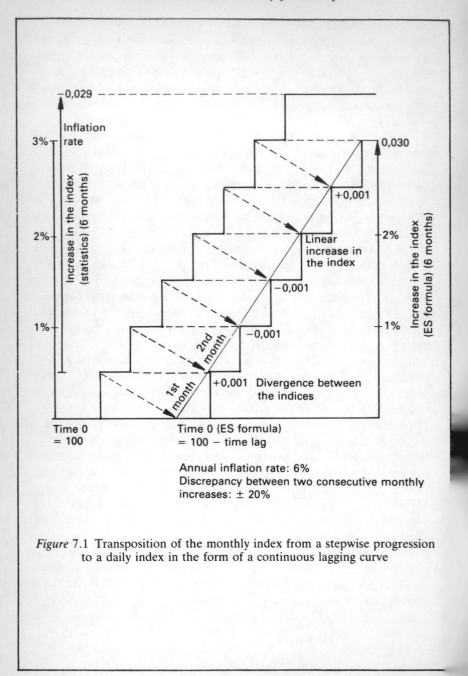

Figure 7.1 Transposition of the monthly index from a stepwise progression to a daily index in the form of a continuous lagging curve

The index stood at 127.00 at time O. On 14 May therefore it will be $127 + 14i = 127.258$, and on 31 May it will be $127 + 31i = 127.50$. The next day, on 1 June, the new growth figure, say 0.6 per cent, becomes applicable, so that the index then stands at 127.520. On 14 June it will be 127.78.

The same calculation will also be made in respect of all the other component currencies.

FROM FIXED VALUE IN NOMINAL TERMS (THE PRESENT ECU) TO FIXED VALUE IN REAL TERMS (ES)

Experience has shown that if we wish to explain the ES and derive its formulae it is not enough to transpose the formulae already discussed in connection with the ECU from nominal to 'real value' terms. No one ever pays a bill with anything but nominal currency; purchases and debts are not settled in 'real value' terms, and least of all with 'constant' value. The nominal value is the envelope and the actual value is the substance.

The human mind is instinctively disconcerted by the idea of a *numéraire* which has all the outward appearances and the practical characteristics of a sum of nominal currency, but which is in fact fundamentally different because substance has replaced the envelope. Nevertheless, a composite currency unit must be looked at from the point of view of value because it is defined in terms of its equivalence to a sum of values (the sum of the values of the amounts of the component currencies).

The fact that these amounts are fixed in nominal terms in the ECU as at present defined means that the value of the composite currency unit, as measured by what it can purchase, decreases each day, just as the amount of goods and services that each of the amounts of component currency can purchase in their countries of origin also decreases.

There is no reason, however, either in theory or in practice, why the amounts of component currency should be kept unchanged in nominal terms. On the contrary, given that the question now is how to define a composite currency, and thus to devise a formula to define it, we might just as well take advantage of this fact in order to exploit the flexibility of the formula and get rid of the handicap that nominal value represents. If each amount of nominal component currency increases each day in parallel with the price index in its country of origin, the quantity of goods and services that it can buy will no longer change. Now, by very definition, what a given quantity of a composite currency can purchase is the sum of what the corresponding amounts of component currency can purchase. If the latter do not vary, the purchasing power, and thus the value, of the composite currency unit becomes invariable. That is the definition of the ES: fixed real value has replaced fixed nominal value.

Let m_A, m_B and m_C be the component currencies at time O (with the index at 100). Let j_A, j_B and j_C be the price indices on the day defined as indicated above in connection with sterling. These indices on day J can be calculated by adding to 100 the figure for the increase in the index as recorded by the statisticians for each amount of component currency in its own country of origin from time O to day J, on the understanding that the daily increase during a month is equal to the last monthly increase recorded in the statistics divided by the number of days in the month.

In order to represent the relationship between the ES and its component currencies we can say that one ES is equivalent in value to the sum of the values of each of the amounts of its component currencies. In order to postulate equivalence of value between sums denominated in different currency units we must select one of them and convert the other component currencies into this common unit.

Let there be three component currencies, A, B and C, with A as the common unit. On day J the sum of nominal component currency A is $m_A \cdot j_A$. The sum of B as converted into A is $m_B j_B \cdot t\dfrac{A}{B}$, and the sum of C as converted into A is $m_C j_C \cdot t\dfrac{A}{C}$, whence

$$t\frac{A}{ES} = m_A j_A + m_B j_B \cdot t\frac{A}{B} + m_B j_B \cdot t\frac{A}{C} \qquad (7.1)$$

Added to this relationship are those that derive from the exchange rates of A, B and C into each other, that is:

$$t\frac{B}{ES} = t\frac{A}{ES} \cdot t\frac{B}{A} \qquad t\frac{C}{ES} = t\frac{A}{ES} \cdot t\frac{C}{A} \qquad (7.2)$$

The amounts of the component currencies and the rates of exchange of A, B and C into each other are the given data; the conversion rates of A, B and C into ES are the variables; they are three in number for three relationships, and are thus 'determinate'.

If we multiply the two terms in (7.1) by $t \cdot \dfrac{ES}{A}$ we get as a corollary the formula which expresses the equivalence of one ES to the total of its components, A, B and C after they have been converted into ES.

$$1 = m_A j_A \cdot t \frac{ES}{A} + m_B j_B \cdot t \frac{ES}{B} + m_C j_C \cdot t \frac{ES}{C} \qquad (7.3)$$

It would have been just as possible to start from (7.3) in order to arrive at (7.1).

AN INTERNATIONAL BASKET OF GOODS AND SERVICES MADE UP OF NATIONAL BASKETS

It is a fact that many minds – and among them some of the sharpest – are unable to accept the very idea of a payment currency with constant purchasing power.

'It is so desirable that if it were possible we should have it already' is what many of them say. If this concept is nevertheless to be accepted, if it is to become a familiar one, it must be extracted from the abstraction that surrounds it and given concrete form.

The value of a unit of money is defined by what it can purchase. There is no getting away from this definition; but there is a multitude of goods and services from which to choose and there are several competing indices, such as the consumer price index, the wholesale price index, the GDP deflator, and so on. Whilst leaving the discussion still open on the final choice of price indicator, let us select the domestic consumption indicator. This is the one that is used in the quantity relationship and which is the theoretical foundation of monetary regulation as it is practised by the monetary authorities today.

The price index therefore is the index of a basket. The composition of that basket, in nature and quantity, results from the statistics on consumption. The rigorous conditions under which the statistics services note down each month, on the market, the prices of the 295 articles that make up the basket cannot but convince any observer who is in good faith of the validity of the published indices.

Within this so carefully defined basket there are agreed quantities of foodstuffs, kilowatt-hours of electricity, underground tickets and even – in minute quantities because comparatively few are consumed – tennis balls. The cost of this basket is measured once a month on the basis of the figures collected in the field, which are first weighted.

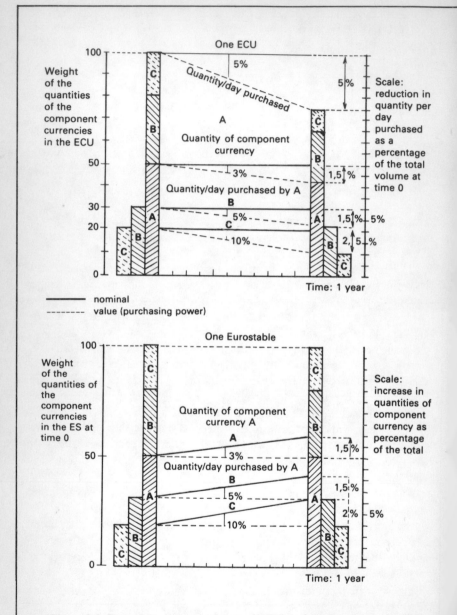

Figure 7.2 From fixity in nominal terms (ECU) to fixity in value terms (ES)

Notes

The shaded rectangles measure the quantities per day of the national statistical basket (containing 258 articles in France) which each amount of the component currencies *A*, *B* and *C* can purchase. The total sum of these baskets represents what one ECU or one ES can purchase.

The annual inflation rates are 3 per cent for *A*, 5 per cent for *B* and 10 per cent for *C*.

On the left: scale of the weights of each amount of component currency, which are identical with the volumes per day purchased at time 0.

The sums in nominal currency are represented by horizontal straight lines, whilst the volumes per day are represented by sloping straight lines, the slope of which is the inflation rate.

On the right: the reduction in the volume per day that each amount of component currency can purchase at the end of the period (one year), measured as a percentage of the total quantity purchased at time 0.

In the case of the ES, the amounts of the component currencies increase each day at the same rate as the inflation rate.

The volumes per day purchased by each of the components of the ES thus do not vary.

The consumption price index on day *J* is the cost, on that day, of the basket compared with its price of 100 on day *O*. What 100 in nominal terms can purchase thus varies in size in inverse proportion to the index. If the day's index increases by one-hundredth of 1 per cent as compared with the index for the previous day, the basket which cost 100 the day before has shrunk by one-hundredth 1 per cent (which is the rate at present in France). This basket and the way it contracts in volume in inverse proportion to the index (in other words, the inflation rate) gives us a concrete image of the value of a national currency, and then, by extension, of an international composite currency such as the ECU.

The basket that a composite international currency is capable of purchasing – which is what defines its 'value' – is made up of an aggregation of all the articles contained in the various national baskets of goods and services which each of the amounts of component national currency is capable of purchasing in its country of origin. This large, common international basket thus contains, side by side, a bottle of French wine (in the proportion that results from the composite currency), a German *Wurst*, some Italian *spaghetti*, and so on. Each of these articles is included in the international basket to an extent, in terms of weight or volume of the component amount, that corresponds to the sum spent on it in its country of origin.

In order to stabilise this international basket not merely in terms of its composition but also in terms of its dimensions, all we need to do is vary every day each of the component currency amounts in line with the movements of the price index of the country of which it is the national currency. This, in a nutshell, is the ES. What one ES is capable of purchasing does not change in either composition or dimensions. Its 'value' is thus invariable.

Now that we have defined the principle of the ES, we must next tackle the question of formulae and figures. This is not the best way of attracting or keeping readers, but the subject of this book cannot be discussed only in terms of generalities: it is important to show that the ES will work, and it will work thanks to its formula. All composite currencies are 'formula' currencies; they are not like other currencies, and the ES is especially unlike other currencies. It is often the case that an idea is in itself enough, but in this case it is not enough. If we confine ourselves to the 'idea' we disarm ourselves in the face of criticism or mere incomprehension. And we should then discover only partially the extent to which the ES can exploit the special properties of the monetary space in which it is intended to function.

A FORMULA CURRENCY WHICH EXPLOITS ALL THE POSSIBILITIES OF THE FORM

The example in figures set out in the following pages is purposely simplified (some similarities may be found, in the choices made, in respect of currencies A, B and C, with the French franc, the pound sterling and the Deutschmark).

$$t\frac{A}{B} = 10 \qquad t\frac{A}{C} = 2.5 \qquad t\frac{B}{C} = 0.25$$

m_A, m_B and m_C are the amounts of A, B and C that go to make up one ES. At time 0, $m_A = 3$, $m_B = 0.2$, $m_C = 2$ (i_A, i_B and $i_C = 1$). The rate of exchange of one ES into A (the amount of A that is equal to one ES) is

$$t^0 \frac{A}{ES} = m_A + m_B \; t\frac{A}{B} + m_C \; t\frac{A}{C} .$$

$$t^0 \frac{A}{ES} = 3 + (0.2 \times 10) + (2 \times 2.5) = 10$$

$$t^0 \frac{B}{ES} = t\frac{B}{A} \cdot t\frac{A}{ES} = 10 \frac{1}{10} = 1$$

$$t^0 \frac{C}{ES} = t\frac{A}{ES} \cdot t\frac{C}{A} = 4$$

It can be confirmed that

$$m_A \; t\frac{ES}{A} + m_B \; t\frac{ES}{B} + m_C \; t\frac{ES}{C} = 1$$

This latter expression represents the unit, in terms of three of its components. It is linked to the first by the exchange rates of A, B and C.

$$t\frac{ES}{B} = t\frac{ES}{A} \cdot t\frac{A}{B} \qquad t\frac{ES}{C} = t\frac{ES}{A} \cdot t\frac{A}{C}$$

Now let us look at how the price indices are involved. Let 0.3 per cent be the last monthly increase for the index corresponding to A (3.6 per cent on an annual basis), 0.6 per cent the monthly increase for B and 0.15 per cent the increase for C; extrapolated to give a daily figure for a 30-day month, these figures become:

$$i'_A = \frac{0.3}{30} = 0.01\%; \text{ over 20 days that gives } 0.002$$

$$i'_B = 0.02\%; \text{ over 20 days that gives } 0.004$$

$$i'_C = 0.005\%; \text{ over 20 days that gives } 0.001.$$

On the twentieth day of the first month the ES formula in terms of A is written as follows:

$$t\frac{A}{ES}^{20} = 3 \times 1.002 + 0.2 \times 1.004 \times 10 + 2 \times 1.001 \times 2.5$$
$$= 10.019$$

$$t\frac{ES^{20}}{A} = 0.0998 \quad t\frac{ES^{20}}{B} = t\frac{ES^{20}}{A} \cdot t\frac{A}{B} = 0.998$$

$$t\frac{ES^{20}}{C} = 0.2495$$

It can be confirmed that

$$m_A \ t\frac{ES^{20}}{A} + m_B \ t\frac{ES^{20}}{B} + m_C \ t\frac{ES^{20}}{C} = 1$$

$$(3.006 \times 0.0998) + (0.2008 \times 0.998) + (2.002 \times 0.2495)$$

Each term in the ES formula in terms of ES, after conversion into A, B or C, is capable of purchasing the same basket of goods and services as at time O. The value of the ES in terms of its purchasing power has thus not changed.

During the following month, which is a 31-day month, the latest monthly increases for the price index used are 0.31 per cent for A, 0.62 per cent for B and zero (inflation rate of 0 per cent) for C.

In Stage 2, the rates of exchange of the component currencies are those that are quoted on the market and are those of the official ECU. In Stage 3 the rates of exchange of the component currencies into each other are fixed.

The daily growth increment for the rates of exchange of A, B and C into ES (g) may be expressed in terms of the weights of A, B and C in the formula and the daily rate of increase of the indices (see the Comment on p. 90).

The weights are $m_A \ t\frac{ES}{A}$, $m_B \ t\frac{ES}{B}$, $m_C \ t\frac{ES}{C}$; that is, 0.3 for A, 0.2 for B and 0.5 for C. The daily rates of increase of the indices are 0.01, 0.02 and 0.025 per cent respectively.

The coefficient g is $(0.3 \times 0.01) + (0.2 \times 0.02) = 0.007$ per cent. During the month the rates of exchange of A, B and C into ES vary in parallel by 0.007 per cent. On the last day of the month immediately preceding ($J = 30$):

$$t\frac{A^{30}}{ES} = 10.0285$$

On the twentieth day of the second month ($J = 50$):

$$t\,\frac{A^{50}}{ES} = 10.0285 + 20 \times \frac{0.007}{100} \times 10 = 10.0425$$

$$t\,\frac{B^{50}}{ES} = 10.0042 \quad t\,\frac{C}{ES} = 2.5060$$

On the last day of the second month ($J = 61$) the daily indices for calculating the exchange rates of A, B and C into ES have caught up with the monthly increases; that is, over two months, 0.60 for A, 1.20 for B and 0.3 for C (all in percentages).

$$t\,\frac{A^{61}}{ES} = 10.0502$$

On the first day of the third month the new daily increases for the indices are as follows: 0.011 per cent for A, 0.022 per cent for B and 0.0055 per cent for C. The coefficient of the daily increment of the exchange rates of A, B and C into ES, determined in terms of the weights of A, B and C in the ES formula, is 0.0104 per cent.

On the nth day of the third month:

$$t\left(\frac{A}{ES}\right)^{61} + n = 10.0502 + 10 \times n \times 0.0104\%$$

$t\,\dfrac{B}{ES}$ and $t\,\dfrac{C}{ES}$ may also be deduced from this.

THE ES LEMMA

The fixity of the exchange rates of A, B and C into each other (Stage 3) means that the conversion rates of A, B and C into ES change each day in parallel with one and the same price index, g, which is established on the basis of the daily increases of the indices for A, B and C, weighted to reflect the weights of A, B and C in the basic formula that links the ES to the three component currencies.

Reference to this index, calculated each month, also shows that the daily increase in these rates is of a comparable magnitude to that of the indices for A, B and C and thus, as a daily figure, minimal. This minimal increase on a day-to-day basis justifies the hypothesis, established for the third stage of development of the ES, of simultaneous dealing on the exchange markets in the ES and its component currencies whilst at the same time not diverging from the conversion rates for one into another as calculated according to the formula. This leads on, in practice, to the possibility of an increased effect on the market by simultaneous combination of the weight of the ES and its component currencies.

Let d and d' be, respectively, the absolute and relative variations:

$$t\,\frac{A}{ES} = t\frac{A}{B} \cdot t\frac{B}{ES} = t\frac{A}{C} \cdot t\frac{C}{ES}$$

$t\,\frac{A}{B}$ and $t\,\frac{A}{C}$ are fixed, so $d't\,\frac{A}{ES} = d't\,\frac{B}{ES} = d't\,\frac{C}{ES} = g$. The absolute variation of $t\,\frac{A}{ES}$ (that is, $d\,t\,\frac{A}{ES}$) may be calculated using the formula that links A to the ES:

$$d\ \ t\frac{A}{ES}\ = m_A\,di_A + m_B\,di_B \cdot\ t\frac{A}{B} + m_C di_C\ \ t\frac{A}{C}$$

If we multiply the two terms by $t\,\frac{ES}{A}$, bearing in mind that $t\,\frac{ES}{A} =$ $1/t\,\frac{A}{ES}$, that $t\,\frac{ES}{B} = t\,\frac{ES}{A} \cdot t\,\frac{A}{B}$ and that $t\,\frac{ES}{C} = t\,\frac{ES}{A} \cdot t\,\frac{A}{C}$, we get:

$$d't\,\frac{A}{ES} = \underbrace{m_A\,t\,\frac{ES}{A}\ di_A}_{\text{weight of }A} + \underbrace{m_B\,t\,\frac{ES}{B} \cdot di_B}_{\text{weight of }B} + \underbrace{m_C\,t\,\frac{ES}{C}\ di_C}_{\text{weight of }C} = g$$

The relative variation of the rates of exchange of A, B and C into ES is equal to the growth of an index weighted in terms of the weights of A, B and C in the ES formula.

If the exchange rates are not fixed but are those of the present official ECU, they move within fluctuation margins (Stage 2): g therefore varies each day and the formula must be corrected by the weighted average of the divergences from parity.

Every day one or two large institutions calculate the rates of exchange of the main currencies into the ECU, using the exchange market figures at the close of business the previous evening. In order to make these calculations, the ECU composition formula is used. The amounts of the component currencies are those that were decided on the last occasion on which the formula was revised (September 1984), that is, 1.31 French francs, 0.719 Deutschemark, 0.078 pounds sterling, 140 lire, and so on. The new exchange rates are then communicated without delay to the main news media and financial centres before the markets open for business. The ES exchange rates will be calculated as indicated above.

Market operators will have no more need to worry about the calculations (which in any case are very simple) than they have to with the ECU. Now that the ES has been defined, we need to sketch out some advance idea of how it will be created and introduced on to the market. During Stage 1 the consortium will have introduced the ECU as a payment currency in international financial circuits. During Stage 2 it will be concerned with introducing the ES, in parallel with the ECU, as a transaction and reserve currency. The sums of component currencies will be those of the official ECU, but in constant units instead of nominal ones, and the exchange rates of the component currencies will be those of the official ECU.

During Stage 3 (see p. 136), the experiment will take on its more specifically European significance. The private interbank office will have been succeeded by a central institution, a European Community body under the tutelage of the Commission. The payment currencies used within the member states will continue to be their respective currencies, but the Community's external and reserve currency will be the ES.

The ES formula will continue to be limited to four or five component national currencies. This is something for which there is a happy precedent. In 1976, Mr de Larosière, the then Managing Director of the IMF, reduced the number of component currencies in the SDR formula from 17 to 5: the dollar, Deutschemark, sterling, yen and French franc. This was a bold and laudable piece of pruning which made the SDR formula more accessible: it was possible to establish a value relationship, and not just on paper. A modicum of reality (and also realism) was thus brought into the definition of a currency unit which was thought by many to be artificial, on account of its composition. The slimming-down of the formula, which was so important for the SDR's future and for the future of monetary matters, opened the door to the definition of a stable extranational composite currency, the similarities of which with the ECU may be set out as shown below:

COMPARISON BETWEEN THE ECU AND THE ES

If it is to have any chance of penetrating a market where its use cannot be rendered compulsory the new currency unit must be of higher quality than its competitors. By its very definition, the ECU is of lower quality than several of the main currencies. The ES, by reason of its composition (and not by a mere effort of its management, which is often dependent on the whims of politics), is exempt from that universal sickness, erosion of value, which affects or threatens all currencies.

A vital characteristic of the new money, one that is rightly sought after more for political than for financial reasons, is intrinsic prestige, something that will symbolise in the eyes of both Europe and the wider world outside, the unity and the 'presence' of the Community. It is enough to reflect on the prestige that sterling, the franc and, more recently, the dollar have conferred at different times on their respective countries and what the Deutschemark represents today for the whole of Germany in order to realise the force of this factor.

In our hypothetical Stage 3 the ES will have become the common external currency of the Community. It will confer on the Community the prestige that will derive from its constant purchasing power, a property that no other currency has ever had, though it has been much sought after. It will help to affirm the identity of Europe and bring together its peoples under a common flag, giving them the feeling that they belong to one and the same Community.

The ECU is a mediocre instrument of measurement because it is dependent on the value of its component currencies. It cannot hope to occupy the illustrious position – vacant at the moment – of a standard of reference that is independent of time and place which the world's monetary systems are crying out for and which, alone among systems of measurement, they lack.

The ES, on the other hand, satisfies the conditions required for a common standard of reference if such a standard is to be able to relate, in space and in time, such diverse factors as exchange rates, inflation rates, the cost of credit, savings, indebtedness, growth, and so on. It is in line with what Maurice Allais has written, to the effect that debts should be contracted and settled in real terms. All the 'inefficiencies that result from the use of economic calculations and accounts in nominal values which are devoid of any real economic significance' would then be eliminated. It would represent an even more desirable step forward in the international monetary universe, where 169 national currencies, each uncertain of its real exchange value and purchasing power, confront each other.

The new currency must also be an intervention medium for the purpose of external regulation (parity support and arbitraging) and internal regulation (maintenance of purchasing power). The ECU is only an indicator. The fluctuation of its component currencies on the exchange markets introduces an element of 'incongruence' into the formula which runs counter to its use as an instrument for intervention and regulation. The ES, in contrast, is used to settle debts and is directly exchangeable on the foreign exchange markets for national currencies. With its component currencies, with which it is linked by fixed conversion rates (Stage 3), the ES will constitute a single currency bloc which, by its very weight, will stabilise the market and eliminate opportunities for speculation.

Adjustment of the exchange parities of the component currencies of the ECU consists of a sudden, single movement and generates both speculation and market disturbance. In the case of the ES, adjustment of the conversion rates would be by gradual, programmed adjustment, spread over a period. It would cancel out any interest and exchange rate differences and would prevent any disturbances in the scale of conversion rates as a result of parity changes.

The main use of a monetary medium is to serve as a reserve instrument for central banks. Reserves are created for the purpose of calling upon them later, at an indeterminate time. The property that a currency unit must have if it is to be used in this way is steady value. One of the prime tasks in setting up any form of monetary organisation is the choice of reserve instrument. The latest such choice was that made at Bretton Woods in 1944, when the dollar was selected. As the risks of using a national fiat money were well known the dollar was required to be convertible into gold at the rate of $35 an ounce. Since 1971 there has no longer been any official international reserve instrument, only an unofficial one: the dollar again, the national fiat money of the United States, the past history of which is well enough known.

At a time when the objective is the foundation of a form of European monetary organisation we ought to learn from the lessons of the past. Once again, the prime question is the choice of common reserve instrument. It cannot but be a form of claim money but it should not be a national currency. In that case choice is limited to one alternative: either this choice is made in favour of a claim money which, by its very composition, is stable, or it settles on one that is not.

This parallel explains why, at the beginning of 1988, and with some fanfare, *The Economist* spoke out in favour of a currency unit identical to the ES, which the paper preferred to call the 'Phoenix'.

In matters of this kind, *The Economist* is more than a weekly news magazine; it is an institution. On several occasions in the past it has anticipated some change in British public opinion or some government initiative. Its opinion and its arguments deserve to be known. That is the subject of the next chapter.

COMMENT

Comment on page 77. The increase in the index, in the case of the ES, during month n is the one that the statisticians recorded for month $n - 1$.

Let us suppose that at the end of $n - 1$ the index stands at 125.000, representing the total cumulative increase since the base time (5 years: index = 100). The index increase taken for the ES during month n is the one for $n - 1$, that is 3.6 per cent on an annual basis (the present rate in France).

The daily increase in the index (for a 30-day month) is $3.6 \times \frac{1}{12} \times \frac{1}{30} = 0.01$ per cent. The index for the thirtieth day of the month will stand at $125.0 + (30 \times 0.01) = 125.30$.

In reality, however, the actual increase in the index during month n turns out to have been not 3.6 per cent but 4.8 per cent on an annual basis, an acceleration in the trend of price rises which has caused some disquiet and has resulted in the authorities' announcing a package of anti-inflationary measures.

If the ES rate had been calculated on the basis of a 4.8 per cent increase, instead of 3.6 per cent, the index would have stood at 1.25 $+ \frac{4.8}{100} \times \frac{1}{12} = 1.254$ instead of 1.253, which represents a discrepancy of less than one in a thousand.

On the first day of month $n + 1$ (a 31-day month) the ES index increases to $1.254 + \frac{4.8}{100} \times \frac{1}{12} \times \frac{1}{31} = 1.254 + 0.00013$. The increase that is then selected is that of month n; that is, 4.9 per cent on an annual basis.

The actual effect of the discrepancy between the indices during month $n + 1$ is confined to the difference between the increase during month n (selected for the ES) and the increase recorded by the statisticians during month $n + 1$. During month $n + 1$ the discrepancy of the previous month is repeated. The difference is never greater than the difference between the increase in the index between two consecutive months and is at its greatest on the last day of the month.

As a purely academic exercise, let us take an entirely improbable extreme example: let us suppose that inflation speeds up to the point of doubling from one month to the next, going from an annual rate of 3.6 per cent to 7.2 per cent. The RPI on the last day of month n would be on the 7.2 per cent base – that is, 1.256 instead of 1.253 – which is what it would be if calculated on the 3.6 per cent base.

The 'real' value (100 at time O) of the ES would then be equal to $\frac{125.3}{1.256} = 99.76$; that is, an underestimation of 0.24 per cent.

As for the nominal currency unit to which the ES is referred, *its* real value has fallen from time O to $\frac{100}{1.256} = 79.61$, or, in other words, a difference of more than 20 per cent.

In actual fact, the effects of any discrepancies between the calculated and actual indices would always be less than one in a thousand and would thus be negligible in comparison with the accuracy of the index measurements and their significance.

This kind of discrepancy obviously offers no opportunity for speculators who might wish to anticipate an inflation rate which they knew to be higher than the one used in the ES calculation. The fact is that there is no likelihood that the interest rate in force will be less than the difference in the increase in the index between two consecutive months (at present interest rates – 11 per cent – the annual inflation rate would need to go from 3.6 to 14.6 per cent during the following month in order to equalise profits and costs).

8 *The Economist* Presents the 'Phoenix'

In September 1974 the Mont Pèlerin Society held its annual meeting in Brussels and the writer was asked to present the ES to the members of the Society, having already presented it to the members of the *Société d'Economie Politique* in Paris some months before (on 12 June). The hundred or so economists of various nationalities who were present at the meeting listened politely and with total incredulity. In an interview published the next day in *L'Echo de la Bourse*, Milton Friedman said: 'The system envisaged by Jacques Riboud is an admirable one. It is well constructed and the idea is very seductive . . . However, I am sceptical as to the ES's chances of success because it is an invented money and the chief characteristic of money is that it is something that develops spontaneously.'

If an 'invented' currency is to have any chance of success, a combination of two new factors is required: a unanimously acknowledged need and an exceptional property. It was probably a happy combination of factors of this kind that induced the magazine *The Economist* to devote its leading article on 9 January 1988 to the prospect of a composite international currency with stable purchasing power, which it called the 'Phoenix':

> Thirty years from now . . . the Phoenix will be favoured by companies and shoppers because it will be more convenient than today's national currencies, which by then will seem a quaint cause of much disruption to economic life in the late twentieth century . . . Preparing the way for the Phoenix will mean fewer pretended agreements on policy and more real ones. It will mean allowing and then actively promoting the private-sector use of an international money alongside existing national monies . . . The Phoenix would probably start as a cocktail of national currencies, just as the SDR is today. In time, though, its value against national currencies would cease to matter, because people would choose it for its convenience and the stability of its purchasing power.

On March 5 *The Economist* returned to the attack on its leader page, arguing that if the ECU is to win the hearts and minds of the

Europeans of tomorrow more than mere encouragement from governments will be called for. What will be needed is a new name for the unit and a purchasing power that 'does not flicker'.

If we are to appreciate to the full this stand by *The Economist* in favour of a stable composite payment currency, we must bear in mind the lack of enthusiasm that this British publication has always shown for monetary innovations, thereby faithfully reflecting the view of the British establishment and British public opinion. In a letter to the author, Mr Rupert Pennant-Rea, editor of *The Economist*, confirmed that this stand had not been adopted without 'a lot of soul-searching', and it had a duly sensational effect.

What *The Economist* has grasped (and what Milton Friedman failed to grasp) is the, as it were, 'commercial' potential of a currency with stable purchasing power, the rapid market penetration that permanence of value would help it to achieve, even though (as a result of the fact that it might not remain very long in any one person's account before moving on) such permanence of value would not necessarily confer any real practical advantage. Millions of investors prefer gold to productive investments. Why? Not for speculative reasons but because they want security. Hundreds of thousands of companies, seeing their cash assets multiply, require their corporate treasurers to perform intellectual somersaults for no other purpose than to conserve the value of those assets in real terms.

That is why it is reasonable to expect that *The Economist's* forecast will come true once a new currency equipped with an incomparable quality image appears on the market, and once the banks responsible for 'selling' this new product are able to put forward the most convincing argument of all: namely that they have a currency that is 'better than any other'.

THE ROLLS-ROYCE OF CURRENCIES

In order to win over importers and exporters in Rio de Janeiro, Bangkok or Le Havre, the banks will need a convincing case or argument. The problem is no different from the kind of problem already mentioned that car manufacturers or airline managers have to solve: namely, the problem of winning over the customers. As *The Economist* says, the prestige of constant value will be such that people will soon forget the artificial nature of a composite currency, the fact that it is defined in terms of national currencies, the use of price indices and the calculations to determine the currency's exchange rate into other currencies. The ES, the European currency *par excellence*, will have become the 'Rolls-Royce' of currencies. In a chapter of *The Case for a new ECU*, entitled 'How to sell a currency', the author wrote in 1984:

A new product which is launched in direct competition with powerful competitors has no chance of establishing itself if it does not very soon acquire a brand image which distinguishes it from other similar products in the eyes of its target customers, the general public, the world of international finance and public administration. What it needs in order to achieve that is a property which will put it ahead of all the others in quality terms.

This is the point of transforming the present version of the ECU into a constant purchasing power ECU . . .

The conversion rates of the ECU will continue to be calculated each day by several large institutions. They will be disseminated by telex, just as they are now, to the main stock markets of the world, to the big banks and to the financial press . . .

The general public know nothing about the details of the manufacture of Rolls-Royce cars, or even how to drive them: nevertheless, the name Rolls-Royce is synonymous with excellence in the world of motoring. The same will be true of the constant ECU in the world of money. The holder of a deposit in constant ECUs will have the reassuring guarantee that when he comes to withdraw at any moment his deposit he will receive in real terms exactly what he deposited in the first place. Borrowers will calculate amortisation costs and interest rates in real terms at an interest rate which will have come back to the traditional level of 3 to 4 per cent. They will thus be able to include the cost of borrowing in their own gross profit margins in all security; such margins have in any case to be calculated in advance in real terms before converting them into their equivalent in nominal terms.

The wish and even the need of a businessman, and even of the Treasurer of a multinational company, is to avoid exchange market speculations. What he hopes for, what he wants, is to be able to protect the value of his assets and not have to make guesses in anticipation of the unknown. If he is to do that, he needs guidance in the shape of a reserve instrument which he can trust. The constant ECU will be just such an instrument for him. What will most impress itself upon him and upon depositors will be the constant ECU's market image. The details of its definition and the way its value is calculated will gradually fade into the background. What will be left will be an awareness of a property which no other currency, not even gold, has ever had: real permanence of value in terms of purchasing power. At the same time the ECU will take on the role traditionally assigned to money but which no modern currency has been capable of adequately fulfilling for some time now, namely that of reliable reserve instrument and standard of reference which is independent of both time and place.

The imaginary or actual territory assigned to the ES is that of the Euromarket. Within this territory, two or three privileged currencies (the dollar, the yen and soon the Deutschemark) act as intermediaries for calculating the exchange rates of the national currencies of 170 states. These privileged currencies are commonly called reserve currencies because countries' central banks need a quantity of liquidity which will function as a 'reserve' for the purpose of converting one currency into another and regulating the rates at which such exchanges take place. The very word 'reserve' is in itself extremely evocative. It points up the attraction that permanence of value would give to a currency unit that was offered on the market as a 'reserve instrument'.

QUESTIONS ASKED BY MEMBERS OF THE PUBLIC IN LETTERS TO THE AUTHOR

Means of payment, reserve instrument, regulator and intermediary between other currencies, and, in addition, equipped with unvarying value in terms of purchasing power: those are uses and properties that we are not accustomed to seeing combined in one and the same currency, something of which we have no experience. Such a proposition evokes doubts and raises questions: shown below are the main ones.

Q. You want to index your currency in order to 'stabilise' it, and yet indexation is recognised as a factor – and even a cause – of destabilisation.
A. The question contains within itself its own reply. In order to achieve stability the ES needs to index currencies which unfortunately are not stable. There are some words that automatically

unleash passions and provoke protests. Indexation is one of them.

It is truc that indexing salaries, and therefore costs, feeds inflation, stirs it up and multiplies the effects of a temporary excess of expenditure which should only be temporary and easily controllable. But before we make value judgements and reject indexation of any kind, we should go further and consider other factors, apart from the indexation of costs. In order to halt a forest fire, fire-blocks are created which lay waste vast areas, but no one concludes from that that deforestation should be the rule in forest management.

Indexation of remunerations is 'vicious' because it carries a past situation forward into the future, the very past situation which it is proposed to correct by indexation. This is so flagrant a contradiction that wage and salary earners (and their elected representatives, which is even more incredible) have been persuaded to accept the freezing, or the partial freezing, of their remunerations, in spite of the severity and injustice of such measures.

The idea of stipulating, as a condition for any progress in solving a problem, that people's living standards (which depend on their earnings) should stagnate or even fall is something that can only be accepted as a part of an overall monetary strategy, which does not in any case concern the ES because it is reserved for a monetary space that lies outside the territory of any state and where, moreover, there is no production, final consumption, or wage and salary earners.

It is an all too frequent shortcoming in economics, and even more so in other fields, to generalise to excess; to submit things, which by their natures are infinitely varied, to the same rules. This particular matter is put in its proper perspective if we bear in mind that indexation acts in reality on money in nominal terms, by reducing each day the volume of what it can purchase.

Although it is inflationary in its effects on salaries, indexation can be anti-inflationary in other sectors, such as credit and interest rates. Non-indexed interest rates, like indexed salaries, have the undesirable property of carrying forward the present situation, the one that is to be corrected, to the future. At the beginning of the 1980s, in the middle of a period of disinflation, it would have been preferable to limit the 'present situation' to the present, rather than carry forward punitive short-term interest rates (needed in order to curb the creation of money through credit expansion) into the future. Such high rates were no doubt necessary, but they had a devastating effect on the economy and also contaminated medium- and long-term rates. That is why the government and large companies are continuing to pay interest on what they borrowed seven or eight years ago at rates which are well above the prevailing market rates.

Savings banks in Europe and savings and loan associations in the United States, along with those who have taken out mortgages to pay for a house or flat on terms which anticipate future inflation at a rate above the actual rate (as subsequently revealed), could all deliver eloquent testimony in support of a stable currency even if such a currency included the price indices in the formula used to calculate its value.

There are also the developing countries to consider. At the beginning of this decade they suffered the full brunt of interest rates that had tripled, on top of their normal debt-servicing burden, and over and above all that there was the extra cost of a dollar that had become twice as expensive on the exchange markets, representing a total additional cost of six times what they had bargained for! Brazil's external debt, which is in dollars (although not much more than one-third of it is owed to American banks) amounts to 90 000 million dollars. There have already been anti-American demonstrations in Brazil.

It is irrational, when something is moving and is causing a nuisance, to reject a mechanism which moves in the opposite direction and thus negates the previous movement. That is what this form of indexation does, involving a currency which can take the place of the dollar. Any exporter who has received dollars in payment for goods exported knows that what those dollars will eventually buy will be slightly less than the value of the goods exported (though the exact amount of the loss cannot be predicted). In spite of this, however, we continue to put off the temptation, the need even, to correct this uncertainty by resorting to a series of measures which, even if they are not called indexation, are related to it (futures options).

Be that as it may, however, my purpose here is not to recommend indexation or non-indexation of borrowings: it is simply to recommend, for use in financial transactions between states, a currency which will offer the merits that gold used to have when used in such cases. This is a comparison which the ES, which is much more a factor for disindexation than for indexation, can justly make use of.

Q. Will not the creation of liquidity in the form of ES by the consortium have an inflationary effect?
A. This liquidity, which is incidentally an inaccurate way of referring to the phenomenon in question, will be destined to circulate not

within a state but merely as a third currency in the extranational space that lies between the frontiers of states.

Inflation, in the popular sense of loss of purchasing power, results from the comparison of final production (the completion of the process of adding value) and final consumption (immediate or deferred destruction of assets). In the extranational space where the ES circulates there is neither final production nor final consumption, and so there is no effect on purchasing power resulting from insufficiency of production as compared with available liquidity, or from excessive production thanks to a superabundance of liquidity. It is within states, and in respect of their national currencies, that the problem of inflation and inflows of liquidities arises. What matters, in this case, is not the volume of liquidity externally but rather the use that is made of it, where appropriate, internally. The ES is not an addition to external liquidity but a substitute for it, and it is one that will be easier to control than the dollar, which can be created at will by the 13 500 banks that make up the American banking system.

It is true that inflation is mainly the result of a vicious process which amplifies the very phenomenon that set it off, resulting in a ratchet effect (the establishment of ever higher thresholds from which there is no descent) and, above all, a spiral of price rises (the rise in costs causing a rise in prices, which causes a further rise in costs and, once again, prices, with an accompanying creation of new money). The instability of the dollar on the exchange markets has repercussions on the circulation of money and helps to set off the vicious, self-amplifying mechanism, upsetting both external regulation (the 'defence' of exchange parities) and internal regulation (protection of purchasing power).

One of the ES's ambitions (during Stage 3) is to 'disconnect' internal and external monetary regulation. National currencies will be supported on the exchange markets by neutral ES, which will be created by an institution that, to a large extent, will be isolated from the effects of circulation within a state. Inflation today, like deflation yesterday, is only the reflection of an inability to maintain the exchange value of a currency unit at a constant level. The incorporation into monetary mechanisms of a factor that is by definition stable will help to correct this deficiency.

What follows is an extract from a letter sent to the author which reveals the extent to which the public, though it is by now familiar with certain economic indicators, is still not clear what they mean.

Q. I have often observed that the figures quoted in the official consumer price statistics have nothing to do with actual prices in the shops, so much so that Le Figaro, for example, publishes once a month the prices of 50 different products by way of example.

A. The indices that result from the statistics are averages. No one person has ever been in an average situation. No matter how carefully they are prepared, no matter how careful the measurements and no matter how finely judged the weighting, no one recognises his own personal case in the statistics. There is no doubt at all that the average *Figaro* reader is not representative of the average of the population at large, any more than the average reader of *L'Humanité* is, which is why it has been suggested that various indices for the various categories of the population should be drawn up. In connection with the question of averages and particular cases, here is a quotation from Alfred Sauvy's *Histoire Economique de la France entre les deux guerres*:

> Just as a situation that is peculiar to a given case appeals to the reader, flatters him and gives him the comfort of having properly grasped what is going on, so the *whole* seems to him to be, if not treacherous, then at least an intellectual trick, the honesty and the intentions of which are less likely to be questioned than the justification and the significance.
>
> Let us take an example: a politician visits a factory. As he listens to the experts who, with their averages and their margins of error, overwhelm him with a flood of well constructed statistics, we see polite scepticism written all over his face. But no sooner has he come across an individual case than his face at once lights up: 'Here is something which I understand perfectly. I love concrete examples.' But this so eloquent individual case may well be an exception, it may be a worker who has been absent from work for two weeks, or one, who, on the contrary, has received some back-pay or some special bonus. The case is certainly a specific one, but it is untypical of the whole.
>
> The price of a steak as one can observe it or thinks one can observe it, or as one remembers it, is 'a definite factor, whereas the price index is only an abstraction'.

Everything is called into question these days, not just the price indices. The fact, however, is that the margin of error in the indices is very small when compared with the rate of depreciation of money.

The notion of inflation is now well established in everyday speech. It is used everywhere without anyone noticing that what they call inflation is nothing more than the consumer price index.

Jacqueline Fourastié has assessed the accuracy of the price indices in her book, *Les Formules d'Indices de Prix*, in terms of changes in production and human behaviour. In this book she illustrates the range of approximation and the margins of error in the figures published by the national statistics services by comparing, for example, the prices of several baskets of goods and services in France (A, B and C) over a period of more than a century (since the beginning of 1840).

Basket A corresponds to the average consumption of a family in 1952. Variations in the prices of articles that have disappeared from use over time or which have only recently been invented are estimated by analogy with those articles that are most similar to them and have remained in use. The second basket, B, is obtained by removing all the articles that did not exist in 1880 and the third, basket C, is obtained by removing all the articles that did not exist in 1840. Starting with the same price for each of the baskets, equal to 100 000 1952 francs, the prices become, respectively, 762, 727 and 752 in 1880 and 621, 611 and 611 in 1840.

This exercise shows that the divergences between the prices of the baskets, the composition of which has been so arbitrarily modified, are very small, which has led some experts to recommend a simpler choice of goods in the baskets (whereas what is contested is rather more the composition of the baskets than the recording of the prices).

Reason dictates that we must make use of the new techniques that progress has made available to us in order to solve the problems of our times. The problems arising from the introduction of a stable reference unit can and must be solved by making use of recent advances in statistical methodology, which have now been tried and tested and have become the norm.

Q. Must we not expect opposition from the strong-currency states to an initiative which will ultimately have the aim of offering competition for their currencies and will thus deprive them of the benefits of seigniorage?

A. The famous economist, Robert Triffin, explains the reasons why the Americans ought to withdraw their currency from use as sole international reserve currency in this extract from a paper he delivered at a meeting of the *Société d'Economie Politique* in 1972:

The first and most obvious reason is that the creation of world monetary reserves ought to be determined in line with the needs of the world economy, and not by the practically unpredictable fluctuations of the balance of payments of a single country.

The second reason is the exorbitant 'privilege' that such a system confers on the reserve currency country, that is, the possibility of financing its deficits through the printing presses of foreign central banks. The United States, which won their independence two centuries ago, are the first to recognise that foreign countries will refuse to finance, at the price of increased domestic inflation, US deficits which are due to policies, or policy errors, in which they have had no say and with which they may sometimes be in total disagreement.

The third reason is that the United States take the view that this exorbitant privilege also constitutes an unbearable responsibility for their economy. Financing their deficits in this way, through the agency of foreign central banks, paralyses the mechanism for adjusting their balance of payments and, in particular, subverts the exchange rate realignments which divergences in the trend of prices and costs make inevitable for all countries from time to time . . . This asymmetrical situation as regards the dominant currency reduces American firms' competitiveness on world markets as well as on their domestic market, thereby undermining their profits and putting their work-force out of work.

For lack of the necessary changes in the foreign exchange sphere, companies and unions will bring almost irresistible pressures to bear on the Administration and Congress.

The German monetary authorities, whose currency at present rivals the dollar as the principal international currency, would not dissent from this view for the same domestic policy reasons, on top of which there are also sound foreign policy reasons. The Germans are well aware that the preponderant position of their currency in Europe, the harbinger of an unacceptable form of economic domination if it develops further, risks breaking up the European Community. Professor Triffin's recommendations have not been put into effect. They are still valid, and they are becoming more and more valid as the lapse of time since 1972 increases, which shows that it is pointless to expect the United States to take the initiative.

Some years ago I was at the annual meeting of the IMF in Washington. Whilst I was there I went to interview the Head of the

European Affairs Department at the State Department. His reply to my question on this matter was unambiguous: 'We lack the political means [that is: domestic policy means] to ensure that the dollar observes the constraints imposed upon it by its international role. It is up to Europe to create a currency of its own and free us of a responsibility that is too heavy for us.'

The time of benign neglect is past: the damage that a yo-yoing dollar can do is now acknowledged. At the beginning of the 1980s an excessively strong dollar, hoisted into the stratosphere by interest rates which had to be high in order to bring inflation down, laid waste entire sections of American industry and agriculture. There is no doubt at all that if it were freed from some of its international responsibilities the American government would be in a better position to collaborate with Europe with a view to stabilising exchange rates than it is at present.

Q. Non-indexation of demand deposits increases the profits that banks make from the interest they earn on loans. The ES would bring interest rates down to the level of 'real' interest rates, and in so doing would deprive the banks of a source of income. How can you expect them to welcome a project which would damage their interests?
A. It is true that banks profit from inflation within a national territory because bank money (demand deposits) is not interest-bearing. But the same thing would not be true of the extranational territory of Euromarkets. The depositors there, large companies and investment institutions, do in fact receive a proportion, which may be large, of the LIBOR, even on short-term deposits.

If we suppose that bank payment money with constant purchasing power could be created within the territory of a state – which it could not – it would indeed be presumptuous to make such a proposal. But the extranational territory for which the ES is destined offers quite other prospects. Outside national frontiers competition is free and bitter. It sometimes happens that the spread (the credit distribution margin) is reduced to 0.5 per cent! And in any case the spread is always far below the real interest rate obtaining within states.

In the Euromarket there is the question of the margin, but there is also the question of prospecting for customers. Why should a Euro-bank reject a product which would give it a better profit margin (because it would also include the seigniorage which it does not receive in the case of the dollar) and which would have unrivalled commercial attractiveness for the bank's customers?

In addition there would also be the official or unofficial support of one or more governments of EEC member states. It is hard to imagine that at least one of these factors would not favour an experiment which would pave the way for a specifically European currency, offered in parallel with a US dollar that has lost most of its appeal. Why would bankers reject a currency which would not be the national currency of any state and would be possessed of incomparable prestige, one that would be the intervention and exchange stabilisation instrument that is at present missing and is needed for a role that the present ECU cannot fulfil?

Q. This constant purchasing power is sometimes criticised. It is pointed out that it would make the currency in question too 'hard' and that a measure of depreciation is necessary in order to promote economic activity by making things easier for the borrower. The suggestion has therefore been made that a coefficient of moderation should be included in the formula.

A. Constant purchasing power is essential and must be kept, for two reasons.

First, constant purchasing power would not mean that the currency would be too hard. It would still leave the borrower the benefit of improved productivity. A really hard currency would be one defined in terms of its equivalence to a constant number of hours of work. The ES, as it is proposed here, depreciates in terms of hours of work at the same rate as productivity increases (2 per cent a year on average).

If a moderating coefficient were introduced into the formula, thus breaking the link between the ES and constant purchasing power, the currency's brand image would be seriously weakened, and a good brand image is necessary if the currency is to compete on the Euromarket with such redoubtable competitors as the dollar and the Deutschmark. Let us suppose that the standard for measuring money was and still is a universal consumer product, familiar since the beginning of time, such as a 1 kg loaf of bread. Let's call it the *K* standard, prices being in multiples of 1 K. In that case there would be no shortage of experts who would consider that this standard was too soft.

In order to understand why, all we need to do is go back to the way this loaf used to be made, and compare it with the situation today: originally, the labourers in the fields, the harvesters with their sickles and the bakers and their kneading-boards; today, in contrast, farmers with their combine harvesters and flour tanker lorries, all representing a reduction in production time of 50 times and more.

We should not go on without also adding that this last question is a very good example of the extent to which we have become used to inflation, prepared to treat it with indulgence and even believe that it has certain merits, provided it is not taken to excess. This is excusable (though we can do better and with fewer risks) bearing in mind the evils of the opposite situation, when the purchasing power of money is rising. There is nothing more fatal for the economy than such a situation and economic history offers some examples, such as the last years of the reign of Louis IV and the 1930s. The best way of tackling a deflation is not to precipitate an inflation, even a moderate one. What is needed is a monetary standard with constant value, in terms of what it can purchase. During the 1930s the purchasing power of gold and thus of the currencies that were tied to it was continually rising, ruining many national economies (see p. 197). A standard of reference with real constant value would have spared the peoples of Europe considerable hardship.

Q. As long as man has used money there has never been a currency with stable purchasing power. A currency of this kind is so desirable that, if it has not yet seen the light of day, there must be some fundamental reason why such a currency cannot be created.
A. This is an extremely important question, the answer to which cannot be given in a few words. It calls for a chapter of its own, especially as the demonstration diverges from the well-beaten paths of traditional economics.

It would be reasonable to expect this chapter to be the next one, but in fact it comes somewhat later in the book (Chapter 14). This chapter, along with two others that also deal with fundamental questions, takes up several pages, too many to interrupt the flow of ideas in the exposition of a project which aims to stay close to the concrete.

The logical order of things has perhaps not been retained here. All the same, it is still a rational approach, after setting out the theory of

a new machine, to put it before the reader's eyes and make it work and show how it opens the whole Euromarket to the ES (the size of the Euromarket is estimated to be some \$2 000 000 million) as well as other international financial transactions.

9 Exchange Risks and Real Interest Rates

Exchange risks are always present in international banking operations. Just mentioning an exchange risk is enough to paralyse initiative even before the possibilities and any financial effects have been evaluated, considered and analysed. In an ES system the risk would be that indexed liabilities might be balanced, on the assets side, by reserves in national currencies or other assets which were not indexed, or the other way around. This would give rise to a situation which could be compared to an exchange risk.

If there is one field of endeavour in the world of banking that deserves to be encouraged (and which is indeed being encouraged), it is the rational appraisal of risks. Too often businessmen have imagined .they saw risks where there were none and, conversely, they have failed to see any where there were indeed some. Some years ago the President of the Chase Manhattan Bank declared that loans to developing countries were 'risk-free' loans: some months back the Chase was obliged to make a provision of some $1000 million to cover losses on such loans. Citicorp, for its part, has gone one better: it has made a provision of $3000 million.

A rational and dispassionate examination shows that the exchange risk that banks doing business on the Euromarket in a stable purchasing power currency would run is tiny, whereas the likely profits they would make would be very high thanks to the seigniorage on the ES they had created and because they would acquire many new customers who would be attracted to them. It must be said, though, that when it comes to risk, people are motivated more by feelings and impressions than by rational examinations.

SHORT-TERM LOANS AND MINIMAL RISK

In the system proposed in this book, the member banks of the consortium would be in a position to transfer the exchange risk to the central office, from which they could obtain refinancing, in national currency or in ES. The exchange risk is thus borne by this office, and

we must therefore evaluate the risks implied by indexation of liabilities exclusively at that level.

The office's role is to offset and even out the member banks' needs in terms of national currency over a period of time. The exchange risk is small because the ES that are put into circulation will be created by loans that must be short-term because the ES thus created soon come up against a customer or a bank which wants them to be converted into national currency. It is unlikely, during the early stages, that an average ES will be involved in more than three or four transactions before being destroyed.

The member banks would risk unbalancing their balance sheets if they granted loans with excessively long maturities compared with the duration of the life of the average ES before it was destroyed (see the simulation on p. 52). The short duration of each ES's active life would give the office all the time it needed, where appropriate, to adopt emergency measures in the event that inflation and its effects, in terms of real interest rates, should threaten disruption. This is in any case a highly improbable eventuality since, throughout the developed world, the monetary authorities have learnt to keep inflation firmly under control by raising short-term nominal rates (and, subsequently, real rates) to levels which are more likely to be too high than not high enough.

In any case, exchange risks only concern a marginal fraction of the total outstanding loans. The consortium's policy must be one of attempting to keep its balance sheet in balance, and thus minimise any items on the liability side that are in other currencies than the ES.

One rule that all Eurobanks follow is that of matching the maturities of the loans they have made with those of their borrowings. The problem would be different for the consortium because it would not have to borrow ES, it would issue them. As regards the liquidity question, it would first have to persuade its depositors to keep their assets in ES; then it would have to find the cheapest possible source of national currency so as to be in a position to meet requests for conversion of ES assets into national currency. During the initial stages, the imbalance will be in the opposite direction in the event of high inflation, as a result of an increase of requests for conversion of national currency deposits into ES.

INFLATION AND NOMINAL AND REAL INTEREST RATES

The so-called 'real' interest rate (which is what will be charged on ES loans) is defined as the difference between the nominal rate of interest and the rate at which money is losing its purchasing power.

Suppose that money is losing its purchasing power at a rate of 4 per cent a year and the interest rate on an initial loan of 100ES (= 100d in national currency) is 7 per cent. At maturity (after a year) the borrower pays back 104d. The member bank meanwhile has received 7E in interest plus 4d to compensate for the loss of purchasing power; that is (ignoring the second order calculations) total nominal interest of 4 + 7 = 11 per cent.

Balancing these loans, there will be payment ES (non-interest-bearing demand deposits), interest-bearing ES deposits (at 3 per cent), and national currency borrowed at the LIBOR of 7.5 per cent. If the sum advanced (and denominated in ES) was paid over to the borrower on request in national currency, the bank has, as a counter-part to its claim, a liability in national currency borrowed from its treasury department or from the interbank institution, or from outside (at LIBOR: that is, 7.5 per cent).

This latter rate may be considered to be made up of the inflation rate of 4 per cent and a real interest rate of 3.5 per cent (4 + 3.5 = 7.5 per cent). The gross margin received on the ES is then equal to (4 + 7) − (4 + 3.5) = 3.5 per cent. In other words, the difference between the interest rate charged to borrowers of ES and the real cost of national currency resources. The widely held opinion that real interest rates might be too low or even negative is entirely unfounded in the case of short-term operations.

Nowadays money is principally bank money, created by commercial banks. From the point of view of inflation, money of this kind and the way it is created involve a form of mechanism that is vicious because its defects are self-amplifying. Payment money is created by bank loans. A real rate of interest that is low or negative can only accelerate the demand for credit.

In the absence of an authoritarian form of credit control, which no one wants any more, the only way to halt this self-aggravating mechanism is to raise the cost of credit to punitive levels. This is what the monetary authorities do, with the approval of public opinion. All surveys of the matter have shown that inflation is − rightly − one of the most feared evils as far as the general public is concerned. It has already been demonstrated that people are prepared for any sacrifice provided that inflation can be conquered. This is why the likelihood that interest rates will again be negative is very low, and even if they were there would be no need to fear a run on the banks (an atavistic fear that haunts bankers and which is caused by a shortage of liquidity). In this case the result would be more likely to be a 'run to the bank' and an excess of liquidity resulting from too many people wanting to make deposits and driven on by panic at the rapidity with which their nominal currency assets were losing purchasing power (so much so that it would be necessary to consider limiting purchases of national currency to a given maximum amount).

As long as the ES has not become well established the situation will be the opposite of what it is in nominal currency, which suggests that forward projections should not relate to particular cases and should cover a long period.

It may happen, though it is unlikely, that real rates will be inadequate, but in any case such a situation would be of brief duration. Inadequate real rates would be compensated for by the real advantages that would be enjoyed in normal times. The member banks of the consortium would have no reason for exaggerating the consequences, especially in view of the fact that high nominal rates would at the same time be making them fat profits.

The (by now) generalised practice of using interest rates to control the growth of the money supply has, as a corollary, real interest rates that are usually considered to be too high. In France during the summer of 1988 typical interest rates on bank loans were around 11.5 per cent whilst inflation was 3.5 per cent, whence a real interest rate of 8 per cent, more than twice the rate that has traditionally been considered normal and compatible with economic growth.

It is also inevitable that the exclusive (or almost exclusive) use of the rate of interest as a weapon with which to defend currencies' parities both externally (in terms of exchange rates) and internally (as regards inflation) will result in overvalued currencies, especially as there are also contrary secondary effects: a rise in the cost of money designed to 'curb demand' also attracts foreign capital and thus results in the conversion of massive quantities of foreign currency into national currency, which in turn results in the addition of large quantities of liquidity to the money that is already in circulation, which has the same effect as the excess demand which the measure was originally intended to damp down.

High real rates of interest are here to stay, however, especially as, contrary to what everyone assumes, borrowers have already got used to them. These high real rates are what will help the banks of the consortium to turn in substantial profits. They should weigh this fact in the balance with the relatively unlikely probability of inadequate real interest rates, which is in any case something against which they can easily protect themselves.

The real interest rate received by the member banks is the nominal interest rate minus the weighted average inflation rate for the various countries of the component currencies. This deduction from the nominal rate of interest is thus, in effect or in actual fact, automatically paid over to holders of ES deposits: it may be considered as included in what is paid on their demand deposits.

The reduced yield on ES for the member banks of the consortium, resulting from the fact that nominal interest rates have been replaced by real rates, may appear to be a cause of lost profit for the banks in question. In fact, however, it will be a source of income, by making depositors less demanding.

In order to protect their assets in real terms against a rate of inflation which they expect but of which they do not know the exact rate, they overestimate. Operating in constant currency rather than in nominal currency will ensure that the interest the Eurobanks receive on their assets (loans and investments in national currencies) will always be greater than the rate of inflation. This interest is available, as are the conditions attaching to it. For the most part, the principal motivation is the desire to protect against the depreciation in real terms of the various national currencies in question. This kind of motivation, which is rather more the fear of depreciation than the actuality of depreciation, would not be justified in the case of ES deposits.

A MARKET TO BE EXPLOITED

There is a potential clientele for the ES which is very large because it covers the whole globe and which consists of people who wish to counteract the depreciation of money in real terms, and to do so without the kind of financial gymnastics that are forced upon the well trained treasurers of the multinationals. This clientele consists of people such as a broker who has just received some commission, an investor who has just sold a hotel, a 'wildcatter' who has just discovered oil, and other such persons. They will be tempted by a Euromarket investment, while still wishing to retain liquidity and reliability and without having to enter into negotiations with their banks concerning options or futures contracts. These investors will be given the reassurance they seek by the ES and will thus be less inclined to look elsewhere for protection of the value of their assets. They will therefore constitute, for the members of the consortium, a source of stabler deposits than the footloose funds, pursued by fears of monetary depreciation, which Eurobanks have to rely on at present.

This, rather than the multinational companies, is the clientele that the consortium must aim for. The number of individuals concerned is greater and they will represent for the consortium new depositors, new borrowers and a new source of turnover which will not be merely in ES but also in national currencies and will derive from the fact that an instrument that is just as useful for transactions as a store of value has been made available to this potential clientele.

The liberalisation of capital movements and the elimination of exchange controls are reforms that are opening up a new area of what are usually called 'investors', although it would be better to call them 'holders of liquidity', to the Euromarket. This new group of investors is practically coterminous with the entire population. A huge group of people whose reactions and motivations are not those of the professional operators will thus gain access to this world-wide market. What these people have in common is that they are all holders of cash, what the statistics classify under the heading 'M1'.

In France M1 (bank notes, postal cheque accounts and demand deposits at the banks) amounts to more than 1 500 000 million francs. The holders of M1 instruments are the creditors of the central bank (as regards bank notes), of the Treasury (postal cheque accounts) and of the commercial banks (demand deposits). They receive not a *centime* of interest on their various claims. At present interest rates (11–11.5 per cent) that amounts to total lost profit of, in theory, 165 000 million francs, or more than 30 times the expected take from the new wealth tax. This continues to be the case in spite of the multiplicity and the variety of the financial instruments which banks and credit institutions are at present offering savers, the objective of which is (and rightly so) to combine high yields with guaranteed liquidity.

The motivation of these passive bearers of 1 500 000 millions' worth of sterile investments needs to be analysed. It should not be confused with that of our mythical treasurer of a multinational company, whose exchange market exploits are the stuff of MBA students' dreams.

The investigation is an easy one: all we need to do is consider our neighbours. There is practically no one who has not on some occasion had to pay interest on a current account advance. Let us ask the mythical Mr Dupont. He receives no interest on an account which subsequently has a creditor balance of 10 000 francs and more, and he takes no advantage of these marvellous SICAVs of which the daily papers are always singing the praises. Why? Because he is undecided, because he is expecting to have to meet some obligation, because he is accumulating some capital with a view to making a purchase, because the effort required to find out and then to take a decision on what to do with his liquid assets, greatly though it has been facilitated, is still simply too much. And so he waits, and resigns himself, although still with a degree of regret, because he is aware that in real terms his asset is depreciating each day.

For these reasons, this category of persons will constitute a vast new market for an asset such as the ES which offers permanence of value without any special conditions. Holders of ES assets will be even less under pressure to take a decision as to how their assets should be put to use than they are with assets denominated in national currencies. And they will also find that the fact that their ES assets increase in value in nominal terms constitutes a form of return which is not available on comparable national currency deposits.

In money matters, even more than in other spheres of human activity, the psychological factors are the decisive ones. They do not affect investors only: they also have an effect on the distributors of bank credit, which justifies the following observation.

A PUBLIC GUARANTEE AS A WAY OF OVERCOMING PSYCHOLOGICAL OBSTACLES

Risks that have been traditionally accepted as inevitable and have thus become ingrained in people's ways of thinking are often hard to analyse rationally. They are excluded from market research, and insurance policies and the law of big numbers ignore them.

This is a psychological question, rather than a political, economic or financial one. That is why it is only prudent to allow for some kind of ultimate guarantee for the consortium and its central institution against the effects of excessively low or even negative real interest rates even though the probability of such an eventuality is almost nil. In order to provide this assurance, an official body may be imagined which would insure the consortium against this risk, in return for a suitable premium (which would be calculated as a percentage of the consortium's profit margin on ES transactions). The model for this body would be the FDIC and the Federal Housing Administration in the United States, or the COFACE in France. All of these institutions have shown that beneficial effects can be expected of an organisation that combines the ability to bear and spread the risk of loss with the merits of private initiative.

10 Adjusting Exchange Rates by the Use of Targeted Creeping Rates

In June 1971, Mr A. Lamfalussy, now managing director of the BIS, wrote:

> We shall never be able to create enough international liquidity to finance the permanent imbalances in balances of payments, that is, to make it possible for international trade to function normally in a world in which the adjustment mechanisms are jammed. It is hard to see how or by what means the process of adjustment could be speeded up if not by accepting greater variability of exchange rates, which does not necessarily imply floating rates. It seems an illusion to hope that governments will abandon their ambitions and devote themselves to achieving internal balance in their economies. This being so, the only way out is occasional variations in exchange rates . . . There is an incompatibility between freedom of international trade and the simultaneous pursuit of external and internal equilibrium; failing exceptional luck, something must give, and by a process of elimination it is clear that what must give is the exchange rate.

It seems amazing that, eight years later, no account was taken of this recommendation in the constitution of the EMS. One of the reasons why preference has been given to fixing exchange rates without using an adjustment mechanism is perhaps that it is extremely difficult to determine this 'true equilibrium' rate.

In the United States at present the theories in vogue arrive at opposite conclusions. The purchasing power parities approach would suggest that the dollar ought to go up on the exchange markets (based on the same prices in a standard basket, which ought, moreover, not to be a typical housewife's). In contrast, if the American trade deficit or the current account balance are taken into account, the conclusion is the opposite.

It is outside the scope of this book to go into this question – which is still in the forefront of economic discussion – in detail. What does emerge from such considerations in any case is that the absence of a common, stable and reliable standard of reference for calculations and comparisons is a handicap and that the use of a national currency (the dollar) as an international means of exchange and store of value is a factor making for disturbances.

There are times when something can be called definitive, permanent and irrevocable, without casting any shadow of doubt. At other times it is necessary to say without fear or flinching that a particular thing is 'temporarily irrevocable'. If this rule had been adhered to regarding the exchange systems that have been adopted since the first international monetary conference, which met in Genoa in 1922, there would not have been so much uncertainty and floating, both of ideas and exchange rates.

What was once thought to be our salvation would not have been so readily denied: floating exchange rates would not have replaced fixed rates (in order to prevent, according to the adherents of the Monetarist School, the effects on the domestic money supply of conversions of national currency from or into foreign currencies); there would have been no need of 'clean floating' (the open intervention of the central banks on exchange markets which are supposed to have been left to the rule of the market) to replace 'dirty floating' (secret interventions by the central banks). It might perhaps also have been possible to spare the EMS its 'fluctuation margins', which deprive it of part of its meaning and merits.

All so-called 'fixed' exchange rate systems have failed in the end for lack of a proper mechanism for adjusting to changing circumstances. The conveniences of a system of fixed exchange rates are obvious, so long as such a system is in harmony with the monetary environment. The need to be in harmony with the prevailing environment means that the trends of the market must be respected. The best way of combining a system of fixed exchange rates with respect for the decisions of the market is a mechanism of organised adjustment. Fixed rate systems in which occasional adjustments are made have not really satisfied this requirement. Such occasional adjustments have always been treated as if they were 'failures' of the system, a 'family problem' which no one wanted to talk about until it became absolutely necessary to make the adjustment and which everyone immediately attempted to forget afterwards.

In the case of the EMS, no attempt has been made to improve

upon this situation by learning from experience: the system set up is merely a 'little less fixed', with exchange rates that are allowed to fluctuate within predetermined margins. Once again, adjusting an exchange parity as compared with the ECU is a painful business. It is done hurriedly, without adequate preparation. The choice of new rates, which is so important, is not carefully thought out, or even properly negotiated, for lack of time. Decisions must be taken quickly because the speculators are at work and such speculation is risk-free because the secret has not been kept.

Once the new rates have been determined, even supposing that they have been judiciously chosen and do represent a new equilibrium, there is no likelihood that this state of affairs will be maintained, that the familiar disparities and distortions will not reappear and be amplified.

Along with these criticisms, we must put one thing to the credit of the EMS: its salutary effect on the chronic exchange rate instability among the EMS members and the fact that it has imposed a minimum of discipline, an obligation to align one's currency with the best managed of the component currencies.

A STABLE INTERVENTION INSTRUMENT TO STABILISE THE UNSTABLE

The spectacle of the foreign exchange markets is one of ceaseless agitation, a kind of monetary Brownian movement, in which it is pointless to look for any kind of guiding principle and in which attempts to create a minimum of order are even more pointless.

In the midst of all this agitation, there emerges, solid and permanent like a lighthouse in a storm, the Deutschemark. How indeed could it be possible to regulate the relations between all these currencies without an intervention medium, a common *numéraire*? This common medium was, and still is – for how much longer? – the US dollar. Its volatility and the American Administration's inability to manage its money are facts that are now acknowledged, along with the abuses to which a national currency is prone once it is invested with the privilege of acting as the key, or reserve, currency for the rest of the world.

The originality of the EMS is that it keeps the exchange rates of the member currencies within predetermined fluctuation margins (2.25 per cent, with 6 per cent for the peseta) on either side of a weighted average of all their exchange rates, otherwise known as the ECU. This definition is fine for the ECU as an indicator but it is not enough to turn it into a genuine currency.

The purpose of these margins is to give a continuing measure of the situation on the exchange markets, to sound the alert and to give the authorities the time to arrive at an agreement regarding intervention. This need to discuss the matter before intervening is easy to explain: the currencies concerned are many and exchange rates are controlled by the market. Demand and supply meet, revealing the prevailing 'trend' only at the last moment.

We have already seen (on p. 70), in connection with the problem of incongruence, why the margins of fluctuation accepted in respect of the exchange rates of the EMS currencies as compared with the ECU involve a risk of incongruence which impairs the use of the ECU as an intervention medium and even as a simple transaction currency. They also have the effect of encouraging risk-free speculation (the rates do not stay for very long at their ceiling or floor), which in turn causes the exchange rate oscillations to increase. In addition to the other problems that regulators have to grapple with, there are also uncertainties regarding the secondary effects of their external and internal interventions. All of these reflections bring out the merits of the neutrality of the ES in the extranational space to which it would be confined; they also justify the elimination of the ECU's fluctuation margins, which would prevent an ECU-turned-ES from being directly exchanged on the market, which is the prime condition that must be satisfied before it could acquire the 'transaction function'.

AN ORGANISED FORM OF 'CRAWLING'

The by now clearly recognised drawbacks to regulation by sudden and drastic parity changes led the former British Chancellor of the Exchequer, Nigel Lawson, to propose a system of what he called 'moving bands'. According to Samuel Brittan, who has discussed the project in the *Financial Times*, advantage would be taken of the fact that the rate of a particular currency had fallen on the market to near to its floor in order to move the fluctuation margin and, in a sense, put the floor where the ceiling used to be (or the other way around).

This proposal reflects the concern to find some more rational form of adjustment mechanism than the present system. But although these 'moving bands' would reduce the depth of the steps and multiply the number of thresholds, they would not eliminate them. It seems preferable to take the line of thought to its logical conclusion and replace this stepwise progression by a form of continuous sliding, and in a straight line rather than a zig-zag.

Such a form of gradual adjustment would fit in easily with the well known concept of the 'crawling peg', but it would have to be adapted and programmed to suit the ES system. In a 'crawling peg' system the rates at which currencies are exchanged vary each day (the 'crawling') and are allowed to find their own market-clearing level. Once this has been found the monetary authorities attempt to keep them there for the day's trading (thus 'pegging' them). In such a system of regulation, the gradual changes of exchanges rates are irregular; since the level is left to the market, no form of forecasting is possible; they eliminate sudden leaps up or down and spread the transitions out in time; nevertheless, they are only a practical way of going from one fixed exchange rate to another, without eliminating any of the inconveniences that may result. Exchange market disorders are not rectified and financial relations between the members of the Community are not harmonised.

The system proposed here for Stage 3 is different, in the sense that the changes in exchange rate parities are spread out over time and programmed; they are in the same proportion from day to day (linear variations), from the beginning to the end of the period.

Such a system is only conceivable, however, because the ES system has a standard of reference that is worthy of the name, with unchanging value. How, in fact, would it be possible to programme and regulate changes in exchange parities for days D, $D + 1$ and $D + 2$ without being able to refer, in order to measure the changes, to a standard of measurement with fixed value that is independent of time and place? Is it possible to imagine a train travelling at a speed which was programmed according to a standard that varied unpredictably from day to day, thus changing the time taken to cover the distance in the same proportions?

SLIDING INSTEAD OF UNPEGGING

Let there be three component currencies, A, B and C. At the beginning of a period of n days the rates of exchange of these three currencies into each other are $t\frac{A}{B}$, $t\frac{A}{C}$ and $t\frac{B}{C}$. At the end of the

same period they are $t'\frac{A}{B}$, $t'\frac{A}{C}$ and $t'\frac{B}{C}$. The daily sliding change in

the parity of A is $p_A = (t'\frac{A}{B} - t\frac{A}{B}) \cdot \frac{1}{n}$. The rate on the xth day will

be $t^x\frac{A}{B} = t\frac{A}{B} + p_A \cdot x$. The lemma of the targeted creeping rate is

as follows: throughout the period during which the rate gradually changes the purchasing power of the ES does not change. The formula that defines the ES in terms of A will therefore be as follows on the xth day:

$$t\frac{A}{ES}^x = m_A i_A + m_B i_B t\frac{A}{B}^x + m_C i_C t\frac{A}{B}^x \tag{10.1}$$

and

$$t\frac{B}{ES}^x = t\frac{B}{A}^x \cdot t\frac{A}{ES}^x; \; t\frac{C}{ES}^x = t\frac{C}{A}^x \cdot t\frac{A}{ES}$$

m_A, m_B and m_C, the indices of A, B and C, and $t\frac{A}{B}^x$ and $t\frac{A}{C}^x$ are the

given factors.

The permanence of the purchasing power of the ES derives from the fact that the three three-variable relationships (10.1) (the rates of exchange of A, B and C into ES) have the following relationship (10.2) as a corollary, which shows that the purchasing power of one ES is identical to the sum of the purchasing powers of the amounts of the component currencies (indexed after conversion into ES), which consequently guarantees its permanence of value.

If in fact we multiply each of the terms of the first equation of (10.1) by $t\frac{ES}{A}$, at the same time taking account of the other two equations of (10.1), we get

$$m_A i_A \, t\frac{ES}{A} \, x + m_B i_B \, t\frac{ES}{B} \, x + m_C i_C \, t\frac{ES}{C} \, x = 1 \tag{10.2}$$

The next example has figures in it and we shall stick with three components (instead of four or five) for the sake of simplicity:

$$t\frac{A}{B} = 10 \qquad t\frac{B}{C} = 2.5 \qquad t\frac{B}{C} = 0.25$$

Let us now suppose that these rates have not changed for two years. After an examination of the statistics for trade and foreign exchange dealings there is a comparison of ES movements in national and other currencies in and out of the reserves of the central office and the central banks. Finally, after negotiations, and with due concern for secrecy, $t\frac{A}{B}$ is allowed to go down from 10 to 9.5 per cent, representing a devaluation of B as compared with A of 5 per cent. At the same time $t\frac{A}{C}$ goes down from 2.5 to 2.4 per cent (a devaluation of 4 per cent).

The period of the creeping adjustment is set at 100 days. On day 0

$$m\frac{O}{A} = 3, \, m\frac{O}{B} = 0.2, \, m\frac{O}{C} = 2$$

The fundamental relation between the ES and A, B and C is

$$t\frac{A}{ES} = m_A + m_B \, t\frac{A}{B} + m_C \, t\frac{A}{C} \left(t\frac{B}{ES} = t\frac{A}{ES} \cdot t\frac{B}{A} \right)$$

If we replace the sums and the rates by their values

$$t\frac{A}{ES} = 3 + (0.2 \times 10) + (2 \times 2.5) = 10$$

we get $t\frac{ES}{A} = 0.1$; $t\frac{ES}{B} = 1$; $t\frac{ES}{C} = 0.25$. On the fiftieth day $t\frac{A}{B} = 9.75$, $t\frac{A}{C} = 2.45$ (given).

Under the effect of the changes in the price indices over 50 days, the amounts of the component currencies have become:

$m50_A = 3.015$ (annual inflation rate: 3.6 per cent)

$m50_B = 0.202$ (annual inflation rate: 7.2 per cent)

$m50_C = 2.0030$ (annual inflation rate: 1.1 per cent)

$$t^{50} \frac{A}{ES} = m_A + m_B t \frac{A}{B} + m_C t \frac{A}{C} = 9.891 \, t \frac{ES}{A}$$

$$= \left(\frac{1}{9.891} \right) = 0.1011$$

$$t \frac{ES}{B} = t \frac{ES}{A} \cdot t \frac{A}{B} = 0.1011 \times 9.75 = 0.987 \, t \frac{ES}{C}$$

$$= 0.2477$$

It can be verified that, on day $J = 50$, the figures in terms of m_A, m_B, m_C and $t \frac{ES}{A}$, $t \frac{ES}{D}$ and $t \frac{ES}{C}$ amount to one:

$$m_A t \frac{ES}{A} + M_B \, t \frac{ES}{B} + m_C t \frac{ES}{C} = 1$$

$$(3.015 \times 0.1011) + (0.202 \times 0.987) + (2.003 \times 0.2477)$$
$$= 1.000$$

ONE REQUIREMENT: CAREFULLY CHOSEN EXCHANGE RATES

This calculation may be compared with the calculation that is made each day for the ECU. It is simpler because all the terms in the formula can be determined in advance instead of resulting from market price quotations for 11 national currencies.

This is not to say that the ECU formula is too complicated. As it is at present, market operators have no need to worry about it: they are content with the figures that are sent to them by the institutions responsible for calculating the value of the ECU.

There is something else that is simpler in the case of the ES: during Stage 3 its exchange rates into national currencies other than the component currencies will be determined on the exchange markets. The rates for converting component currencies into foreign currencies may be deduced from these ES rates. In contrast, the exchange rates of the ECU into other currencies do not result from comparisons of supply and demand on the market, but are derived from the exchange rates of the nine component currencies. As a result it is necessary, when parities need to be adjusted, to follow the

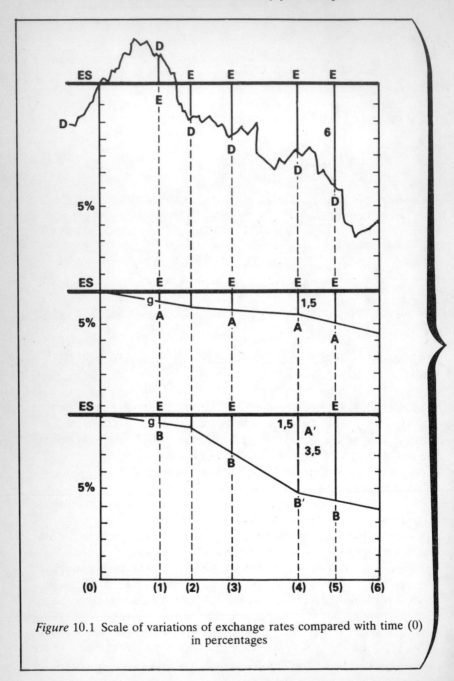

Figure 10.1 Scale of variations of exchange rates compared with time (0)
in percentages

Notes

The relative exchange rate variations from time (0) between D (the dollar) and the component currencies A and B are represented by vectors.

The relations between these rates (see p. 78) are such that we can say that the variation in the exchange rate of D into A or B (the amount of A or B that is worth one D) is represented by $\overrightarrow{AE} + \overrightarrow{ED} = \overrightarrow{BE} + \overrightarrow{ED}$.

$t \, {}^{A}_{B}$ is fixed outside the periods of adjustment between (2) and (4).

The A and B slopes are thus parallel from (0) to (2) and from (4) to (6). They diverge between (2) and (4). These slopes fall away from the ES's line by g, the weighted index of the ES formula (in the graph this is represented as constant because it changes very little and only slowly).

At time (2), on the scale shown, the variation of the exchange rate of D into A or B is AE + ED, that is, $1 - 2 = -1$ per cent. At time (2), therefore, the dollar has fallen by 1 per cent since time (0) in terms of A and B.

At (2): controlled fall of the rates of exchange of B into A, equal to A'B', that is 3.5 per cent over an adjustment period equal to (2) to (4). The same equations apply for the purpose of determining the exchange rates during this period (the ES lemma: see p. 119).

From (4) onwards the A and B slopes become parallel and fall away by g from the ES line. At time (5), for example, the variation in the rate is:

The dollar (D) into A: $\overrightarrow{AE} + \overrightarrow{ED}$: that is, $2 - 6 = -4\%$

into B: $\overrightarrow{BE} + \overrightarrow{ED}$: that is, $5.5 - 6 = -0.5\%$

The dollar has fallen by 4 per cent in terms of A and by 0.5 per cent in terms of B. It can be seen that the difference between the two (that is, $-4 + 0.5 = -3.5$ per cent) is identical to the one that was targeted.

Figure 10.1 shows the regulating and stabilising effect that could be obtained with a specifically European Community currency that was freely quoted on the exchange markets and to which the other Community currencies were linked by predetermined exchange rates. It also shows how easily these rates could be adjusted by a form of 'targeted creeping'.

procedure adopted by the EMS of stepwise adjustment from one level to another, instead of gradual creeping adjustment over a period, which could be announced in advance and carefully prepared and negotiated. The result is a flow of huge quantities of capital from one part of the market to the other. Sudden parity changes cause foreign exchange to flow into the reserves of the country of the currency which has just been devalued. Governments do not devalue twice in one and the same year, which means that foreign capital is sure to be able to make handsome profits, at no risk and for a long period of time, thanks to higher interest rates. A TCR system would deprive them of this opportunity for risk-free profit. At the moment the capital is repatriated, the sliding adjustments to exchange rates will have cancelled out the interest rate differential.

As they will be protected against untimely inflows of foreign capital and the increase in the money supply that results from the conversion of foreign currency into national currency, the monetary authorities will be in a position to stick to their money supply growth targets, especially as these targets were taken into consideration when selecting the new parities and the rate of creeping adjustment.

The chosen rates of change of the exchange rates of A, B and C reflect the interest rate and inflation rate differences between their respective countries. They will correct the distortions that result from these differences, the consequences of which will be all the more serious when internal markets in the member states cease to be protected by tariff barriers.

The rates at which currencies are exchanged for each other are an essential factor for trade in goods, services and capital. The graphs drawn by the OECD to illustrate what it calls 'loss of competitiveness' are extremely instructive. Such losses, in the case of France, increase after each devaluation. On occasion, at times of high inflation, loss of competitiveness has reached 10 per cent, which goes some way towards explaining the country's annual 40 000 million franc trade deficit with Germany.

The rates chosen for the conversion of a currency into others and the way those rates are determined and changed are of such importance for the European Community that the right sorts of procedure need to be devised and introduced.

Not only does the way that prices are determined in ES for foreign trade not interfere with the free operation of the market, but it also eliminates the causes of the sort of disturbance that prevents it from carrying out its function as a means of forecasting and returning the situation to balance.

ELASTIC (NOT FLUCTUATING) FIXITY

It now remains for us to examine the conditions for the practical application of this principle and the effects, where appropriate, of certain factors. These result from an examination of Figure 10.1.

The fixity of the exchange rates of the component currencies A, B and so on is represented by the fact that the straight lines which represent the variations, d', of their conversion rates into ES are parallel:

$$t \frac{A}{ES} = t \frac{A}{B} \cdot t \frac{B}{ES} \; ; t \frac{A}{B} \text{ fixed; } d' \, t \frac{A}{ES} = d' \, t \frac{B}{ES}$$

This fixity (or parallelism) implies that interest rates in the countries of origin of A and B must be similar otherwise speculators could take advantage of the risk-free option of converting at sight at stabilised rates so as to invest funds in the country where rates are highest and thus upset the sought-after states of equilibrium.

Rates that fluctuate within given ranges (such as those of the component currencies of the ECU) create a situation of uncertainty regarding the exact rate at which funds invested abroad will be repatriated, which has the effect of curbing speculation and engenders a degree of tolerance in respect of interest rate disparities. Merely from the point of view of the mechanism proposed here, a question must be asked: is there not a need, in certain cases, to allow for fluctuation margins for the exchange rates of the component currencies into each other, on the model of the EMS?

We have seen (p. 68) that the EMS component currencies are quoted on the exchange markets directly, independently of each other, and that this kind of procedure has had the effect of preventing the ECU from being used as an intervention medium and has reduced it to a mere indicator. If it were to copy this practice of fluctuation margins for its own component currencies, the ES would not suffer from this handicap because its component currencies would not be directly quoted but only via the ES itself, to which they would be linked by predetermined exchange rates. The margins for the exchange rates of the ES component currencies into each other would not result from market fluctuations but would be predetermined by the authorities. By varying the rate from one day to the next, they would be recreating and amplifying a factor of uncertainty which would act as a curb on any speculation centred on disparities between interest rates, without, however, compromising the use of the ES as a means for intervening in the exchange markets.

Speculative capital is short-term capital. An interest rate difference of 4 per cent a year would only result in a gain over two weeks of 1 cent on each US dollar at an exchange rate of 6 francs, not much more than an option premium and enough to facilitate the central banks' counter-offensive designed to discourage speculation: the manoeuvre is akin to what is known as 'countering' in football. The trick is to let the opposing player get out of his depth and then take advantage of the fact that he is defenceless in order to teach him a lesson. In this case, the 'lesson' would be a predetermined rate of premium for the currency if the speculator was betting on a discount.

During the period of creeping adjustments a manoeuvre of this kind would have the effect of artificially increasing the extent to which interest rates could be allowed to diverge (because they were not inviting speculation) and thus accelerate the process of creeping adjustment and reduce its duration.

The ES's constant purchasing power – its fundamental feature – would not be affected. At any given exchange rates of component currencies into each other, this purchasing power depends exclusively on the quantities of component currency included on day O and on the weighted price index, neither of which is modified (see the TCR lemma on p. 119). This 'controlled' elasticity ought to make it possible to 'regulate' the creeping.

As regards the outside world, it is the ES that is freely quoted in dollars or yen. The efforts to regulate the conversion rates into these currencies are well known, and are strictly limited by the central banks' resources. The ES's value in terms of dollars fluctuates, just as its value in terms of yen and other national currencies fluctuates (or, rather, let us say that if one currency has stable value and other currencies do not, it is they that fluctuate, although national currency fluctuations against the ES would not be so wide-ranging and inconsistent as those that can be observed on the exchange markets at present).

If a mechanism is made up of component parts that move freely and are not interlinked, there cannot be anything other than a state of chronic, disordered and sometimes violent agitation, even if the movements of some of the parts are limited, as is the case with the EMS. This situation can be mitigated by linking up certain component parts, which is what the EMS does. Some adjustment is still necessary, however, so as to take account of the fact that some of the cogs and levers are not properly adjusted. This is true of the interest rate and exchange rate cogs, whence the need for a degree of flexibility which will palliate undesirable effects.

By announcing a slope coefficient which offers market operators the chance of profit, the creeping process is speeded up, whereas the eventuality of predetermined rates which depart from the slope curve acts like a brake. Manipulation of both forms of motivation ought to make it possible to control the creeping without jeopardising the reserves of the central office or the Community central banks.

THE CONSTRAINT OF CONGRUENCE

It is because it is related to its component currencies by predetermined exchange rates that remain fixed for the whole day that the ES is able to satisfy the conditions needed for it to function as an instrument of exchange market intervention, both against foreign currencies and amongst the Community national currencies. In the event that A, B and other component currencies should be quoted directly and independently the ES would no longer be suitable for intervention operations. The arbitrage process is not an instantaneous one (see p. 129) and the ES would be subservient to it rather than in control of it; what is more, the risk of incongruence is always there (see p. 129). Once it was excluded from the role of intervention currency the ES would have only a remote chance of achieving the status of an international payment currency: something that is in any case not easy to achieve.

If a neutral European currency with stable purchasing power could be offered in place of the dollar the foreign exchanges would be relieved of their greatest handicap. The only thing that would matter then would be the ES's exchange rates into foreign currencies: the component currencies' exchange rates into national currencies would be no more than the corollaries of these rates. Contracts, prices, imports and exports would all be listed, invoiced and paid in ES. Conversions from or into national currencies would be brought forward or postponed in accordance with the entering into or the conclusion of forward market operations. In this way the interference of divergent interest rates would be reduced.

The stability of the ES in real terms would be transfused to international financial relations and would give them a consistency that intranational relations do not possess.

A FIXED POINT OF REFERENCE FOR A FINANCIAL UNIVERSE THAT IS IN A STATE OF FLUX

On the exchange markets, the ES central institution and the central banks will freely exchange their ES for foreign currencies (Stage 3). They will also exchange the constituent national currencies for foreign currencies. The effect on the market will be the same as would result from sales or purchases of ES, since the ES and its component currencies are exchanged at sight, at rates that are fixed and predetermined during the day's business (see the formula).

It may be supposed that the rates of exchange of the ES into the principal currencies, and therefore also the rates of exchange of the component currencies into other currencies, will be subject to some kind of international agreement. The present trend is towards a return to order in the exchange markets, and an attempt to stabilise rates. Each day the volume of trading on the Tokyo, New York, London, Frankfurt and Paris foreign exchange markets is in excess of $200 000 million equivalent. The size of this volume and the market agitation and effervescence are encouraged by the absence of a fixed point of reference, a common standard according to which the value of each currency could be measured. There are 170 states and 169 national currencies; it is otiose to hope that all of these currencies will be able to arrive at suitable cross-rates on their own without at the same time precipitating disorder.

It is possible to imagine that once the ES has been introduced on to the exchange markets it will become the fixed standard of reference that has so far been missing, because in the minds of market operators (as also in the minds of the members of the public) its value will be known. What is more, people will know that that value will not vary. For the first time ever, there will be something available on the market, a *numéraire*, with a value that will no longer be expressed only in terms of its equivalence in other currencies, all of which are as changeable in value as such a *numéraire* would be, but rather one that has a consistent value which does not change.

Whatever progress may be made towards unification by the member states of the European Community, wealth, attitudes and policies will continue to differ. In theory – and this was the great originality of the EMS – the commitments entered into with regard to the other member states of the Community are supposed to have the effect of moderating wage demands and imposing a salutary measure of discipline. The prospect of 'Europe', 1992 and the opening of frontiers provides some evidence: up to a point. One question arises, however, and it cannot be deflected or evaded with calls for union and 'dialogue'.

European unification has its merits and its problems. They must be looked squarely in the face. We are entering a system that is fundamentally liberal (in the Smithian sense of the term) in which liberalism, competition and the law of the market are not practised by companies only but will also apply increasingly in relations between states.

The French have no very great experience of such liberalism and probably have little taste for it either. Time and gradual adaptation will be necessary. Only a flexible system of monetary regulation will be able to prevent dangerous discord and distortions; a system that does not presuppose the completion of the political unification of Europe, with its crowning achievement, the creation of a single European currency; a system that will ignore disputes about the future European central bank and its independence, taking advantage instead of the real qualities of the ECU, along with its handicaps and its prospects.

THE ES AS ARBITRAGE MEDIUM

The use of a composite currency unit as a medium of exchange market interventions poses problems if the mutual exchange rates of its component currencies are decided by the market (the case of the ECU) instead of being fixed (the case of the ES). This observation also applies to arbitrage operations with a view to aligning exchange rates and making them 'compatible'.

Currency X is worth two of Y; Y is worth three of Z. If mathematical congruence is to be maintained, X must be worth six of Z: when it does not, opportunities for arbitrage arise. Unlike the monetary authorities, arbitrage operators are motivated by a desire to take advantage of these discrepancies, when the value of X and Z is incongruent, in order to make a personal gain. In the language of economic science, arbitrage interventions of this kind are called 'virtuous', something which is bound to gratify, and perhaps also surprise, the operators themselves. But it *is* virtuous, in the sense that intervening in this way corrects a distortion by realigning rates. At least, that is what most usually happens, but there are exceptions.

In order to grasp the mechanism of arbitrage, let us consider an extremely simple case, that of currency U as the common medium between two other currencies, A and B. If $t\frac{A}{U} = 1$ and $t\frac{B}{U} = 2$, equilibrium requires that $t\frac{A}{B}$ must equal $t\frac{U}{U} \cdot t\frac{U}{B} = \frac{1}{2}$. On the market, $100U$ will buy $100A$, $100A$ will buy $200B$, and $200B$ will buy $100U$. The initial quantity of $100U$ can be found at the end of the circuit.

For one reason or another, one of those rumours that are always going the rounds on the stock exchange results in a weakening of the exchange rate of A, whilst B remains firm. $t\frac{A}{U}$ goes up by 10 per cent: $100U$ will now buy $110A$, $110A$ will buy $218B$, and $218B$ will buy $108U$. For the arbitrageur, this situation represents a source of $8U$ of profit, which causes further speculative purchases of A and B and a movement towards a new equilibrium: $100U$ will now buy only $108A$, $108A$ will buy $214B$, and $214B$ will buy $105U$, representing potential profit of $5U$.

A third series of arbitrage operations brings the rates back into line, so that, when the cycle is completed, the dealer finds himself back with the $100U$ he started with.

The main instrument of arbitrage on the markets is, quite naturally, the dollar, and it is even used as the intervention medium for operations involving the EMS currencies. The ECU, for the reasons that have already been pointed out, is unsuitable for this role (the exchange rates of its component currencies may vary independently of each other). But the instability and the volatility of the dollar are good reasons for wanting to replace it in this use.

The exchange rate discrepancies that arbitrageurs exploit are, as is well known, extremely small. The rapidity with which buy and sell orders can be transmitted and the low cost, together with the extension of such transactions to all the world's financial centres, multiply the number of occasions for such activities, which explains the vast volume of foreign exchange transactions on the market, estimated at

20 times the volume of actual transfers of funds for purposes of investment or payment for supplies of goods or services. In addition to the fickleness and the sensitivity of the market mechanism, there is also its psychological vulnerability and the tendency to overreaction and exaggeration. Government ministries, opinion research organisations and many other bodies are not slow in producing figures or statistics; the stock exchanges of the world react in unison using the dollar. These are not the conditions required for an effective arbitrage medium.

Let us go back to the previous example: *A* weakens and *B* looks like a safe haven from *A*'s problems, but without – because time is needed for a return to equilibrium – a relaxation, as there should be, in the tensions between the exchange rates of the two currencies. Arbitrage in this case would consist of selling *U* for *A*, then *A* for *B* and finally for *U*.

However, *U* (the dollar) is tending to rise on the exchange markets. If our arbitrageur listens to the rumours, he will not be tempted to buy *A*, which is falling, in exchange for *U*, which is on an upward trend. If, on the contrary, *U* tends to fall, the arbitrageur will be discouraged from buying it in exchange for *B*.

The discrepancies that determine which currencies the arbitrageur should buy and which he should sell are very small. In the space of an hour variations in the dollar rate may upset his forecasts. In addition to the instability of the system that is to be regulated (the exchange rates) there is also the instability of the regulator (the dollar).

The use of the American currency as an instrument for regulating the exchange rates of European currencies is in itself a paradox. But to use, for that purpose, a currency unit that is chronically unstable is even more of a paradox. The ES would certainly be a more European intervention instrument than the dollar and also a more effective one, thanks to the fact that the exchange rates of its component currencies would be fixed *vis-à-vis* each other and its value in real terms would be stable.

SOME THOUGHTS ON THE USES OF A 'FORMULA CURRENCY'

Now that we have reached this point, and before we go on to Stage 4, let us pause for a moment's reflection. Money is used to pay for things. It is a right to something. The amount of that something is what determines its 'value'. The problem of how to guarantee and maintain that value is one of the things that have been at the forefront of man's preoccupations since the earliest times. For centuries man used a precious metal, either directly or indirectly, and the reason was the intrinsic value that was locked up in such payment instruments.

Claim money, which is the only kind of payment money in use today, can only have an uncertain value because the person or institution for which it is a debt, the issuer of the money, is at liberty to discharge that debt by handing over another form of claim money representing a claim on a different institution. From one form of claim money to another, the 'holder' of the claim changes debtor, but what he holds continues to be nothing more than a claim.

A lot of time and many unfortunate experiences were needed before men decided not to stabilise the purchasing power of money, but simply to attempt to do so. This delay was due less to a lack of willpower than to the backwardness of men's understanding of money matters.

On p. 145 the reader will find a re-evocation of the dreadful years of the 1930s, which saw the major economies of the world collapse, plunging the populations concerned into despair and then into criminal folly. That was over 50 years ago. In the late 1970s we knew rather more about these matters, but that did not prevent money matters getting out of hand once again, resulting in a situation that could only be overcome at the price of a painful period of disinflation.

In spite of the advance of technology and the broadening horizons of knowledge, societies continue to be ignorant of how to organise the monetary system on which the success of the economy depends. This justifies giving attention to a new kind of money: formula-based composite money. This is a new kind of money and there is no precedent for using it as a payment currency. It opens a vast and promising field to investigation, and is one that the ECU has not adequately explored.

For the first time in the history of money we are in a position to control the instrument, instead of being controlled by it. At this point I can almost see the smiles on my readers' faces (smiles of indignation as well as of amusement). 'Manipulating money is exactly what we are criticising, what we fear and what we are trying to stop.' Here, once again, the words are deceptive: money these days is indeed manipulated, for better or for worse. Monetary regulation is an attempt to manipulate it for the better, but such regulation attacks it, as it were, from the outside, without having any effect on its constitution. In such cases money is like a ball for which various players are struggling; a game that the authorities attempt to organise and discipline, but without attempting to affect the instrument itself, or its nature and composition.

This new type of composite money – 'formula money' – can be controlled from inside, precisely because it is defined by a formula. But that is only possible under certain conditions and provided that the environment is right. A neutral environment, without final consumption or production, such as the one surrounding the ES, is favourable to such an initiative. How to exploit this fact and the benefits, material and otherwise, that may be expected from it, are what constitute the subject matter of this book and this project.

COMMENTS

Comment on page 126. Only experience can determine the most suitable way of accommodating a creeping system to the interest rates at present in force and to market operators' behaviour (the elasticity of the fixed rates in force under the Bretton Woods system was 1 per cent).

The use of predetermined 'elastic' rates which depart temporarily from the chosen slope ought to eliminate most opportunities for speculation. But that is not what matters most: what matters is that the exchange rates of *A*, *B* and the other component currencies into each other and in relation to the ES should be 'controlled': that is to say, not left to the market. That is the condition the ES must satisfy if it is to be suitable for use as an intervention instrument and, beyond the world of the stock market and foreign exchange dealers, for the role of payment currency in international finance and commerce (see p. 119).

On day *n*, before the Community's financial centres open for business, the central office's managers establish and disseminate the predetermined rates at which the Office is prepared to exchange the component currencies for each other and for ES. If the creeping rate slope that they have chosen is 4 per cent over 200 days (that is, 0.02 per cent a day) and the variation in the weighted price index is 0.01 per cent (equal to an annual inflation rate of 3.6 per cent), the theoretical creeping of the rate on day n as compared with day $n - 1$ is 0.02 per cent for the exchange rate of A into B and $0.02 + 0.01 = 0.03$ per cent for conversion of A and B into ES.

Instead of these figures, the central office disseminates for day n the rates ruling on day $n - 1$ adjusted by 0.2 per cent (that is, ten times greater) for conversions of A into B and $0.20 + 0.01 = 0.21$ per cent for the exchange rate of A and B into ES. $t\dfrac{A}{ES}$ and $t\dfrac{B}{ES}$ are thus predetermined and 'stretched' above or below the slope of the creeping rates (0.01, in order to stay within the conditions for maintaining the ES's purchasing power). During the day the ES is quoted in terms of the dollar (D) at $t\dfrac{ES}{B} = x$, and the resulting conversion rates of A and B into the dollar are:

$$t\,\frac{A}{D} = x\,t\,\frac{A}{ES} \qquad t\,c\,\frac{B}{D} = x\,t\,\frac{B}{ES}$$

Comment on page 127. The first thing that must be aimed for in order to achieve some progress in the field of foreign exchange matters must be a substitute for the dollar as a medium of exchange and standard of reference. This alternative must not be a national currency, no matter how many virtues it may have. That has already been tried, on two previous occasions: in 1922 at Genoa, when an international conference attempted to construct a replacement for the gold standard by adding, to gold, in the role of standard of reference and reserve currency, first the dollar and sterling and then the dollar alone; and then at Bretton Woods in 1944 when, in order to organise the financial system of the post-war world, an attempt was made once again, so strong was the conviction that a monetary system needed to be based on a 'powerful economy', which could only be national.

The time is now past – or at least let us hope it is – when pre-eminence was thus given to the currency of a particular state to act as the 'queen' or 'sun' in the monetary firmament, around which the other currencies, of other states, were required to revolve, like satellites. Such an attitude was already mistaken, even when the dollar was the very symbol of financial solidity; today it is a mere aberration.

Comment on page 130. Money is an indispensable instrument at the service of the economy, but it is also an uncertain instrument, subject to periodic crises. In order to interpret the measures used in monetary regulation, the most convenient and most reliable approach is to refer to the quantity relationship, as expressed in terms of relative variations (see p. 179): $d'M + d'v - d'P = d'p$ (where M is the money supply, v the velocity of circulation, p the price level and P the rate of production in volume terms).

In order to control d_p, dM is used as a lever. But there are two other variables, dv and dP, whence an indeterminate state. And there are also exogenous factors (the rise in the level of wages, oil prices, and so on). Milton Friedman never tires of advising the American monetary authorities (the Federal Reserve) to take as their monetary growth target a rate calculated by adding together the growth coefficient in volume terms of production, say 3 per cent, and the acceptable rate of inflation, say 2 per cent, and to stick to the resulting figure of 5 per cent come what may and whatever the effect of exogenous factors on the level of prices.

The quantity relation shows that a price rise due to exogenous factors has the effect, if $d'M$ is not modified (for example, by putting more money into circulation), of causing production to fall and thus increasing the risk of an economic crisis. Milton Friedman's reply to this is that it is domestic production that falls, freeing a quantity of production for exports, the very one that is needed to compensate for the rise in external prices.

Milton Friedman is at his ease in macroeconomics, but diverting production to exports may take some time. It is true that it is imperative that the start of an inflationary price–costs spiral should be prevented, and it is also true that the velocity of money offers the fortunate surprise, when it is studied, of varying in a continuous, linear and therefore predictable fashion over a given period of time. This is something that Milton Friedman was responsible for discovering and he has, of course, turned it into an argument in support of his thesis.

Nevertheless, the monetary growth target must be capable of being calculated on a basis that includes internal exigencies as much as external effects. The progress of statistics makes it possible to refine the choice of economic targets, including monetary ones. But this kind of exercise is rendered impracticable by the volatility of the currency unit in which foreign trade is denominated (namely, the dollar). It is only possible if such measurements are made in a stable monetary unit.

11 Stage 3: On the European Scene

If we step back a little to look at things in perspective, it is impossible not to be struck, when considering the fantastic progress that has been achieved in so many fields of human endeavour, by the total lack of progress in one of them, namely monetary matters. This is all the stranger as there is no area where progress is more important for the economy and the welfare of nations, and the history of the world since the beginning of the present century provides eloquent testimony to the consequences that monetary disorders can have on the happiness and the life of mankind.

One conclusion is self-evident: the system must be overhauled. But the very need for an overhaul implies, once things have been allowed to degenerate beyond a certain point, the need for innovation. The term 'non-system', used ironically to describe the international monetary system, indicates the state into which it has been allowed to decline. As with a machine that is not working properly and is getting worse and worse, the causes must be found and, once they have been identified, parts must be replaced, changed and repaired. To do that, imagination and a willingness to experiment are called for, and it is here that the problems arise. Of course, imagination and creativity are highly honoured qualities, but it is not enough to praise the merits of such qualities: it is just as important to be fully aware of the special conditions that must be satisfied if they are to be allowed free play. In the case of the international monetary system, unfortunately, these special conditions have not yet been satisfied.

At this point it may be objected that we have indeed witnessed a recent successful monetary innovation in Europe: namely, the creation of the EMS and the ECU. That is true, but the example of the ECU seems to me to illustrate better than any other how difficult it is for a government, let alone a group of governments, to innovate for the benefit of the public, and explains why it is a waste of time to expect governments to indulge in the kind of experimentation that is necessary before an innovation can be adopted.

As a unit of account, the ECU represents a big and useful step forward: in a turbulent monetary universe, it offers an element of stability and certainty. But a transaction currency is an entirely different thing from a unit of account. No one can be required to use the ECU as an international transaction currency: it must be freely chosen. For this purpose, therefore, it has become a private unit. That word 'private' is very evocative. There is a public ECU, used in the accounts of the European Community, and there is a private ECU, which private financial institutions are attempting to launch as a means of payment. Between these two ECUs there is no connection, no relationship, apart from the fact that they share the same value definition.

Now, the ECU will never be a genuine currency until it is used for making payments, and not just payments by one central bank to another, but payments by the man on the street, by everyone. That is what the aim of the EMS should be. All the same, the Community authorities have had no hand in the enterprise: it is purely the concern of the private sector (whence this strange-sounding term 'private ECU').

It is pointless and unfair to blame national governments and finance administrations for this unfortunate divorce between the official and the private ECUs. Such a separation is in the nature of things. As regards monetary matters, some of the best brains are doubtless to be found at the Bank of France, and it is not short of ideas and projects. But it lacks the political and administrative means to try them out even at national level, still less at international level, where it would depend on the goodwill of 11 other national governments.

In order to innovate successfully, one needs first at all to experiment, correct and rectify; one needs the right to make mistakes. The governments of the world do not have any such right, and this observation has been one of the guiding factors behind the project set out in the pages of this book.

During Stages 1 and 2 initiative was allowed free rein, without directly involving the responsibilities of one or more governments or public administrations. In this way the experiment has the benefit of the flexibility that it needs. But a Community currency, even one that is only used for external purposes, cannot remain a private affair for very much longer. Once the experiment has shown, during Stages 1 and 2, that such a currency is feasible, the ES will acquire an official status during Stage 3. That is the expectation – and the assumption – with which this chapter deals.

It may seem presumptuous to suggest that the Community may one day be prepared to change its policy and replace the present ECU with a constant one. Certainly, this will not happen straight away, merely on the strength of the merits of the ES: but it may happen on the evidence of a growing market that is developing before the eyes of the public, whose opinion on the matter national governments will not be able to ignore.

If that happens, a new stage in the process of monetary unification will have been completed. It will have started where it had to, where it could, with the EMS and the ECU, and it will have concluded where it had to, with the creation of a Community currency that is better than any other, for use in trade between member states and with non-member states.

Thus no one should be offended by the following pages, which anticipate, propose and unfold a canvas which will be useful for those who wish to add to it, remove from it or otherwise innovate.

FROM PUBLIC TO PRIVATE: A TESTED PROCESS OF DEVELOPMENT

During Stage 1, the project has been in the hands of a consortium of Eurobanks with the unofficial support of a national government. The consortium has endeavoured to develop the use of the ECU as a transaction currency for international financial relations, but without solving the problems regarding quality, definition and composition that the ECU poses. For this reason, as soon as circumstances permit it, the ES, in its turn, will be introduced and offered to market operators (Stage 2), and for this purpose it will be enough to replace nominal national units, in the same official ECU formula, by constant national units.

Introducing the ES will be a source of further profits for the members of the consortium. At the same time it will demonstrate the power of attraction that a stable currency can have and will show how it is suitable for fulfilling the transaction and reserve functions that are required of an international means of payment.

The demonstration in question, as it is imagined for Stage 2, can only be on a modest scale, but that will be enough to show the public, the professionals, the theoreticians and the practitioners, in government and public administration, the reality of an exceptional currency unit, so that its advantages can be seized upon.

I admit that this type of approach is not entirely satisfactory; some of the stages could be skipped. But the pragmatism that is the basic principle of this project requires recourse to private initiative because it is hard to imagine that the consensus among national governments necessary for an almost revolutionary enterprise such as the adoption of the ES as the Community's currency unit could ever be achieved. The need for an innovation that abandons well trodden paths in order to achieve some progress towards European monetary unification has not yet been properly recognised.

Only deeds, examples before people's very eyes, will have any chance of overcoming refusals, of shaking faith in existing principles and forms of organisation, no matter how defective. The forces of resistance to change grow exponentially in proportion to the number of governments whose consent must be obtained in order to undertake the project; whence the path proposed here, which is perhaps tortuous, but which offers a chance of success because it appeals to kinds of motivation (the desire for profit and prestige) which are known to be effective and takes advantage of an opportunity which is unprecedented and known to be very promising.

THE ES SYSTEM TRANSPOSED AND OFFICIALISED

The pivot of the system would be the central institution, under the authority of the Commission of the European Communities. A number of Community currencies – four or five at the most – would participate in the ES system and would be selected to act as the component currencies of the ES, not just because of their importance in international financial relations but also because they were well managed currencies. The other national currencies of the Community would retain their independence outside the ES system, perhaps within the EMS.

The central ES, which would be issued and managed by the central institution, would be used exclusively for transactions between the latter, the Community central banks, non-Community central banks and commercial banks affiliated to the consortium. They would not be in the hands of the public.

The central institution would not make any loans or purchase any debts. During Stages 1 and 2 it would dispose of a quantity of working capital in central ES, created as claims upon itself and lent to the consortium member banks. During Stage 3, after being officialised at the European Community level, it may be expected that, in common with other international institutions such as the IMF and the

FECOM, the central institution will issue central ES against payments of national currency, readjusted from time to time.

The central banks of the Community member states, which will be members of the ES system, will divide among themselves some of the functions that were peculiar to the consortium's interbank office. The ES banking system proper will be made up of Eurobanks from the consortium described in earlier chapters of this book. Each of them will be connected (affiliated) to one of the central banks of the system (that of the country in which it is domiciled if that country is a member of the ES system and that of a neighbouring country if it is not a member). Thanks to this organisation (priority affiliation), the member banks of the consortium will be able to retain the benefits of their initiative and the advantage they will have acquired by launching their enterprise in the purely private-sector Euromarket ahead of any competitors.

Each affiliated Eurobank's ES transactions will be reflected in its account at the central bank to which it is answerable. The ES operations of the affiliated Eurobanks are those that were described under Stage 2: they will make loans in bank ES and will exchange national currencies for ES. They will clear their mutual debts and claims each day, first via their central banks and then via the central institution. The clearing system will thus be global and will include all the banks that are affiliated to the ES system (clearing in tiers, see p. 205).

The bank ES will not circulate as means of payment within states: they will be used exclusively for the purpose of making international payments. They may, however, be held by residents, just like other financial instruments. The Community member states will continue to use their own national currencies for internal payments.

The central institution will be responsible for regulating the ES on the exchange markets. It will cooperate with the other central banks in order to stabilise exchange rates. The national currencies that are members of the ES system will be quoted on the foreign exchange markets, but subsidiarily to the ES, and will be linked to it by pre-announced rates which will be independent of their exchange rate with non-Community currencies. Non-Community banks will create 'Euro-ES', which will be claims upon bank ES created by affiliated banks.

There is no need to go any further with this description of how the ES banking system will function: it represents a faithful transposition to the scale of the Community of the consortium system described in an earlier chapter, ignoring the purely political and administrative aspects of the organisation; with the exception, however, of the question of the independence of the future European Central Bank (which, curiously enough, has agitated public opinion much more than the technical question of how to devise an appropriate mechanism to set up such a bank and help it work). The subject is an interesting one and provides an opportunity to clarify some aspects of a monetary 'accident' which has had the most alarming consequences. Conclusions may be drawn from this episode which go beyond the question of the independence of the European Central Bank: namely, that proper monetary analysis is the condition *sine qua non* of good management, and of innovation.

ONE POINT OF VIEW ON THE 'INDEPENDENCE' OF CENTRAL BANKS

This book is concerned first of all with monetary mechanisms that are yet to be put together, and much less with the forms of administrative organisation needed in order to ensure that they work properly. All the same, it is worth pausing a few moments in order to consider one aspect of this form of organisation so as to show that it fulfils one obligatory condition: respect for national sovereignty and maintenance of the autonomy of the national central banks.

Our central institution is not in fact a bank. Like the interbank office of Stages 1 and 2, it must be looked on as a body set up in order to carry out a task that without any doubt is part of the responsibilities of the European Commission: that is, the promotion of an external European currency and the stabilisation of exchange rates.

The central institution will issue central ES in return for national currencies. It will not make any loans. Its resources will be obtained from borrowing on the market or from swaps. The door will be firmly closed to any kind of laxity, which is rightly feared in cases like this. In this way it should be possible to avoid, during Stage 3, the contentious question of the independence (or lack of it) of the future European Central Bank.

A central bank in a given country has a variety of roles. The management of the currency is also the management of the economy. This latter management is a synthesis of fiscal, wage and social policies and hence the position of Valéry Giscard d'Estaing, who sees, in a European Central Bank, the crowning stage in a process of gradual unification of Europe, but one that is still some way off and which leaves plenty of time for experimentation, adaptations, corrections and innovations, without really raising the question of a European Central Bank, whether or not exclusive, whether or not a federal institution.

All the same, people continue to discuss the question of the independence of this putative European Central Bank, and do so heatedly. The Bundesbank, fortified by its successes in the monetary field, is intransigent. A European Central Bank, it maintains, must be independent of any political influence. The management of a future European currency (but which one?) must be left to the 'technicians'. It is a pity that some consideration is not given in this context to the past and to the difficulty of drawing lessons or a rule of conduct for the future from past experience.

The Bundesbank owes its form of organisation and its independence to the Americans. Both were imposed on the vanquished by the victors and were naturally based on the situation of the American Federal Reserve System. As is well known, the Governor of the Federal Reserve System is appointed by the President for a period of six years. He is in effect independent of the President but is required to account to Congress twice a year for his management of the Federal Reserve and his plans and projects (the monetary targets). In order to understand the 'independence' of the Federal Reserve we must look at the situation prevailing when it was set up. At that time, in 1913, what was most feared and what had to be prevented at all costs was uncontrolled use by the government of the 'printing press', in response to difficulties and demogogic pressures. There were still very vivid memories of the monetary explosion which, during the Civil War, had ruined the finances of the Confederacy. The intention was a laudable one, but it did not take account of the fact that issuing money was no longer the exclusive privilege of the central bank and, as time passed, was becoming less and less so. On the contrary, it was now the privilege of the banking system as a whole and was destined to become more and more so.

Sixteen years later, the independence of the Federal Reserve had disastrous consequences by preventing the Washington government from correcting the psychological effects of the 1929 stock market crash. Once the stock exchange had collapsed there was panic. The banks, which were many, small and isolated from each other, succumbed to a fear of shortage of liquidity and called in loans, at the expense of consumers and small businesses. In three months the velocity of circulation fell by 36 per cent and industrial output by 20 per cent. Not long after that, the volume of outstanding loans contracted and, with it, the money supply.

The experts of the period had not apparently realised that bank money, which already accounted for a sizeable proportion of the money supply, does not follow the same rules as central bank money. Whereas central bank money, once it has been put into circulation, stays there (unless it is locked up in Keynes's 'liquidity traps'), bank money needs to be constantly renewed through bank credit. Suddenly cutting off bank credit had the result of withdrawing money from the economy, which was just like withdrawing blood from a living organism. The American economy did not get over the shock and it took the Second World War and massive injections of money to get it back on its feet.

Roosevelt, and even his predecessor, Hoover, had looked into the bottomless pit into which the economy was falling and had realised the need for an urgent injection of new money. The Federal Reserve, however, fortified by its 'independence', remained faithful to its dogmas, which required it to stay outside 'market effects'.

Once the creation of money is no longer the privilege of the Sovereign and has been extended to include the whole commercial banking system, there is a problem of discipline. This discipline can be more effectively imposed by the government than by the monetary authorities.

Resistance to inflation requires control of public finances and a curb on wages and salaries. Both are the prerogative of the central government: the central bank has no say in such matters. If a central bank is given an excessive amount of independence and an exclusive role in monetary matters, it is given responsibilities which only a government is able to discharge. The risk then is that they will be neglected. In Washington today the way in which the executive and legislature escape their responsibilities in connection with the budget deficit shows the truth of this. It is better to combine power and responsibility than to separate them.

Would it not be better, in connection with the Community Central Bank, to leave the question of its 'independence' aside? Would it not be better to find the means of making some progress without arousing opposition and diversions over an institution for which there is no fundamental need, at least in the present scheme of things?

At the Community summit meeting in Hanover in July 1988, Mrs Thatcher refused even to allow the matter to be mentioned. The final communiqué thus omitted all reference to a European Central Bank. As for the Germans, although they did not go so far, they evinced little taste for such an initiative (but they are too concerned not to offend their neighbour's sensibilities to express an opinion and it is perhaps enough for them to know that the project is a long-term one and that time is working in favour of the Deutschemark and the Bundesbank).

This project confines itself to proposing the creation of a central institution which will not be a central bank, even if, in the ES system, it will be responsible for external regulation (exchange rates) and will make a contribution to internal regulation (maintenance of the purchasing power of the currency and development of ES business) whilst freeing the authorities who are responsible for it from the side-effects of regulating the exchange rate as they manifest themselves at present.

DISCONNECTING INTERNAL AND EXTERNAL MANAGEMENT

In order to disconnect internal and external management what is needed, first and foremost, is an instrument for exchange market intervention which will not be one of the national currencies at present in use and one that will be selected for itself, because it is better than the others.

External regulation seeks to stabilise exchange rates and internal regulation seeks to stabilise purchasing power; two related but distinct objectives, which are often divergent and sometimes in opposition.

The criteria according to which a regulatory mechanism is judged, whether in economics or mechanics, are selectivity and reliability, aptitude to take effect where the effect is needed and not somewhere else, and the ability to respond rapidly and with magnified force (leverage).

Interest rates, as regulatory mechanisms, do not satisfy these criteria. On the exchange markets, as a medium, there is a national currency, the currency of a foreign country, which spreads the contagion. As a mechanism there is the rate of interest, which is expected to do too much. Externally, it is expected to regulate the capital flows, whilst internally it is expected to control the growth of bank credit, the main source from which the mass of means of payment (purchasing power) is increased. In addition, it is also supposed to promote economic activity and investment. All of that (and more besides) results in a leverage effect working in the opposite direction: in order to keep monetary growth to the range 100–105, instead of 100–110, the cost of borrowing is raised, not just on the 10 that is to be restrained but on the original 100 as well.

No real progress will be made in monetary management so long as external management of the exchange rate has not been disconnected from internal management, which is concerned with the purchasing power of money and economic growth. But disconnecting them will not be possible so long as a national currency (one, moreover, that is afflicted with chronic instability) is used as international means of exchange. It *will* be possible with a neutral currency that is not the currency of any particular state and has stable purchasing power.

COMMENTS

Comment on page 143. The Great Crisis of the 1930s has been analysed in all its aspects by the science of economics. The roles of credit and investment have been criticised in abundance (by Keynes). But the main role was not played by credit as such. The sudden shortage of bank credit did, it is true, contribute to the slowing-down of the economy, but it does not explain the extraordinary speed with which the paralysis spread, as if like a haemorrhage in a living body. A mere glance at the graphs for economic activity at the time in the United States are enough to show that in a matter of months, weeks even, the economy collapsed.

It takes time to put bank credit into effect. Calling it in, or an absence of credit, is quicker to take effect. Only this sudden withdrawal of bank credit from the mass of available payment money can explain the brutality with which the crisis affected the economic system; one which, moreover, was destitute at that time of any shock-absorbers, such as unemployment benefit. The events of the 1930s also highlight the very special nature, which even today has not been adequately explained, of the fact that the constant renewal of bank credit continually pumps up the money supply: not enough in the 1930s and too much in the 1970s.

The transfer of 90 per cent of the privilege of issuing money from the government authorities to a group of commercial banks is one of the great events of the monetary history of the last 100 years, but its consequences have not yet been adequately explored.

Comment on page 144. We have just seen a typical case of interference and confusion of effects. It is a very recent one and has already been quoted but it is worth quoting again because it provides a demonstration, not of a mistake of analysis as in the case previously mentioned (1929), but rather of the inability to manage things properly, and look for the means of so doing, by an appropriate form of monetary organisation.

During the early years of the 1980s, in the United States, interest rates on bank loans reached unprecedented levels (21.5 per cent in December 1981) in order to absorb an outbreak of inflation which had been aggravated by the rise in the price of oil (but which was much higher than the oil price rise could have been responsible for 'quantitatively'). This was followed by a rise in the exchange market value of the dollar, as a result of the inflows of foreign capital attracted to the United States by the high returns. This capital was converted into dollars at the Federal Reserve and added to the dollars that were already in circulation, which was the exact opposite of what the authorities were aiming for by stifling the growth of bank credit. The consequence was a diversion of spending on to imported goods and rapid growth of consumption, the collapse of certain sectors of industry and agriculture and an explosion in the foreign trade deficit. Abroad, various economies, principally those of the developing countries, were shaken in their turn.

The main topics of the moment are continually before the eyes of the public, and in well chosen and imagined terms: the 'battle' against inflation, 'defence' of exchange rate parities, 'development' of investment, 'protection' of savings, 'encouragement' to acquire property (in the case of housing), the 'indebtedness' of the developing countries, the foreign trade 'imbalance', and so on and so forth.

The press, the radio and the television, with their talkative and well informed commentators, have familiarised the general public with these terms, which cover all forms of action, like a treatise on military strategy. But does the public realise that behind all that, in order to 'regulate' everything that the commentators say needs to be regulated, there is one instrument – and almost one only – which moreover is full of imperfections: namely, the rate of interest?

The central bank's intervention rate is supposed to take effect thanks to the banks' needs in terms of central bank money, so that they can convert deposits into bank notes. This need is continuing to decrease because of the growing share of bank money in the total money in circulation, and because it is lost in the continuous movement of conversions from and into foreign currencies. In addition, there is also the process of osmosis between the short, the medium and the long term, which is amplified by the various kinds of 'financial instrument', creators of liquidity if ever there were any, such as unit trusts, SICAVs and so on.

The result of all this is that the nominal interest rates of the moment, instead of real rates (as with the ES), are carried forward into the future; a sure recipe for prolonging inflation and inequality.

12 An Internal Currency and an External Currency

States have internal currencies for use in paying bills within their own territory and external currencies which are used for paying overseas debts, currencies that they share with other states and which function as forms of financial intermediary.

An importer domiciled in Paris with a bill to pay from a supplier in Spain asks its bank to purchase a given quantity of pesetas which are then transferred to the exporter's account in Barcelona. The importer's account in Paris is debited in French francs and the exporter's account is credited in pesetas. But this can only happen after an intermediate currency has come into play between the French franc and the peseta.

In order to obtain the pesetas for its customer, the French bank has had to dip into its dollar reserves and it used those dollars to pay the bank which sold it the pesetas. It is also possible, alternatively, that it used those dollars to pay the bank in Barcelona directly, which then either converted them into pesetas or, more probably, transferred them to its reserves, at the same time as it credited its customer, the Spanish exporter. The following day, the bank in Paris, in its turn, receives a transfer of pesetas, which it sells to another bank in exchange for dollars.

This basic pattern is open to numerous variations. It shows the reality – and the necessity – of a monetary medium or intermediary for financial dealings and payments between states. It also shows the need for a 'pool' of liquidity denominated in this medium, into which the sums received are paid after conversion from national currencies and from which the sums that are to be paid out may be drawn. This 'pool' occupies the extraterritorial space which has been frequently referred to in this book and which is the natural territory of the ES.

This territory has no physical limits, but it does have conceptual, administrative and fiscal limits and, above all, monetary limits. It is used for depositing the assets of non-residents and the reserves of central banks. It is the preferred choice of Eurobanks. In geographical terms, it is coterminous in many places with national territories, where the stock exchanges, the banks and the treasury departments of big international companies operate. This immense area is criss-crossed by international financial dealings. It is an area which many financial flows cannot help but cross; where, in addition to a market, footloose funds can also find refuge, substitutes and the pool of liquidity mentioned above. The total 'money supply' to be found in this area amounts to several million million dollars.

IN ORDER TO CREATE A POOL OF LIQUIDITY AND RESERVES: A STABLE CURRENCY

When we consider the purpose of this pool and its monetary unit it is easy to see why it operates mainly in dollars. The dollar's pre-eminence has resulted from the need for a common medium of exchange between national currencies. That is the main reason, a much more important one than its position as the national currency of the most powerful country in the Western world, and without any doubt more important than any intrinsic qualities fitting it for this role; such qualities have indeed long since disappeared.

The dollar is an international medium of exchange but it is also – and primarily – the legal tender currency within the territory of the United States. There is no reciprocal effect between these two uses. The dollar as an international currency has no direct effect in terms of purchasing power on the dollar as national means of payment (this matter is dealt with at some length in Chapter 14). But the contrary is not true: the bouts of inflation to which the domestic dollar is subject and the American state's budget deficits do have direct effects on the value of the external dollar. And it is indeed one of the paradoxes of our times that the currency unit that is most frequently used as an international medium of exchange and standard of reference should be one of the most unstable of the principal currencies of the world.

These days everyone is aware of the dollar's instability and of the fact that it is dependent on the whims of a government and a people who are both to a considerable extent indifferent to its role as an international currency and to the responsibilities which that involves. The dollar's place is now starting to be taken by the Deutschemark and the yen and the beginnings of a system of monetary zones can be glimpsed: the dollar for the Americas, the yen for Asia and the Deutschemark for Europe.

It would be much better for the member states of the European

Community if they had, as their external currency, a specifically European *numéraire* which was not the currency of any one state and which was, in addition, equipped with a special property: the special property that is most desirable for a medium of exchange and reserve instrument destined to form a pool of liquidity.

That special property is constant value in real terms. The very description of the use for which this pool is destined implies the need for this *numéraire* to retain its value from the moment assets are stored in it until the moment they are withdrawn from store. Without such a special property it is doubtful that any European currency will succeed in going beyond the narrow role of unit of account, whether official or private.

In contrast, the stability of the value of the ES ought to induce other states, outside the European Community, to choose it as their external currency, thereby enlarging the 'pool' which will be needed for the purpose of facilitating international financial relations. An exporter in Taiwan, an oil producer in Arabia and a bank in Nigeria all use the dollar, as does a financial intermediary in Peru. Now they are considering using the Deutschemark instead. They will be tempted by a European currency unit that is a by-word for stability. Who can doubt that such a quality will be truly remarkable in a monetary universe where everything is constantly shifting and subject to countercurrents, where all currencies either lose their value or are in danger of losing it?

The European Community would then have achieved two objectives: it would have affirmed its unity by identifying itself with a currency, its own, and only its own, which would be better than any other currency; and at the same time it would have equipped itself with an effective instrument for stabilising exchange rates and orientating trade flows towards Europe. Prices would be listed in ES instead of being listed in dollars. Importers and exporters would know that prices listed in the ES would not be likely to be raised or bowled over by a groundswell of funds rushing into the dollar, upsetting cost prices and opening and closing sales outlets.

The currency unit that the central bank of a particular country keeps for the purpose of regulating and adjusting trade flows between that country and the outside world is known as a 'reserve unit'. This is one of a central bank's main functions: hence the name 'Federal Reserve System' given to what is in effect the central bank of the United States.

Reserve units are stored up when there is a trade surplus and they are used to feed demand when there is a trade deficit. The main property that such a reserve function calls for is stability of value; in addition to that, reserve units also function as reference units.

In a system where goods and capital circulate freely there is a need to maintain a minimum of parallelism between changes in currencies' exchange rates and changes in their purchasing power. A trade imbalance between two countries cannot last for ever. Correction of the trade imbalance will eventually be followed by an alignment of purchasing powers, by inflation of one currency or deflation of the other.

One remedy to this situation would be continuous, parallel development of exchange rates and purchasing powers; the advantage, from this point of view, of a standard of reference for trade defined in terms of international purchasing power such as the ES, is thus clear.

TOO MANY UNPREDICTABLE VARIABLES ON THE EXCHANGE MARKETS FOR A DEFECTIVE MEDIUM

The new European Community currency must be not only a means of payment and a reserve instrument but also a tool for interventions on the exchange markets. It must be used to express and correct any imbalances between member states and it must also be the medium used for the purpose of calculating the position of the main member state currencies on the exchange markets *vis-à-vis* foreign currencies.

The ES will be directly quoted on the exchange markets. The component member state currencies will be linked to the ES by conversion rates that will be independent of the market. They will be exchangeable into ES at these rates on demand. Their value in terms of foreign currencies will thus be calculated in terms of the ES, even in cases where they are directly quoted (it will be remembered that the conversion rates for the ES into the component currencies increase each day, in line with the weighted price index in the formula: that is, on the figures for summer 1988, a daily increase of about 1/10 000).

The two functions of the ES, as an instrument for making payments and holding reserves and as an intervention tool, go hand in hand and will help to assert its presence on the markets.

In the EMS, as it operates at the moment, each component currency in the ECU formula is quoted on the markets directly against every other currency. The member state central banks intervene on the markets in order to maintain exchange rates within the agreed fluctuation margins, as compared with a weighted average (which is what defines the ECU). Problems of coordination and harmonisation – and about what steps to take – do arise. The French government complains of the 'asymmetry', as it sees it, of the responsibilities and the objectives that are implicit, for the central banks, in the need to maintain the exchange rates of the component currencies with regard to each other within fixed fluctuation limits, as well as their positions *vis-à-vis* other currencies, first and foremost the dollar.

The ECU is not used as such for market intervention. The Community's exchange rates are defended by the national currencies, together, separately, sometimes divergently and sometimes even against each other.

In the spring of 1988, in an internal memorandum on European monetary union, Mr E. Balladur, the then French Finance Minister, said: 'Whatever the extent to which the joint credit system is perfected, the onus for financing market interventions rests systematically on the central bank of the country whose currency is least sought after. This anomaly would be quite clear in the event that the country whose currency was appreciating the most should depart the furthest from the previously agreed objectives.' He goes on to recommend that 'steps must be taken gradually to ensure that no major non-Community currency or a single Community currency comes to be used as the *de facto* intervention and reserve currency for the EMS as a whole'. In these few words, Mr Balladur thus condemned both the present procedure for regulating exchange rates *vis-à-vis* the dollar and the rise of the Deutschemark as European currency *par excellence*.

The asymmetries in the EMS with which fault is found are such that they threaten the whole system, and first of all the simultaneous floating of the EMS member currencies, even within their fluctuation margins. In order to calm the markets and counteract the agitation which grips one, two, three currencies and soon ten or more, an intervention medium which is equipped with very special properties is indispensable. The most important of these special properties is an organic resistance to floating by the 'effect of mass'. This effect can be obtained in the case of the ES thanks to the fixed conversion rates that link its component currencies. Furthermore, there is a factor for stability, a value in real terms that is clear and familiar to market operators.

The theoreticians of floating exchange rates thought that the levels at which currencies would settle down on the markets, once they were freed of the shackles of fixed exchange rates, would faithfully reflect the relative positions of their respective economies and the trade situations of the countries concerned and, by arriving at a position of 'equilibrium', that would help to align them.

Market forces have enormous virtues, but if we wish to put them to good use we need to know their limits. Even in a marketplace where goods are sold by open outcry, the equilibrium price is not always achieved. On the exchange markets we are very far from achieving it. It is excluded by the extreme fluidity of the market, its natural instability and the enormous masses of capital involved. The theoretical point of market-clearing equilibrium is overturned by waves of buying or selling that are inspired purely by gut feeling, rumour and uncertainty, as well as expectations (providing in addition profitable opportunities for speculation). The position of equilibrium that the theoreticians of floating exchange rates seek would be brought nearer if dealers' feelings and expectations could be based on a reference that clearly defined 'real' values.

In monetary matters, the psychological factor is preponderant; more so than in other matters. One of the most striking examples is that of the gold standard, as it used to function in the nineteenth century, particularly during one of the crises that periodically used to affect Western economies; another is the Great Depression of the 1930s.

In both cases it was psychological reactions that played the decisive role. In the first crisis (the crisis of the nineteenth century), negative reactions by the holders of money, who were perturbed by rumours and hearsay, often lacking in any foundation, were what caused the trouble. In the second case (the 1929 crash), it was negative reactions on the part of the distributors of bank credit faced with the prospect of a run on the banks.

One of the main objectives of monetary regulation is to monitor price levels. For this purpose, attempts are made to curb increases in costs (wages and salaries) and expansion in the money supply. In fact, the main cause of disorder is not the direct effect of exogenous actions but the way they are amplified by psychological reactions on the part of the masses. Here is an example. Movements on the exchanges add (or subtract) means of payment 'quantitatively' (an endogenous reaction of one of the parameters on the other three). Movements of around 13 000 to 15 000 million francs are needed in order to cause prices to move by 1 per cent, and only after a lapse of 18 months. A rise in the oil price of $3 dollars, up to $20 a barrel, has a 'quantitative' effect on prices of no more than 1.5 per cent, which is far below the effects observed as a result of price or cost spirals or the precautionary measures that are precipitated by such a price rise.

One powerful psychological factor is the natural desire of all holders of money to protect the value of their asset whilst keeping it simultaneously instantly available. This factor could be usefully exploited by an external monetary instrument with stable purchasing power which, when used domestically as an alternative savings instrument, would syphon off excess liquidity in national currencies after they had gone through the credit circuits and before they were used for consumption.

Monetary systems have the rather unenviable characteristic of being unstable by nature, of involving a multitude of parameters and of depending on choices made by innumerable users, as their fancies take them. That is why there is a need, in order to control monetary systems, to attempt first of all to control people's choices, and to do so by indirect processes of which none are very satisfactory. The need to organise, to rectify and to repair the disorder is recognised, along with the need to innovate in order to do so. One very happy innovation would be to introduce into a system that is intrinsically unstable one component which by *its* nature was fixed and to which choices and fancies could cling.

A WEIGHTY CONGLOMERATE TO DAMP DOWN AGITATION

The ES intervenes directly on the markets and would constitute, along with the component national currencies, a conglomerate which would be able, thanks to its weight and power, to damp down disorderly market movements, whereas the EMS allows its component currencies to float freely within specific margins.

One may wonder why an institution such as the EMS, set up in order to create stability, should include so many unstable parameters, even allowing for the fact that variations within these parameters occur within defined limits. The components of the system do not go through the floor or the ceiling, but they are in a situation of chronic instability, which is a factor making for disturbances to the system. It is likely that this 'limited floating' was seen at the time (1977) as a compromise between fixed and floating exchange rates, each of which had its merits (and its demerits); doubtless it also represented a compromise between respect for the 'market' and the need to correct the market's abuses (a dilemma that is still with us today, and not just in connection with the economy and money). At the same time, the architects of the EMS thought that this kind of floating would show which way the market was heading and that it would give the central banks time to arrive at a common position and harmonise their market interventions.

It is not certain that, at the time, anyone realised that it might happen that the central banks would need to intervene in opposite directions in order to arrive at a 'harmonised' position (one selling dollars which were immediately purchased by another). In addition to this concession to the market, there were also hesitations – and, it may be supposed, opposition – regarding the creation of a real intervention instrument, which would quite naturally have become a fully-fledged payment currency: the Community's own currency.

The degree of 'play' between the component parts of the EMS mechanism (the fluctuation margins) acts as a brake on the use of the ECU as a tool for exchange market intervention, just as it is hampering its development into a payment currency. At the same time, its instability in terms of value, which is due to its components, is preventing it from being used as a reserve currency. This is the reason why the ECU must be seen as a promising initiative but only as one stage in a process, the stage that has set in motion a process which must lead up to the creation of a currency unit of the same kind: that is, a composite currency (which it will have the merit of familiarising the public with), whilst at the same time making full use of the possibilities inherent in a 'formula-based' currency and in the extranational monetary space within which it will be used.

The ES, with its component currencies, will constitute a mass of means of payment which by its sheer size will restore correct exchange market imbalances. The desired aims of harmonisation and stabilisation will be more easily achieved than with a variety of different currencies, each floating independently, each subject to the whims of market operators and speculators, each pushed along or held back by its central bank and its monetary authorities who, in their embarrassment, are torn between their external monetary responsibilities and their domestic responsibilities.

The ES and its component currencies will eliminate the problems of asymmetry, divergence and decentralisation of decision-taking. There will simply be one Community central body which will be responsible for deciding whether to buy or sell ES against dollars or yen.

A *NUMÉRAIRE* AND A POOL

The conditions will by then have been met for the spontaneous use of the new European currency as a medium of exchange not just between states but in all the financial centres of the world. In this way a 'pool' of liquidity will develop for use in financial transactions between numerous currencies, of varying size and often with no counterpart. In the space that lies between the frontiers of states there will be an M1 money supply that will be peculiar to that space, just as there is in every state, behind its frontiers. The creation of this stock of money will offer opportunities for growth and profit to the member banks of the ES consortium; they have already been mentioned in connection with the seigniorage (see p. 18).

The seigniorage which accrues to the issuer of a payment currency is nothing more than the price that holders of that currency agree to pay for the right to spend the unit of money when, where and as they like. The profit from seigniorage is all the greater if the unit of money is well suited to being used simultaneously as both a payment instrument and a store of value, the one role being interlinked with the other. In addition, there is also the role of standard of reference, for the accurate measurement of value.

For banks, as also for market operators, the need to ensure that every unit of money is rapidly redeployed so as to earn further interest and counter the loss of purchasing power which, as is well known, eats away at its value each day, is a constant concern. This consideration inclines them towards one solution and away from another, especially as in the international market the choice is free: no one currency *has* to be used. The security which the ES will offer, thanks to its constant value, will remove the need for haste and instant investment decisions. It must also make it preferred to other currencies, none of which can offer the same guarantee.

At another level, the extension of the use of the ES to all the world's financial centres will do more than any speech-making to tell the world that the European Community is a reality. It will illustrate the progress that has been made towards European union, by associating the various national currencies, which will be retained for domestic use, with a specifically European currency which will be used for external transactions.

THE YAWNING GAP BETWEEN THE FERTILITY OF TECHNOLOGICAL IMAGINATION AND THE STAGNANCY OF INSTITUTIONAL IMAGINATION

It is necessary – indispensable even – for an external currency, much more than for internal currencies, to unite the characteristics that have traditionally been required of money: namely, the ability to function as a standard of value, means of exchange and reserve instrument.

The main attribute of money which unites all these characteristics is stability of value in real terms. We shall see later, in Chapter 15, why it is that a national payment currency is constitutionally incapable of acquiring such an attribute so long as it is used for internal payments. Stability of value in real terms can only be achieved with an internal currency at the price of considerable discipline, with results that are always open to risk. In contrast, an external currency that is reserved for international financial transactions in the extranational territory of the Euromarket may be conceived in such a way as to enjoy the privilege of constant value in real terms.

It is a very rare occurrence that such stability should be guaranteed precisely where there is greatest need of it, and what is more a very happy occurrence, in sharp contrast to the depressing ambiguity of the world economic summits, whether held in the Plaza Hotel in New York, at the Louvre in Paris or at other equally high-sounding addresses. The scenario is always the same: at the end of the summit solemn undertakings regarding exchange rate stability are announced to an expectant world. Everyone knows that they will not be honoured, in spite of the 'concerted' intervention of the main central banks. This is not the fault of those who entered into the undertakings, but rather of a system centred on a national currency that is vulnerable (as are all national currencies, ultimately).

It is an amazing spectacle to observe the various 'satellite' currencies of the international monetary system, as they intervene in concert in order to support or, on the contrary, restrain their fallen 'sun currency'. According to a monetary expert writing in the *Financial Times* of 3 January 1989, they cannot achieve these aims:

No period of growth since the Second World War has ever died of old-age because demand had finally collapsed or stocks had accumulated sky-high. Everyone was afraid that growth would lose its dynamism in 1985 and again after the crash of October 1987. Everyone was wrong. In fact, periods of growth have come to an end when they were strangled by the Federal Reserve on the pretext of fighting inflation. That is what happened in 1958, 1967, 1970 and, above all, in 1979 and 1980 . . .

A number of indicators suggest that the dollar ought to fall, and by at least 20% if the current account deficit is to be brought back into balance, but that is ignoring the fact that inflation in the USA is four points higher than in Germany or Japan. If we include this factor in the equation, the result is a depreciation of 40% compared with the Mark and the Yen if the American trade balance is to be brought back to equilibrium without a recession.

It would be hard to give a clearer illustration of the extent to which the position of the dollar depends on America's domestic policies, its uncertainties, its embarrassments and its digressions. Similarly, it would be hard to find a better illustration of the disorder that the national currency of the United States, because it is also the main international currency, is capable of creating in the monetary affairs of the world.

At the moment, the world is at the mercy of such disorders: with a neutral, stateless, stable currency in the place of the dollar, it would no longer need to be.

13 By Extrapolation: Stage 4

We have followed the project that is set out in the preceding pages as far as its Stage 3. At this point it has achieved most of what is required for the European Community's monetary organisation. It has its own currency, which is equipped with an exceptional property – namely, constant value – a factor that will confer prestige as much as it will make for economic unification and progress. This currency will be issued and managed, under the aegis of the Commission, by a central institution which will function as a link and a regulator, linking the national currencies of the member states to each other and to foreign currencies. Each member state will retain its own central bank and its own currency; within its territory, only its own national currency will circulate and be used for payments.

The component currencies of the ES will be exchanged for each other at fixed rates of exchange and these fixed rates will be adjusted from time to time. Parity changes will be achieved by a system of targeted creeping rates and the ES will also be bought and sold for foreign (that is, non-Community) currencies on the foreign exchange markets. The exchange rates of the national component currencies in terms of foreign currencies will be calculated by deduction from the ES rate, using the daily conversion rate (coefficient g, see p. 84) of each component currency into ES, as it results from the composition formula.

Stages 1 and 2 (the consortium and its interbank office) prefigured the kind of monetary organisation that would result from the official introduction, as the Community currency, of a neutral currency with purchasing power that would not vary over time or from place to place, as well as the advantages that would accrue to the Community from such a currency.

However, whereas Stages 1 and 2 depend upon private initiative, Stage 3 will require an agreement among governments. It may be expected – it may be hoped at least – that the practical demonstration of the system before the eyes of the public will have had its effect, that innovations which previously had been rejected will have been accepted and that a consensus of governments will have been achieved.

The objections that are made to monetary unification, to the ideas of a single currency and a European Central Bank, will have become pointless. There is no unification, only a form of organisation. There is no single currency, because each member state will retain a national currency under this scheme. What there will be, over and above these things, will be a new currency for the use of a political entity, the European Community, which is itself new. There will be no European Central Bank, whether dependent or independent. There will simply be a central institution, which will be a technical organ, responsible for regulating the Community currency and its exchange rates into foreign currencies. It will protect the national currencies from external disturbances. It will not make any loans, nor will it interfere with the management by each member state of its own currency, except for the purposes of providing guidance and support.

Why should the Community not be prepared to replace the American dollar in transactions between its member states and with the outside world by a currency unit that would be specifically European and would have been purged of those vices to which no currency is immune?

Let us now allow our imaginations free rein in these areas. There is still a lot to discover.

ONE FUTURE (OR FUTURISTIC?) POSSIBILITY

Let us first suppose that Stage 3 has been reached. The central institution has been set up and the ES is quoted on the markets. The national currencies are tied to the ES by their conversion rates. A new OPEC-type of oil cartel is set up and oil prices shoot up. Arab oil producers invoice their crude oil in ES, in preference to keeping their accounts in dollars. What matters to them is not just what they can buy in return for what they have sold but also what they can put into reserve. In order to be able to keep accounts, plan and accumulate reserves, they need a reliable and stable currency unit: for these reasons the Arab oil producers have chosen the ES. The Community oil importers' banks purchase ES for national currency from the central institution at the rate resulting from the ES formula so as to be able to pay the import bills.

Now let us suppose that the price of oil is multiplied by ten. The effect, after dilution in the national economies, is an average rise in costs of 1.5 to 2 per cent, which is reflected in the conversion rates of the ES into the national currencies. The experience of using a national currency, the dollar, with an indeterminate value in real terms has caused fears that a price–cost–price inflationary spiral will be set off by contagion from that currency: the isolation provided by a neutral currency like the ES has, in contrast, helped the authorities to halt the epidemic.

The rise in costs is a modest one, so the central banks of the Community member states do not take any especially urgent steps to safeguard the situation. They take the view that there is no need to raise the discount or open market rates. All the same, the central ES institution points out to country *D* that it has allowed its prices to drift upwards beyond the average level; this discrepancy in *D*'s price index has an effect on the weighted price index in the formula. The conversion rates of the national currencies into ES, it will be remembered, vary in parallel. They are affected by the unsatisfactory performance of *D*'s currency in proportion to its weight in the formula.

In the event that *D* should not succeed in restoring its position to balance and prevent its currency from drifting down, the sanction applied to it would be to exclude *D*'s currency and replace it in the ES formula by another Community currency.

Second, let us suppose that the dollar comes under strong upward pressure. Both resident and non-resident ES deposit-holders (the ES cannot be used for making internal payments but it can be held in domestic deposit accounts) are tempted by the high interest rates paid in New York in order to 'stifle inflation and prevent the economy from overheating'. ES are changed into dollars at the central institution's offices. Part of the resulting outflow of foreign currencies is replaced by investments, which are switched away from the dollar because of its instability and the risk of inflation. The commercial banks recycle the ES that are deposited with them and take part in issues of ES-denominated bonds.

The upheavals to which the exchange markets are prone from time to time offer tempting opportunities. At the same time they are also the cause of much anguish, sending depositors in search of a refuge for their assets. Hence the ebb and flow of masses of capital and, each time, opposing trends into and out of the ES, which serve to neutralise the disruptions.

Exchange market disorders are a universal disease. One may suppose that the example will have been followed, and that an Asian monetary zone, modelled on the European one, has been created in the Far East, at the initiative of the Japanese. An agreement will be in the process of being negotiated between these two monetary zones in order to regulate the exchange rates of the ES into its Asian equivalent.

The stability that would be achieved in this way for European economies is not an impossible ideal. As much must be admitted once we are prepared to accept that the mighty earthquakes that have devastated them did not really originate in upheavals of production, consumption or trade but rather in the inability to organise a reliable means of international exchange and to stabilise its value in real terms.

A STAGE 4 WHICH IT IS AS YET TOO EARLY TO ORGANISE

That is the way monetary matters are likely to develop during Stage 3. Beyond that, the door is wide open to suggestions (and objections). That is why it is better, at this stage, to deal only briefly with the opportunities that are likely to arise, including the replacement of national currencies in internal circulation in the member states by a single common means of payment. A replacement of national currencies in this way ought not to raise any insoluble technical problems, given that national currencies will be freely exchangeable at fixed rates of exchange – and will have been so for a long time – and that changes in price indices will vary little from one country to another.

On the other hand, the advantage of a single internal payment currency for all the states of the Community is not evident. A single currency that was introduced prematurely would have the defect of depriving the laborious process of unification that is taking place right now of one of its last adjustment mechanisms; one that is likely to remain even after the abolition of customs tariffs and other compensatory devices.

In any case, what we are speaking of here belongs to an as yet distant future, one that will be shaped by experience and the results that have been achieved. It is better not to go into details, even as an academic exercise, because this is where criticism, scepticism and hostility will be concentrated, whilst all the intermediate stages and the progress achieved and the lessons learnt will be overlooked. Prudence suggests that it is better not to enter prematurely upon ill marked and potentially risky paths.

What matters, what is of predominant importance for a European currency, is its external status much more than its internal status. The ultimate success or failure of a European currency depends on its use – or non-use – privately, as a means of exchange and a reserve instrument between the various national currencies and in dealings with non-member states. The prestige of sterling and the dollar as international currencies (which will soon be the prerogative of the Deutschemark) was not due to their merits as domestic currencies within their own territories. What prestige they had was acquired in their use as international currencies.

Although Stage 4 is indeterminate, however, the steps leading up to it are, in contrast, clearly defined and accessible, by a gradual, stage-by-stage process. These intermediate stages may be entered upon without delay. Initially, a group of Eurobanks which enjoy the support of one or more member state governments will set the ball rolling. By the time they arrive at Stage 3 they will have behind them a successful experiment which will carry public opinion with it, not to mention the Community governments.

This scheme of operations has been conceived so as to be capable of being launched without delay. There is not much time left, and deeds will speak more loudly than intentions and desires.

Whatever the merits of the EMS, whatever the merits of the ECU – and they are considerable – neither will achieve the aim that has been forced upon them both: that is, to create a European payment currency that will be freely chosen in preference to others.

The constitution of the ECU and the way the EMS operates, some aspects of which are the consequences of that constitution, do not give either the ECU or the EMS any chance when faced with the Deutschemark. As things stand at present, the future European currency will be the Deutschemark. Already, the American Secretary for the Treasury goes to Bonn without visiting Paris when he has to settle some world monetary problem. In November 1987 the *International Herald Tribune* revealed that the Germans were proposing that the Bundesbank should become the future European Community central bank.

In France, awareness of this is only just starting to dawn. Some people are starting to give thought to a policy for 'monetary unification', the creation of a 'European central bank', 'financial harmonisation', and so on. The least that can be said of such reflections is that they were not sufficiently thought out before being aired (the same could be said of many other major projects). In the newspaper, *Le Monde*, of 13 December 1988, in an article spread over four columns with the headline 'The trap of monetary union', an anonymous senior civil servant spoke out against a policy which was leading France to subordinate itself 'with a kind of joyful willingness, to the Bundesbank'.

Once public opinion has become aware that France has become, monetarily, financially and economically, what some will call a 'satellite' of the Germany and what others will call its *brillant second*[1] then there will be a revolt.

If that happens, the whole process of European unification will be threatened. Of course, people will refuse to accept responsibility. They will blame the Germans for not being 'European enough' to prevent their currency from continuing to rise on the exchange markets. They will blame the Americans for not having reduced their budget deficit and the Italians for having for so long kept the lira in the EMS with a fluctuation margin of 6 per cent above and below its parity, the width of which deprives the system of part of its validity; and finally they will blame the British for having refused to join the EMS.

There is something else, something that is independent of questions of nationality, or, if you prefer, nationalism: whatever the advantages of convenience that may be advanced in favour of using the national currency of a given state as an international means of payment and reserve instrument, using it in that way confers upon the state in question considerable economic, commercial and industrial advantages which it rivals may find intolerable.

It is not healthy for an association whose members claim to be equal if one of those members derives excessive profit from the *de facto* exclusivity conferred upon its currency in a use which is for the common benefit. To accept that would be to repeat the mistake, which is now fully recognised and has been denounced over and over again, of adopting the national currency of the United States, which is subject to all the vicissitudes of that country's domestic policies, as the central currency in the international monetary system.

To allow any one of the Community's national currencies to achieve this kind of dominance would be the wrong way to try to forge European union and it would also be to let slip the opportunity of equipping the Community with a currency that is worthy of it, one that can be the instrument of a rational and consistent common monetary policy.

---

1. This expression was used in France to describe the position of Austria-Hungary *vis-à-vis* Germany before 1914.

THE FUTURE OF THE 'PHOENIX' AS SEEN BY *THE 'ECONOMIST'*

Monetary disorder constitutes an obstacle to progress and harmony in the relations between peoples. Governments' inability to cope with monetary disorders is one of the great scandals of this century. One of the prime causes of their impotence is inadequate knowledge of monetary mechanisms, of which this book has already quoted several examples. In this connection let us quote, once again, the words of Valéry Giscard d'Estaing. There is no other quotation which better expresses the obstacles that stand in the way of any progress in monetary matters (which explains the importance given in this book to demonstrations and proofs rather than to entertaining the reader):

> It is a conviction shared by many distinguished economists that the real problem is not one of willpower. It is a lack of knowledge . . . This impotence in the field of economic theory is largely due to ignorance of economic and monetary reality . . . In international matters, I am convinced, like M. Denizet, that only a system founded on the issue of an additional currency in addition to gold has a reasonable chance of success. The creation of such a currency will test the ability of politicians to innovate, and thus protect the world economy and mankind in general from the dangers of ignorance and incompetence. (Preface to *Monnaie et inflation*, by Jean Denizet, published by Dunot)

Since writing these lines, Mr Giscard d'Estaing has more recently added, in a television interview on 29 May 1989, his conviction that European unification is not something that can be taken for granted and has only a two-in-three chance of success, so that the measures taken to achieve this aim need to be very carefully thought out.

It was perhaps a similar order of reflections that led *The Economist* to make an exaggeratedly pessimistic forecast regarding the future of its 'Phoenix' (alias ES). It concludes the article from which large extracts have already been quoted in Chapter 8 in the following terms:

> Several more big exchange-rate upsets, a few more stock market crashes and probably a slump or two will be needed before politicians are willing to face squarely up to that choice. This points to a muddled sequence of emergency followed by patch-up, followed

by emergency, stretching out far beyond 2018 – except for two things. As time passes, the damage caused by currency instability is gradually going to mount; and the very trends that will make it mount are making the utopia of monetary union feasible . . .

As the next century approaches, the natural forces that are pushing the world towards economic integration will offer governments a broad choice. They can go with the flow or they can build barricades . . . Let us pencil in the Phoenix for 2018 and welcome it when it comes.

Thirty years: must we really wait as long as that? Perhaps, if we take the official paths, but the official paths are not the ones that this book is counting on. They are not the ones that are proposed and recommended here.

What we must first find for the European Community is an *external* currency, long before an internal one. Why? Because it is by using a common external currency that Europe will show the world that it is united; because there are fewer obstacles outside the boundaries of nation states and also because that is where the need of a new *numéraire* for use in transactions between states is most urgent. Inside their frontiers, states have learnt – or almost learnt – to 'control' their currencies; outside those frontiers lies disorder. Outside those frontiers, also, governments are impotent: they cannot impose their will. Whatever means of payment are used outside the frontiers of states are freely chosen. If the Community's currency is to be freely chosen for such a role it will have to be 'promoted'.

That, however, is something that it is vain to expect from the officials of the European Community: their function is a different one. Promotion of the European currency for an international role must be the work of private initiative, with the unofficial support of at least one government.

If that were to happen *The Economist*'s pessimism would be seen to be unjustified, because once a new enterprise can be seen to answer an existing need, one that has been demonstrated to be unsatisfied, there are no precedents that suggest that launching such a new enterprise would not succeed, especially when it has an open road ahead of it, free of the impediments which would hinder it within the borders of a state, and, finally, when it requires only a negligible amount of investment (negligible anyway when measured against the prospect of prestige and profit to which such an enterprise may lead).

This brings us to the last of the various problem areas that have been raised with the author by members of the public (see Chapter 8), namely: 'If these arguments are valid and a constant external currency has still not been created there must be some hidden fundamental reason which stands in the way of achieving it.' This point has frequently been aired. 'A Letter to a sceptic' was penned in reply, and is reproduced at the beginning of the next chapter. This letter provides the opportunity to go to the very heart of the real nature of money, an essential factor in the form of monetary organisation into which the ES must fit. The reply is then completed by a further study on this topic.

14 The Theoretical Foundations of an Extranational Composite Currency with Stable Purchasing Power, and their Implications

A LETTER TO A SCEPTIC: IS IT POSSIBLE FOR THE ECU
TO HAVE STABLE PURCHASING POWER?

You say that you are doubtful, that my demonstration of the theoretical foundations of the ES does not convince you, that a currency unit capable of retaining its value in real terms is 'contrary to the nature of things'. And then you add: 'Everybody admits that there is a need for a reliable standard of measurement, and therefore for a currency with a purchasing power which, to quote *The Economist*, "will not flicker". If such a thing were possible', you argue, 'the fact would be known and such a currency would already have been created; it does not exist because no currency has ever been capable of resisting the pressure of costs, the effects of supply and demand and the law of the market.'

The answer to that is that the very notion of a composite currency is a new one, just as is the idea of a payment currency that is exclusively for external use (for example, the ECU and the various Eurocurrencies). Only since the creation of the Euromarket have we been able to observe forms of claim money with full payment powers that do not circulate within the frontiers of any state. And the idea of distinguishing between claims denominated in a national currency and that national currency itself (the distinction between a claim expressed in Eurodollars and actual US dollars) is also a recent one.

In actual fact, it is not the theoretical demonstration set out in this book that you are questioning: rather it is the mental representation of what a constant payment currency would mean, the attempt to imagine how it would be used, that is causing you embarrassment.

We are all by now so accustomed to the real value of money being shrouded in uncertainty that we cannot imagine things being otherwise. The experience of the distant past is opposed to the very concept of stability of purchasing power in the case of claim money. The notion of a constant currency is anyway not properly understood, even when restricted to statistics and economic research. The 'housewife's shopping basket', the 240 articles that go into it, the price statistics, in short, all the items that go to make up the RPI – as well as a constant purchasing power currency – are hidden from view behind the rate of inflation, which *is* clearly perceived.

A constant currency unit will, by definition, have the same purchasing power, as defined by the statistics, on day n as on day O. Its value in terms of nominal currency on day n will be its rate of conversion into nominal currency on day n. This rate can be deduced from the inflation rate on day n (which is itself determined on the basis of the latest monthly increase in the index, divided by the number of days in the month).

The idea of a constant composite currency derives from the same notion. It can be more readily accepted if we start with the proper definition of a composite currency, ignoring the image of a shopping basket which distorts the reality of the situation. A composite currency unit is one whose value (that is, its purchasing power) is defined by adding up the separate purchasing powers of several fixed sums of national component currencies. In the case of the nominal ECU, its purchasing power is the sum of the purchasing powers of the amounts of nominal currency that make it up. The constant ECU would have the same definition as the nominal ECU, but the sums of component national currency would be sums of constant national currency, instead of nominal ones.

A currency is an internal-use currency if it is used in dealings between two residents of a country. It is an external-use currency if it is used in dealings between a resident and a non-resident or between two non-residents. An exclusively external currency may be defined in such a way as to conserve its purchasing power intact.

An internal-use currency, in contrast, cannot, and neither can it when it functions simultaneously as an internal and external payment currency (such as the Eurodollar) because its external value is the same as its internal value. The difference between an external and an internal currency is based on the fact that within a national territory production (adding value) and consumption occur. If that consumption is final, by destruction *or* possession, the sum of money used in the payment remains in circulation. It confers the right to a further act of final consumption (or possession) on the next holder of it, whereas this right has already been made use of once. In contrast, when a sum of money passes from one holder to another the counterpart to this movement may be an addition to production which is then available for consumption. Within a national territory, therefore, the exchange value of a currency unit depends on factors which are refractory to definition. This is not true of a currency which is exclusively external in its use because the space within which it circulates and effects payments has neither final production nor final consumption. A simple example will illustrate this property of an exclusively external currency, which permits it (if it is properly defined) to conserve its purchasing power.

Let there be three national, nominal currencies, a, b and c. The corresponding constant currency units are (a), (b) and (c). The purchasing powers of these currencies are defined by the baskets of fixed quantities of goods and services that each one is able to purchase in its country of origin.

On day O the constant currency and the nominal currency both have the same purchasing power:

$100(a) = 100a$, and both will buy 2 kg of P and 4 kg of Q
$100(b) = 100b$, and both will buy 8 kg of R and 12 kg of S
$100(c) = 100c$, and both will buy 4 kg of T and 8 kg of V

On day n, the value of (a)'s basket (the value of 2 kg of P and 4 kg of Q) has become $105a$, in terms of nominal currency. The value of (b)'s basket has similarly become $103b$, whilst (c)'s has grown to $106c$. The respective inflation rates in the countries concerned are 5 per cent, 3 per cent and 6 per cent. The price index readings (1.05, 1.03 and 1.06) are the conversion rates on day n of the constant units into the nominal units on day n:

$100(a) = 100 \times 1.05a$

Let us now suppose that there is a composite currency unit, U, which is defined by its equivalence in value terms (purchasing power) to the sum of the values of three amounts of (a), (b) and (c), taking by way of example amounts of component currency equal to $50(a)$, $25(b)$ and $75(c)$.

The formula for the composition of U as a constant composite currency unit is $100U = 50(a) + 25(b) + 75(c)$. (a), (b) and (c), as constant currency units, will together purchase the same basket of goods and services on day n as they could on day O. This basket is made up of 1 kg of P, 2 kg of Q, 2 kg of R, 3 kg of S, 3 kg of T and 6 kg of V.

So far we have only considered for each unit what the basket as defined by the national statistical services will purchase. Let us go beyond these limits and 'purchase' a quantity of currency X; in other words, let us convert U into X. The exchange rate of U into X is determined by the quantities of X which each sum of component currency can buy. The sums of X which $50(a)$, $25(b)$ and $75(c)$ can buy depend on the value of $50(a)$ in terms of a (that is, $50 \times 1.05a$) and on the exchange rates on day n of a into X (See Chapter 7 for the formula).

The relationships between the constant composite currency unit and the data of the moment in nominal terms are thus given, and $100U$ will always be able to purchase the basket of goods and services defined in the previous paragraph, provided that the composition of the basket and the territories within which the purchases are made are those that have been agreed. That said, an overseas importer builds up holdings of $1000U$ in the Euromarket (that is to say, 'off shore', outside national frontiers, the U being issued against foreign currency or in the form of a loan). The purpose of acquiring this quantity of U is the purchase of a quantity of goods, M. The first transaction is the purchase of $50M$, for which the importer pays the exporter $200U$. The latter exchanges the $200U$ for the equivalent quantity of his national currency, X, at that day's exchange rate, which is disseminated by an official institution and calculated as described above.

For the purchaser and the seller, the 'real' value of the goods purchased for $200U$, expressed in terms of other goods, is a sack full of 2 kg of P, 4 kg of Q, 4 kg of R, 6 kg of S, 6 kg of T and 12 kg of V. After the $200U$ have been paid over the cash balance remaining will be $1000 - 200 = 800U$. Its constant value, expressed in terms of P, Q, R, etc, may be calculated by multiplying by 800 the quantity of P, Q, R, etc that $1U$ can buy, which is invariable. It can also be calculated by subtracting the value of $200U$ in terms of P, Q, R, etc from the value of $1000U$ in terms of P, Q, R, etc. The two figures are naturally the same.

These calculations of stocks and balances are only possible because there is within the U money supply no spontaneous addition (final production) or destruction (final consumption) of P, Q, R, etc. Off shore, in the Euromarket, increases in stocks or losses are registered as indicated above, without upsetting the accounting equilibrium.

Let us suppose, on the contrary, that the 1000U have been created and are circulating within a national territory and are used to make payments in the same way and on the same conditions as the relevant national currency. The mechanism of production and destruction affects the value of U in terms of P, Q, R, etc as it affects the exchange value of the national currency. The 800U balances will not have the values in terms of P, Q, R, etc determined above; the two ways of calculating the balance in terms of P, Q, R, etc will no longer have any meaning.

An even more convincing demonstration of the difference in nature between a currency that is exclusively external and one that is used internally is provided by the technique for controlling the money supply which is used at present in all countries in order to 'combat inflation'; in other words, in order to maintain the real value of money. The 'target' that is aimed at by this technique is the rate of growth of the stock of means of payment. This is one of the main objectives of economic policy. The rate is broadly aligned with the expected rate of increase of the GDP in volume terms, to which certain other factors peculiar to the country in question are added. This process of targeting takes no account whatsoever of any use that may be made of the national currency outside the country's borders.

Total assets denominated in US dollars and held outside the territory of the United States (in the Euromarket) by companies or by Eurobanks (banks domiciled outside the territory of the United States) are estimated to amount to 2000 million million dollars. The transaction volume that is confined within this off-shore space is thus considerable. It does not, however, affect the exchange value of the dollar, which is determined solely by the uses that are made of it within the national territory. Nor is this huge mass of Eurodollars taken into account by the Federal Reserve when it comes to select its monetary targets.

This is very precisely what makes the aligning by definition of the exchange value – and the inflation rate – of an extranational currency such as the ECU with the exchange values – and the inflation rates – of national currencies so paradoxical, when it could by definition be, as it were, 'organically' immunised against them.

The notions of added value and final consumption are amongst the most fruitful of the new ideas that have enriched economic science during the last 50 years. Thanks to these concepts it is possible to interpret and guide the management of claim money. They help to cast light on the differences between the constraints to which, by their constitution, national and extranational currencies are subject. They also show how these differences may be turned to account so as to equip the European Community with a currency that is worthy of the name of European currency.

It is flying in the face of all logic to identify a purely external currency (such as a Eurocurrency or the ECU) with one or more national currencies. To do so is simply to transfer to the external-use currencies all the vices of the national currencies in which they are denominated, whereas the way such currencies function renders them independent of the national currencies. The monetary mechanisms are the weakest links in economic systems. Whereas society has continued to progress in so many fields, in the monetary field it has regressed. Today, even more than yesterday, society is in search of a payment and reserve currency which will also function as a standard of value that is independent of time and place.

The reader will find that the arguments that have just been set out in this 'Letter to a sceptic' are looked at again in the following pages from a different point of view, beginning with the quantity relationship. This relationship elucidates the profound difference between internal and external circulation of money and sets out the theoretical foundations for this difference. In addition, it helps to show how and why this new type of monetary unit, known as 'composite', provides the means for creating a monetary reference standard that is superior to all those that man has made use of since money has existed.

It is true that no currency – gold no more than any other form of claim – has ever succeeded in retaining its value, in resisting a rise (or, more frequently, a fall) in its purchasing power. The value of currencies is determined on the marketplace: it has never been possible to determine it arbitrarily, still less to impose it on a free market. That has been true in all epochs, and that is where the special – and novel – property of a composite currency exclusively reserved for circulation between states and excluded from circulation within a state comes in.

In financial exchanges, the ES would function as just such an intermediate currency, operating as a link between currencies. Thanks to that fact it would be neutral and stateless, permanently isolated by two exchange offices, one of which (upstream) would be the payer's office while the other (downstream) would be the payee's office. These two offices would seal the ES off from the internal market. The price of any traded commodity would ultimately always be paid in national currency by the purchaser and similarly the seller would ultimately always receive payment in his own national currency. It is only thanks to this feature, one that has never before been exploited, that the ES could retain constant purchasing power.

In order to illustrate this property, I compared the ES in a previous book to a canal reach that is kept at a constant level between two locks. The locks correspond to the ES's exchange offices. Upstream there would be the purchaser's currency, with its purchasing power, and downstream the currency of the payee, with its purchasing power. The level of the reach of water between the two locks is kept constant whatever the undulations elsewhere in the circuit.

This image failed to convince many experts; on the contrary, it aroused their suspicions. For that reason, I shall now give a more intellectually severe exposition of the thesis in the hope that the scientific rigour of this explanation will satisfy the most demanding reader. It is based on a fruitful (and unexploited) concept of monetary analysis which was set out at some length in my book *The Mechanics of Money* (Macmillan, London, 1980) and is known as *prélèvement* (called 'reduction' in *The Mechanics of Money*). The natural corollary of *prélèvement* is its opposite, *restitution*, known as 'restoration' in the previous book.

This notion of *prélèvement* is the key, thanks to which it is possible to dismantle the mechanism of price formation and show how it depends on production and final consumption. It also shows why it is not possible to guarantee constant purchasing power in the case of a currency that is used within the territory of a state, and why it *is* possible to guarantee it in the case of a currency that is confined to the extranational territory within which the ES will circulate. It thus gives a solid foundation to the principle on which this proposition is based.

This concept of *prélèvement* takes us straight to the notion of *seigniorage* (see pp. 18ff). It also, at the same time, gives its fullest meaning to the quantity relationship (in terms of relative variations) and thus provides a reliable instrument for analysing present-day techniques of internal and external monetary regulation.

A PRINCIPLE OF ECONOMIC LIFE: FINAL CONSUMPTION
OF PRODUCTION

Prélèvement in value terms occurs on all units of money that circulate
and are used in payments within the territory of a state. In the case of
a unit of currency that circulates between the territories of states
there is no *prélèvement*. That is where the difference lies and that
difference is what the ES exploits.

The proper function of money is to be used to effect transactions.
In exchange for a commodity which he has just sold, or for a service
which he has just supplied, an economic agent receives a unit of
money or a claim on an institution which takes the place of that
commodity or service and which he will make use of later in order to
purchase something in his turn. The unit of money that he then
spends has been 'earned' because in order to obtain it he has produced something, or received payment in the form of a salary, or
used the proceeds of an investment or perhaps even of a piece of
speculation, as a counterpart of all of which another economic agent
has relinquished something that he too had 'earned'.

The situation is different if the unit of money in question has been
put into circulation by means of a bank loan. In that case, the first
user of the money, the borrower, has not 'earned' what he buys with
the money: in order to obtain it he did not make any counterbalancing contribution to production which could compensate for what he
receives, consumes or invests.

Let us suppose that a bank makes a loan of 60 000. It enters its
claim on the borrower on the assets side of its balance sheet and its
obligation towards him on the liabilities side. The borrower purchases a new car with what has been borrowed. A quantity of goods
and services that have been produced and supplied are thus 'consumed': the borrower has the benefit of something that has been
made by others, hours of work that have been worked by others.
Who makes the counterbalancing contribution to balance the equation? It is not the garage owner who sold the borrower the car,
because with the money he receives in return he buys another car.
Neither is it the builder, who, with the money he receives from the
garage owner, boosts his bank balance and pays his employees and
suppliers. Nor is it the employees and suppliers, because they use
what they receive to purchase the wherewithal to live and work. No,
the cost of the goods and services consumed in the form of the new
car can only be borne by the entire community of holders of M1

money, whose purchasing power is proportionately reduced to the extent of this specific operation.

Nothing comes of nothing. If a commodity is consumed without having been 'earned', there must somewhere be economic agents who 'provided' it and who, because they received nothing in return, have suffered a *prélèvement* on the purchasing power of their money assets. As a corollary, a net restoration of purchasing power to the holders of money assets is made when a unit of money is destroyed or is placed in a savings account and thus loses its 'transaction function'. In order to procure the unit of money that he puts into his savings account, the saver had to produce something. He receives no goods or services in return if the unit of money really is destroyed (through the repayment of a loan to a bank) or is only temporarily incapacitated, as it were (if it loses its transaction function). There is thus a net contribution of value, which may be seen as a restoration of what was taken from the holders of money assets at the moment the unit of money was created.

The difference between the amount of money that is created and the amount that is destroyed gives the measure of the net *prélèvement*. Opposite this *prélèvement* (or restoration) through consumption there is the rate of production in volume terms. If it rises or falls, the effect is the converse. The final *prélèvement* on the value of the unit of money can be deduced from it.

The creation of a unit of money always has the effect of a *prélèvement* in value terms on the purchasing power of the M1 money stock, and conversely the destruction of a unit of money has the opposite effect of restoring purchasing power. This holds true whether there was any counterpart to the new unit of money when it was created or not. Similarly, it holds true whether the counterpart, if there is one, consists of a quantity of gold, foreign currency, a claim or a raw material or finished product.

This can be verified by comparing, when gold is purchased, foreign currency is exchanged, a bill is discounted or a bank overdraft is opened, the equilibrium in terms of production and consumption, according as the unit of money used in the exchange was earned (by adding production) or, on the contrary, was created *ex nihilo* for that express purpose and added to the mass of existing M1 money by the user of the new unit of money.

Issuing paper money as a counterpart to the purchase of a quantity of gold is the archetype, according to traditional teaching, of a 'backed' money, representative of a commodity, and one that symbolises 'genuine' rights. Let us compare this contribution of goods and services and consumption of them in two cases: in the first, an economic agent buys a kilogram of gold and pays for it with money which he has earned, taken, for example, from his money assets and thus representing a number of hours of work; in the second, the same kilogram of gold is bought by the Bank of England, which pays for it with bank notes which it prints. In the second case there is an amount of purchasing power over and above what there is in the first case, supplementary, unearned purchasing power corresponding to the new bank notes, which, once they are introduced into circulation, will result in a proportionate *prélèvement* on the value of assets denominated in transaction money.

If, instead of gold, foreign currency had been sold to the Bank, the sum credited to the seller's current account would have enabled him to purchase and consume a quantity of production over and above the quantity that would subsequently be imported and consumed with the foreign currency that he sold to the Bank of England.

The same procedure and the same conclusion apply to all cases of creation of money, *without exception*. In order to show that this is so, it is convenient to compare consumption (*C*) after the creation of a quantity of money and production (*P*) in volume terms purchased by that same quantity. There is a situation of equilibrium when *C* is equal to *P*. If *C* is in excess of *P*, there is a *prélèvement*; if *P* is in excess of *C*, there is a *restoration*, or net addition to purchasing power.

Let us suppose, for example, that a quantity of production, *P*, corresponds to a bill which is discounted: *P* is the amount of goods delivered in exchange for the bill. There is *C* consumption by the purchaser of the goods, and also by the seller of the goods with the money that he receives when he discounts the bill. If this latter sum is made up of new money created by a monetary intermediary there is then 2*C* for 1*P*, resulting in a *prélèvement* equal to *C*. If the sum is transferred to his account by a non-monetary intermediary, and the corresponding purchasing power is withdrawn from the original depositor of the sum in question, there is then $2C - 1C = 1C$ for 1*P*, and thus equilibrium and no *prélèvement*.

In order to purchase a quantity of gold, an economic agent had to produce *P*. He sells the gold to the Bank of France and receives in return a sum in francs. There is then 1*P* and 2*C*: that is, a quantity of gold held by the Bank of France and consumption by the seller. If the Bank of France then sells the gold, a quantity of bank notes enters its coffers. The purchaser of the gold from the Bank of France had to produce P in order to obtain those bank notes, whence a loss of possession by the Bank of France and additional possession by the purchaser, altogether $-1C + 1C + 1P = 1P$. The new owner of the gold sells it to another economic agent: production and consumption (in the form of possession) are then in balance. Trade in existing goods, even at fluctuating prices, has no effect on the purchasing power of the currency unit.

Figure 15.2 gives a more complete representation of the phenomenon of *prélèvement* (or restoration) by addition or subtraction of claim money, plus an example, on p. 184, of the process of restoring balance by extra (or less) annual production (equal to $5C$), which gives some idea of the disruption that is caused by adding $S = C$ to the money in circulation.

The *prélèvement* on the money supply is carried out progressively through the agency of new units of money as they gradually spread through the economy. It ceases when it balances out the initial quantity of consumption for which there was no corresponding amount of production, at the moment the unit of money was created. The period during which this process of amortisation takes place is generally estimated to be slightly more than 18 months.

The effect of this *prélèvement* on the purchasing power of money can be compensated for by increasing the rate of production, in which case the *prélèvement* in value terms on the holders of payment money takes the form of lost profit, failure to reap the benefits of increased productivity.

Figure 15.2 and Table 15.1 illustrate this phenomenon. The explanatory notes facilitate the transition from the abstract to the concrete which is the subject of Chapter 15.

PRÉLÈVEMENT IN VALUE TERMS ON UNITS OF MONEY THROUGH FINAL CONSUMPTION (NON-EXISTENT IN THE CASE OF AN EXCLUSIVELY EXTERNAL UNIT)

Let us go back for a moment to the *ex nihilo* creation of a sum of money by a financial institution for the purchase of a quantity of goods. Consumption occurs twice: first, the consumption of the goods purchased with this sum of money, and then what the seller consumes with the sum of money received from the institution. In contrast, there is only one quantity of production, the production that the seller was obliged to supply in order to obtain the goods he sold to the institution, which makes $2C$ for $1P$, resulting in a *prélèvement* equivalent to $1C$ which takes effect on the money supply as the new units of money gradually spread through the economy (and which ceases once C has been compensated for by the *prélèvement* on the purchasing power of the unit of payment).

This *prélèvement*, which balances out C, is the sum of various partial *prélèvements*. It is convenient to represent them by analysing the production–consumption operation into a series of sequences.

At the end of sequence n, a worker receives $100M$ in payment for the amount of production (that is, $100UP$, or units of production) which he supplied during sequence n. During the following sequence $(n + 1)$ the worker spends the sum he has just received. In a stable system (before new money was added) he would consume as much in value terms as he had produced (that is, $100UP$).

Introducing new money into the system has the effect of causing a unit of money during sequence $n + 1$ to withdraw, say, a fraction $(1\ UP)$ of production from the amount available for purchase with the $100M$ issued to the worker at the end of sequence n. As a result, the $100M$ are no longer capable of purchasing $100UP$, but only $99UP$. There is a further partial *prélèvement* during the following sequence, and again during the next one and so on, until the worker reaches the stage of receiving $100 + XM$ for each $100UP$ that he supplies. During the following sequence he will thus be able to obtain for consumption as much as he supplied ($100UP$). The *prélèvement* will then be at an end and will have balanced out the amount of 'unearned' consumption by the first user of the new unit of money.

All of this, however, is only true provided that the consumption in question is *final consumption* (annihilation of the goods). If it is 'intermediate' consumption, value is maintained or added and then passed on at the end of the sequence, with no form of *prélèvement*. This is what happens in the external market.

THE QUANTITY RELATIONSHIP AND ITS VALUE FOR THE DEMONSTRATION

Let dM be the sum of payment money added to the money that is already in circulation, at constant velocity and rate of production. The value in money terms of the *prélèvement* resulting from final consumption can be measured by $M \frac{dp}{p}$, where p is the value of consumer price index; $dM = M \dfrac{dp}{p}$.

If there is no final consumption (destruction of goods or failure to make further use of a service) but only intermediate consumption, there will be no causal relationship between dM and $M \dfrac{dp}{p}$. The conclusions regarding v, the velocity of circulation (income velocity), and P (the rate of production in volume terms) are the same.

If P and M are frozen and v is varied by $\dfrac{dv}{v}$, the volume of the transaction for final consumption will vary by $M \dfrac{dv}{v}$ and the *prélèvement* will be $M \dfrac{dp}{p}$.

If we then freeze M and v and let the rate of production in terms of volume, P, vary, the effect will be the opposite from what results from a variation of M when P is unchanged, whence $\dfrac{dp}{p} = -\dfrac{dp}{p}$.

Variations in each of these three terms, M, v and P, will only have an effect on p if there is a *prélèvement* for final consumption. In cases where there is none (in an extranational area) there is no relationship of causality between the variations of M, v, P and p.

If, on the contrary, there is final consumption (within the territory of a state) P in national currency will be affected. If we free the three variables, M, P and v, and add up the effects on p, we get:

$$\frac{dM}{M} + \frac{dv}{v} - \frac{dP}{P} = \frac{dp}{p}$$

This is the quantity relationship in terms of relative variation.

This relationship thus has a definite effect within the national territory of a state but has no effect outside the boundaries of a state. In both cases the demonstration is a decisive one. It has the advantage of being founded on a solid and incontrovertible base, because nothing comes of nothing. In order for there to be final consumption there must be an equivalent contribution in value terms and therefore a source and a transfer mechanism. This is an unexceptionable postulate which leads straight to the quantity relationship. The solidity of the demonstration dissipates any doubt as to the neutrality of the ES.

In the extranational monetary space which the ES will inhabit the absence of final consumption or production has, as a corollary, the absence of any of the effects that final production and consumption have on prices. From this it follows that it is possible to fix the exchange value of a unit of money that circulates in that space.

It is precisely because the reality of this extranational space has for long been ignored that something which could be so fruitful continues to be ignored as well. Once it is admitted that there is a need to equip the international monetary system with the stable standard of reference independent of time and space that is indispensable for any measurement system, it would be logical to turn to advantage the singular properties of a non-national currency, whilst at the same time taking advantage of the benefits of the progress that has been achieved in the modern science of statistics. In this way, a European currency could be given that incomparable kudos which stability in terms of real value, something that has always been desired but never achieved, would confer upon it.

15 From Abstract Theory to the Reality of Practice (with the ES in mind)

In order to provide the demonstration that was set out in the previous chapter we had to descend to great depths of abstraction, and I have often had the occasion to observe that that is not a journey of exploration which appeals to many pilgrims. However, it could not be ignored or got round: in order to put the ideas that are propounded in this book on a solid base it was necessary to go beyond appearances, and not merely stay on the surface. Now that we have come back up from those depths of abstraction we are in a good position to make the transition from the abstract to the concrete, to interpret the ES and assign it to its rightful position alongside the other great currencies of the world, as a payment and reserve currency.

ONE VARIABLE (IN NATIONAL CURRENCY) AND ONE DATUM (THE ES)

The main characteristic of money, the one that takes precedence over all others, is its value in terms of what it can purchase. What matters is maintaining that value over time. And this latter requirement is the consequence of the three functions that are expected of money: those of means of exchange, reserve instrument (or store of value) and standard of reference and value measurement.

Means of exchange? Someone who has produced something or supplied a service has acquired a right to something, in return for what he has parted with, and that right will be made use of later, at an indeterminate time and in an indeterminate place, for the purpose of acquiring something of equivalent value to the product that was sold or the service that was rendered. Reserve instrument? The very terms implies constant value, just as does the function of standard of reference, but a currency cannot satisfy those requirements unless its value is independent of time and place.

It may be superfluous to remind readers of these facts, but it still seems necessary to point them out because the habit of regarding money as an instrument of uncertain value, which it is most usually losing, is so deeply ingrained. This uncertainty of value is the lot of all forms of claim money these days. It is an integral part of units of payment, an aspect of their very nature, the direct consequence, within the confines of a state, of the process of conversion of production into final consumption through the agency of money.

Immediately, a single glance at the quantity theory is enough to reveal that one variable, the level of prices, is balanced against three parameters, the velocity of money, the rate of production in volume terms and the money supply. And there is already an 'indeterminate' element, in the mathematical sense of the term; the value of money cannot be linked with any certainty to any one of the other three parameters: it depends on all three of them at once. And this is only the beginning, because each of the three parameters is subject to forces, pressures that move it forward or hold it back, which are called 'exogenous' and the list of which is almost limitless. There are costs, wages and salaries, productivity, imports, so-called natural phenomena, moods, fears, attitudes, and so on. And then there is also politics. Hardly any aspect of the economic situation at any one time is without some effect on the value of money. That is the central problem of monetary regulation.

The theoretical study set out above will help us to represent this variability of the value of units of money in terms of a graph (Figure 15.1). A dotted line shows the variations in the purchasing power of a unit of national currency, whilst another (a straight, horizontal line) indicates the value of the ES in both cases as they result from various types of monetary operation, such as creation of money, investment and repayment. First, let us take a case of creation of money: at (1) a sum S is introduced into circulation by a bank loan. The borrower consumes a quantity of production valued at S which he has not earned. The purchasing power of S gradually falls as it spreads through the economy (this phenomenon is analysed on p. 186). At (2) it can be seen that the effect of bringing S into circulation has been amortised. The stability of the purchasing power of S has been restored, but at a lower level than it started with. The other operations are closely similar, but with variants.

The usually accepted period of amortisation is one to two years. The slope representing the loss of S's purchasing power should therefore cover this period of time. This slope can be compared with another that we have already encountered, the one that represents

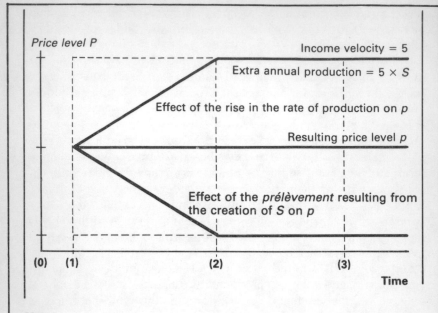

Price level P

Income velocity = 5

Extra annual production = 5 × S

Effect of the rise in the rate of production on p

Resulting price level p

Effect of the *prélèvement* resulting from the creation of S on p

(0)   (1)   (2)   (3)

Time

Notes

The effect of the *P* rise in production on *p* is symmetrical with the *prélèvement* by *S*.

The disparity between the effect of the *prélèvement* by S on p and the annual rise in production needed to compensate for it (5 *S*) shows why it is necessary to control it at source (bank loans).

The use of the interest rate as a regulator has the defect of affecting both the money supply and, indirectly, the exchange rate (through inflows of foreign capital). This leads on to the idea proposed here of replacing national currencies as instruments for exchange rate regulation by a neutral currency such as the ES.

Figure 15.1 Compensating for the *prélèvement* by a modulated rise in the rate of production (*P*) (within a national territory)

the gradual slide of exchange parities in a TCR system. It will be remembered that in the ES system proposed in these pages the reciprocal exchange rates of the ES's component currencies will be fixed from time to time and 'adjusted' according to a special process of 'programmed creeping'. This latter will have the effect of spreading changes in the exchange rates of the national currencies into each other over a period of time until the point when the selected rates are reached.

In monetary matters, as in many others, there are advantages to moving from one state to another gradually, to replacing a sudden fall or rise by a regular adjustment, thus making adaptation possible. There may be moments in the political or economic life of a country when circumstances require, or merely result in, a monetary realignment which will eventually lead, after a period of amortisation, to a fall in the purchasing power of the currency (as in France in June 1968, after the generalised rise in wages and salaries). The value of a currency and its exchange rate are linked. It is possible to make use of the period of amortisation needed for the money in question to reach a new stabilisation threshold, and also of the period of gradual adjustment under the TCR system in order to establish a degree of correspondence between foreseeable changes in purchasing power and exchange rates, thereby sparing the economy the distortions of the two with which we are familiar.

After this use, where appropriate, of the value slopes that characterise a national currency, we now come to the question of how the ES would behave, which is revealed in Figure 15.2. This shows how the ES would react if it were subjected to the same banking operations: the graph line is a straight, horizontal line. The ES is thus one of the 'data'. Its 'determinacy' protects it from the effects of multiple, changing and uncertain parameters, which condition the value of a national currency.

THE LIFE CYCLE OF A NATIONAL CURRENCY REVEALS ITS VULNERABILITY

Table 15.2 on p. 186 shows the accounting states that represent the life cycle of a unit of money. The banking operations indicated on the opposite page complete the representation. Between two movements, a unit of money remains in a current account, as part of its holder's liquid assets. Below are outlined the stages in the circuit.

First there is the birth of the unit of money, which is endowed with the transaction function, from a bank loan or the purchase of a quantity of foreign currency. Then there comes a transfer from one bank to another, for the purpose of effecting a payment. At the end

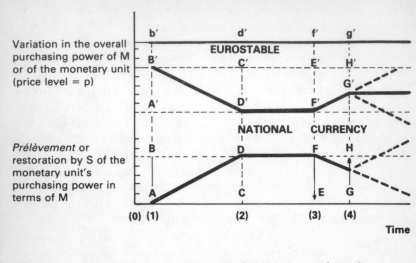

Time (0):   Purchasing power of M stable (all parameters frozen)
     (1):   Creation of sum S; consumption of 'unearned' final production: AB

from (1)
to (2):   *Prélèvement* AD, symmetrical fall in the overall purchasing power of M or of the monetary unit; AB=CD=C'D'

     (2):   The *prélèvement* has reached the equivalent value of the issue of S (that is, AB)

from (2)
to (3):   The *prélèvement* has ceased: M + S continue to effect transactions. Purchasing power is stable

     (3):   S is placed in a savings or time deposit and loses its 'transaction function'

from (3)
to (4):   Gradual restoration of AB purchasing power to M

     (4):   At G the time deposit is revived (or an equivalent sum is created). Simultaneous effects of the continuing restoration and the *prélèvement* set off by the revival of the time deposit (identical to the effect of creating new payment money)

Figure 15.2 Comparative effects of the creation and destruction of money in the case of a national currency and the ES (v and p frozen)

National currency: The rate of production in volume terms is constant.

The overall purchasing power (production consumed per period) of the means of payment does not vary: M from (0) to (1); M + S from (1) to (3); M from (4); none varies.

Ignoring the second order calculations, it can be seen that the line B'D'F'G' represents equally the purchasing power of the monetary unit and the overall purchasing power removed from or added to M alone (S is not integrated).

This latter interpretation singles out the overall purchasing power that is removed from or added to M as being identical to the sum S that is created (1) or withdrawn (3).

ES: The same operations as with the national currency: the line is straight and horizontal (there is no *prélèvement* or restoration).

Comment: Only those transactions which, in national currency, convert final production (completion of the process of adding value) into immediate or deferred consumption (investment) are taken into account. These account for about one transaction out of every ten, the other nine being limited to simple transfers of goods or services. All the ES transactions come into this second category (see p. 200)

---

of the cycle there is the repayment of a loan, the purchase of foreign currency or an investment in a term or savings account with the corresponding destruction of means of payment, or extinction of the payment function. The life cycle of the unit of money has then come full circle.

In order to make it easier to relate this accounting diagram (Table 15.2) to the purchasing power graph, a distinction has been made between units that have the transaction function and those which do not, no account being taken of any intermediate stage between these two.

A basic distinction as clear-cut as this is not, of course, in accordance with statistical practice, which recognises intermediate states between those of money and non-money (such as 'near money'). But our analysis would run the risk of being invalidated if we were to introduce into the argument categories of the 'semi-living' (or, if you prefer, the 'half-dead'). There exist living units of money, and their existence is contained within the limits of birth and death. When they

Table 15.1 Claim money: a life cycle

Banks	X	Y	Z	
		Beginning of cycle: creation of transaction function		
R Reserves in central bank money	(1) 100	100 (1) (1) 100	100 (1) (1) 100	100 (1)
D of foreign currency	....	.........(2) +100		
C claims	(2) +100	....	.........(2) 100	
A Deposits with without		+100 (2)	+100 (2)	+100 (2)
B The transaction function				
		Movements		
R	.........(1) 100 (2) −100	100 (1) (1) 100 (3) −100	100 (1) (1) 100 (3) −100	100 (1)
D	....	.........(2) 100		
C	.........(2) 100	....	.........(2) 100	
A		100 (2) .... −100 (3)	100 (2) .... −100 (3)	100 (2) −100 (3)
B				
		End of cycle: extinction of transaction function		
R	.........(4) + 80	100 (1) (4) + 90	100 (1) (4) +120	100 (1)
D		.........(2) 100 (5) − 90 = 10		
C	.........(2) 100 (5) − 80 = 20		.........(2) 100	
A		+ 80 (4) .... − 80 (5)	+ 90 (4) .... − 90 (5)	+120 (4) −120 (5)
B				+120

Notes

Beginning of the cycle: X and Z: A loan is made by entering 100 in the customer's current account (2)

Y: Sale of foreign currency by customer who has received the 100 (2)

Movements: X, Y and Z: Transfers to external banks to make payments (3)

End of the cycle: X: 80 of the loan is repaid in the form of a deposit (4) and (5)

Y: Purchase of foreign currency in return for a deposit of 90 (4) and (5)

Z: Deposit of 120 (4) and entry in deposit account (5)

At the end of the cycle the net balance of payment money created = 300 − (80 + 90 + 120) = 10

Hence a gradual *prélèvement* of a proportionate amount on the purchasing power of the monetary unit. This *prélèvement* is independent of the nature of the operations that gave rise to the current account deposits (payment money) and their counterparts. The general nature of the way bank money is created by financial operations is thus highlighted, and the effect of these operations (which is nil in the case of the ES) on the value of the money can be deduced.

are born there is a *prélèvement* on the purchasing power of other units of money, and when they die there is a restoration of what was originally taken away. This clear-cut distinction, with no nuances, makes it possible to arrive at a net balance at the end of the cycle (10). This final balance corresponds to the *prélèvement*, which will continue until the end of the process of amortisation.

That said, however, and for reasons other than this analysis and this connection with the particular monetary phenomenon that we are studying, the variety of categories of money used in statistics is justified. Whether we are talking about expectations of the effects of certain factors, such as the velocity of money, or more simply of the definition of a monetary aggregate, changes in which are related to the behaviour of the mass of means of payment, such distinctions have their justification.

Prélèvement and restoration of purchasing power in the case of existing units of money depend directly on the addition of completely new units of money to those in circulation or, conversely, on their withdrawal from circulation. The accounting entries make this clear, but there may be some ambiguity regarding the creation or destruction of units of money. In order to remove this ambiguity, we need to go back to the form of analysis used on p. 177, by comparing production in volume terms (P) with consumption of that same production (C). According as C is larger or smaller than P, there will be *prélèvement* or, on the contrary, restoration regarding the purchasing power of the unit of money.

The comparison between 'unearned' claims used for consumption and 'earned' claims not used for consumption is an aid to untangling the knots into which monetary analysis gets itself when it has to cope with such diverse concepts as 'liquidity and the multiplier', 'intermediation' and 'disintermediation', financial deregulation and, in its wake, the cortège of new financial instruments, such as SICAVs, unit trusts, credit cards, money-market paper, futures, options, commercial paper, Eurobonds, and so on.

Not so very long ago, the sign over the door gave a clear indication: there were banks and there were non-banks. Today savings banks are

allowed to issue cheque-books to their customers. The Head of the
Caisse des Dépôts can make statements such as this (from *Le Monde*,
20 December 1988):

> When the *Caisse des Dépôts* or any other bank makes a loan to a
> local authority money is naturally created . . . Only part of the
> sum lent eventually comes back to the institution that created it (in
> the form of a deposit in a type A savings book in the case of the
> *Caisse des Dépôts*) and can then be re-lent. The 'credit multiplier'
> thus ultimately depends on the quantity of liquidity injected by the
> central bank, which can be used to refinance loan operations,
> whether they were originated by the *Caisse* or by any other bank.

In fact, however, there is, or is not, a net creation of money
according as the unearned claims on production (such as deposits at
the Caisse des Dépôts) are or are not excess of the earned claims,
use of which is forgone by the holder when they are deposited.

Money is a claim on production, and the only claims that matter
are the ones that 'absorb' (or destroy) goods and services that have
been produced or supplied, to the exclusion of all those that are
merely exchanged for other units of money. If a cheque drawn on a
savings bank is exchanged for central bank or bank money, the
transaction is ultimately effected by that central bank or bank money,
not by the claim on the savings bank. The 'unearned' claim thus put
into effect is counterbalanced by an 'earned' claim which has been
temporarily 'frozen', or forgone. The savings bank is then operating
like a non-monetary intermediary and there is no creation of new
money.

If, on the contrary, the cheque drawn on the savings bank is sent in
for clearing at the clearing house (see p. 205), a more or less large
fraction of 'unearned claims' corresponding to the cleared cheque is
used. This time money *is* created (in addition to the money created
by the banking system) and it is created by the savings bank. The
clearing mechanism has put a claim on the savings bank into circulation as a payment instrument, whereas in the previous case it was a
claim on the banking system, even though the cheque had been
drawn on the savings bank. If all cheques drawn on the savings bank
are included in the money supply, without discriminating between
those that go through the clearing and those that do not, there is a
risk that creation of money will be assumed where none exists. Here
again we come up against the basic precept that *payment money*

should not be confused with a *right to payment money* (see p. 199).

This case of a cheque drawn on a savings bank has been dealt with at length because it is a good example of the subtleties of monetary analysis. It also shows why an unprecedented monetary innovation such as the ES has for so long been held back by traditional monetary lore, which adopts other approaches.

This discussion of the life cycle of a unit of money confirms our observation regarding the vulnerability of claim money, by very reason of its nature, in respect of its value. Through the process of destruction of production by consumption, which is one of the essential functions of money within the territory of a state, the value of the money in question is made dependent on a multitude of factors. Maintaining that value, adjusting it in line with a constant factor, attempting to restrain it when it comes under downward pressure, or, much more infrequently, when it is being pushed up: these are the dominant preoccupations of monetary policy, and they cannot be avoided. There is no undiscovered, magic way of ensuring that a payment currency, in a national monetary system, can acquire guaranteed value of itself, independently of the circumstances, the environment and employment conditions. When the matter is looked at from this point of view, it is easy to see why claim money did not appear on the scene until relatively recently in monetary history. From the beginning of time men have preferred a quantity of precious metal as a representation of the claim on production that they received every time that they sold something, without, however, completely eliminating thereby the effects of extraneous factors on the purchasing power of their metallic monetary unit.

Figure 15.2 provides the best illustration of this inherent instability of claim money as a means of payment. The line B′ D′ F′ G′ represents the purchasing power of the monetary unit as it results from the disruption that is caused by the creation of new means of payment, AB, which is added to a stable system. The graph may be completed by representing the variation that would be needed in one of the other parameters in order to compensate for the disruptive effect. Let us take, for example, production in volume terms per unit of time as our compensating parameter. Variations in this parameter starting from time (1) would then have to follow the line B′D′F′G′ symmetrically, increasing as from (1), stabilising from (2), going down again at (3), and so on.

The need for so severe an adjustment in order to maintain the value of the monetary unit brings out its congenital instability more than a practical demonstration. The final consumption must be compensated for somewhere, in dM, dv and dp (see p. 180), by a factor which balances out its variations. The graph shows the fragility of the state of equilibrium on which the value of the monetary unit depends. It also gives an idea of the scale of the effects of a disruption, by measuring the extra total annual production that would be needed in order to balance out the effect of adding S. This extra production is equal to five times the amount of 'unearned' consumption that follows from the creation of S' (income velocity = 5).

The disparity between the disruption and its effects explains why monetary regulation is concerned with controlling the creation of money using an instrument with well-known imperfections (the rate of interest). It would be even more appropriate to reduce the sources of such disruptions, other than bank credit, namely: foreign currency conversions, which originate in the level of exchange rates, and the 'defence' of parities. Defending parities with a neutral currency, rather than with a national currency, would result in fewer disruptions. To this a simple, 'mechanical' observation may be added. In order to reduce the amount of agitation in a system a shock-absorber may be introduced. That was the role assigned to gold in the nineteenth century. It is hard to see why, given the importance and the difficulty of the problem, those who should know better continue to ignore the stabilising factor which is made available to us by the extranational sector, precisely because the process which this instability feeds on (that is, the final consumption of production) is not to be found in the extranational sector.

Within the frontiers of states, the business of adjusting the means of payment so that they accurately match a quantity of production that is continually being renewed is always uncertain; outside national boundaries the same financial operations of purchasing, lending, repaying, and so on can be conducted without the need for any kind of adjustment.

A PARADOX: DOES THE ES CHALLENGE THE LAW OF THE MARKET?

An ES that retains its real value without being affected by demand and supply for it? This is something that may seem strange and arouse doubts. If there is one field where the law of supply and demand are omnipresent it is the field of money. No theoretician or manual of economics fails to explain that prices fall or rise according to the quantity of money that is demanded or supplied, and that the authorities attempt to maintain prices at a constant level by regulating the supply of money so that it stays in step with demand. That is the very basis of monetary regulation in all countries these days.

The ES seems to be an exception to this rule. It retains its value in terms of purchasing power without any need to compare the amount that is 'demanded' and the amount that is 'offered'. This paradox may be explained by looking at claim money as what it is: a vehicle for transporting purchasing power from the purchaser to the seller, after which, after a brief stay in an account, the seller (having in turn become a purchaser) transfers that same purchasing power to someone else. The law of supply and demand does not apply to the vehicle but rather to the 'transport cost'; in this case the rate of interest.

A company despatching goods by road does not need to buy the lorries they will travel in, or, if they go by rail, the goods waggons. Instead, it purchases so many 'ton/kilometres' per day (the rate of interest per day). Naturally, the number of vehicles used and their cost are factors that do have an effect on transport costs, but that effect is greatly reduced in the case of the creation of bank money by the simultaneous entry of a claim amongst the bank assets and a credit to the customer's account. All the same, there are factors involved which, within national boundaries, do curb the creation of bank money: namely, the purchase of central bank money by the sale of a claim for the purpose of converting bank notes, reserve requirements, liquidity ratios, and so on.

In the case of the ES, the need for foreign currency liquidities in order to guarantee convertibility will impose a limit on the creation of new ES which otherwise might become excessive, given the absence of the restrictions imposed on national currencies where excessive monetary creation undermines the purchasing power of the existing money stock.

The interest rate which an ES borrower would be asked to pay could not diverge very much from the rate in real terms that is charged for the main world currencies. If it were significantly lower it would encourage borrowing and conversion of the proceeds into national currencies, which would siphon off the consortium's resources and create a loss as a result of the interest rate differential; if it were significantly above the going rate for national currencies, it would be a disincentive for potential borrowers.

The ES money supply should not be looked on as a closed circuit;

on the contrary, it should be looked on as an intermediate reservoir equipped with an overflow to remove (in national currency) any excess supply (by conversion into national currency). The permanence of value which the ES is assured of thanks to its definition will set off automatic regulators which will control the level of liquid in the reservoir, whereas in the case of a national currency it is the level which determines the purchasing power of the currency.

In any case, what matters commercially for the producer of ES (the consortium) is the market share it will take from the Eurodollar, without any effect on the (enormous) mass of Eurocurrencies in circulation.

ANOTHER PARADOX, EXPLICABLE BY THE ABSENCE OF ANY ALTERNATIVE

The American Administration is very generous with statistical data. They provide an abundant source of material for press commentary and market expectations, not to mention speculation, although not intentionally in this latter case. Each week the latest figures are anxiously awaited. At the time of the great inflation, the latest figures for M1 and M2 were published every Friday afternoon. These days, the figures that are awaited with greatest interest are those for the United States' trade with the rest of the world; just recently the unemployment figures are similarly in the limelight. Once they became known, the figures for November 1988 sent bond prices plummeting on Wall Street. Why? The figures were excellent. The reason was 'fear of overheating', resulting, in order to keep inflation under control, in higher interest rates, and hence further falls in bond prices.

Let no one say that financiers do not take the long view! And that provokes the thought that, contrary to appearances, London bankers who manipulate hundreds of millions of dollars, borrowing them, lending them, circulating them around the globe, must sometimes wonder about the use they are making of 'sick' dollars, suffering from domestic ills in which they have no say.

The Federal Reserve, for its part, takes no account of dollars used abroad when it comes to fix its monetary targets. It treats Eurodollars as if they did not exist. Payment by an importer in France to an Arab oil exporter, using dollars borrowed in London, has no effect on the dollar in the United States. A Eurodollar only becomes a normal dollar again when it is used to pay an American resident.

The paradox of the dollar, which projects its domestic disruptions on to the outside world (a movement which is strictly one-way, moreover) ought to provoke reactions on the part of Eurobankers. The only way to account for their apathy, which is decidedly unexpected coming from such alert operators, is to assume that it is because there is nothing else available to them as an alternative to the Eurodollar; they are lacking a product whose only chance of success would be the fact that it was guaranteed to be better than the dollar, and not just for the moment.

The fact remains, however, that the Eurocurrency *par excellence*, the dollar, is not one that allows the Euromarket to take advantage of all the possibilities that would be open to it if it had a currency of its own. Eurodollar banks are in effect allowing the banking system in the United States to keep a good proportion of the seigniorage arising from the creation of dollars. They would find themselves at a disadvantage to the member banks of our ES consortium as regards quality of product (constant value in real terms), profit margin (seigniorage in addition to the normal Euromarket spread) and quantity constraints (procuring funds by monetary creation rather than by borrowing).

Eurodollar banks are in the position of a taxi-driver who, instead of owning the taxi he drives, hires it from someone else and is obliged to pay over to that person or firm a proportion of what he earns for transporting people from A to B. This approach may be justifiable for a small operator, where the equipment hired calls for a large investment, but it is much less justifiable in the case of a product like bank credit, which has a very small production cost in issued money.

We now come to the second paradox, after the paradox concerning the law of supply and demand: Eurobanks make use, for their transactions outside national frontiers, of a currency which itself is a national currency and, as such, is subject, by its very nature, to instability of value (something to which an extranational currency would be immune) and which, in addition, requires them to pay over a part of the profits they make from using this sick currency to those who produce it.

It is without doubt paradoxical to be borrowing something less good than you could make yourself from your competitors and pay them for the privilege into the bargain, instead of making something better yourself which costs you nothing. This paradoxical situation can only be explained by the history of how the Euromarket grew up.

Its creation and development are a marvellous example of the enterprise and imagination of the British banking sector. It was not, however, the product of any carefully considered approach to the problems it was meant to solve and there was no rational plan, taking due account of the monetary phenomena involved.

For a variety of reasons, including the need to disguise the identities of the real owners in some cases (for example, the Russians, at the beginning of the Cold War in the early 1950s), holders of liquid dollar assets (claims on US banks) not resident in America made them available to British banks, which naturally began to lend them out. The rapid growth of international financial transactions and greatly improved communications and transfer facilities then helped to swell the initial bubble to its present immense proportions. That in itself is a good thing, but it leaves certain factors with enormous potential for commercial development completely unexploited.

Whether in the fields of mechanics, physics, chemistry or medicine, or even in a simple commercial operation, it is not possible to construct, rationally, something quite different from what already exists and, eventually, on a large scale, if one does not base one's actions from the outset on solid theoretical foundations. That is what this book sets out to provide and that is what, in my view, justifies the space accorded to them here.

The gradual progress from the abstract to the concrete throughout this chapter will help us to place the ES in its rightful position in the panoply of monetary instruments, a necessary first step when one is attempting to introduce something very different for which there are no precedents. We shall begin with gold (something that has long been familiar) and conclude with the SDR (which is very recent and not as familiar).

A FORM OF PAPER MONEY WHICH IS HEAVIER THAN PRECIOUS METAL

The only example of a stable currency (familiar to the public and the experts) from history is precious metal, whence the (justified) nostalgia for the gold standard, the hope (which is not justified) for its restoration and the incredulity and even hostility (which are even less justified) in the face of any attempt to regain, and even surpass, this marvellous property of stability using 'mere paper' (the contemptuous term used to describe that very useful artifice we call claim money).

The history of the various attempts that have been made since the Genoa conference of 1922 to restore the stability which the world's main currencies enjoyed in the nineteenth century is very instructive. It reveals once again how little is understood of the way monetary systems function, and even how little the gold standard (with which, however, all the participants were familiar) was understood. In the circumstances, therefore, there is nothing surprising about the fact that the new form of money that composite currencies represent is also greatly misunderstood. This will be clear from the comments quoted later in connection with the SDR.

Precious metal, the idea people had of it and its convertibility at a fixed rate into paper money (and vice versa) helped to stabilise the purchasing power of national currencies during the nineteenth century.

However, contrary to a popular and deeply rooted idea, once a precious metal is linked at a fixed conversion rate to claim money, if that convertibility is more or less conditional, and sometimes even if it is unconditional, it is just as much the purchasing power of the claim money that determines the purchasing power of the precious metal as the converse. As a consequence of this idea not being grasped, mistakes of monetary management have been committed during this century which have had disastrous consequences. At the beginning of the 1930s, the purchasing power of the money in circulation – which was paper money – was rising, dragging the purchasing power of gold up with it. This rise in the purchasing power of claim money in the United States (and then bit by bit in other countries too) has already been discussed in these pages: it was due to a reduction in the volume of new loans, and then of the amount of money in circulation, by American bankers who were afraid they would be short of liquidity with which to cope with panic rushes on deposits as a result of the stock exchange crash.

The high priests of orthodox finance did not, however, see this. They had not realised how important was the role played by bank money in the total money supply: in their eyes, as in those of the public at large, the purchasing power of money was determined by the purchasing power of gold. Some thought it should be accepted with resignation. That was the case in France. Others (in the United States) thought that the dollar's link to gold should be broken, whence, in 1934, a devaluation of the dollar of 40 per cent, which had practically no effect. There was a good reason why it should have had no effect, because the devaluation did nothing at all to correct the withdrawal of money from circulation that resulted from the calling-in of loans and the failure to renew outstanding lines of credit.

After the war the reverse occurred: the fall in the purchasing power of the dollar dragged gold down with it, until on 15 August 1971 President Nixon broke the link to gold. The result was a sharp fall in the exchange value of the dollar and a gold price which, once free of the link to the dollar, shot through the ceiling.

At the time President Nixon, and with him the whole of the United States, was severely criticised. Later, he and his country were held responsible – and still are – for the inflation that followed.

It is, however, still true that even today there is a widespread and firmly held conviction that the (presumed) stability of the purchasing power of money can only be restored through a return to convertibility into gold (which however is excluded as a possibility because of the phenomenal growth of claim money). An easier and less risky result could be achieved (confined to external usage, admittedly, but that would already be something) by making use of a composite unit.

A NEW TYPE OF MONETARY UNIT TO BE EXPLORED: THE SDR

At the annual IMF meeting in September 1988 several governments, including the French government, recommended 'making better use of the SDR' as a reserve currency. In *Le Monde* (dated 4 October 1988) Paul Fabra indignantly denounced 'the idea that a country, instead of taking the trouble to earn its currency reserves, could now, with the help of one or two others, cause them to rain down from the sky like manna'. And Fabra then went on to refer to General de Gaulle, who 'mocked the notion of paper gold'. Here, once again, we see the intellectual confusion to which claim money (paper money) gives rise as far as theory is concerned.

The initial reason for creating the SDR was to reduce the use by central banks of the dollar as the basic raw material of their reserves. Awareness of the inconsistency of using a national currency for the specifically international functions of *numéraire* in payments between states and as an intervention instrument in the foreign exchange markets does not date from yesterday.

In fact, the SDR is not used directly for the purpose of making payments in the place of the dollar. It is confined to causing movements of dollars, countries with surplus dollars being induced to lend them to deficit countries in return for SDRs. By accepting SDRs they have both a guarantee of repayment by the IMF and a means of exchange which they can use, in their turn, to procure dollars in the event that they should need them.

Here we have a loan transaction for which it is easy to find the basic paradigm: country A obtains from country B, in return for SDRs, dollars which have been earned by country B but not by country A, the recipient. This is exactly the same as what happens when a savings bank lends funds deposited with it by customer B (who has 'earned' them) to customer A (who has not 'earned' them).

Let us suppose that an institution which needs the public's savings decides to offer an insurance policy, which it calls an SDR, to borrowers so as to protect both depositors and the savings bank against default and thus encourage saving. Would we then say that such an SDR constituted a form of liquidity?

It is possible to avoid confusing what is payment money (the dollar) with what is not but which confers the right to payment money on its holder (a Eurodollar) by referring to the precepts for monetary analysis set out in my book *The Mechanics of Money*, (Macmillan, London, 1980), some of which have already been quoted in this book.

The relevant precept here is that a right to something is not necessarily of the same nature as that thing itself. If we mix them up we end up counting two things, where there is only one in reality. The right to claim a sum in order to make a payment should not be treated as being the equivalent of that sum. Unlike the sum of money, the right may well not have the 'transaction function'.

All of this may seem to be self-evident, but all the same it has not been accepted as self-evident by modern monetary analysts; hence the continuing confusion of money with near-money and the uncertainty regarding the meaning of the indicators, doubts about whether to choose, M0, M1 or M2, controversy as to whether or not the Eurodollar banks are monetary or non-monetary institutions and misunderstanding regarding the real nature of the SDR.

The SDR itself, which anyway is not much used, should not be the target of criticism, which should rather be directed at the abuse of credit that may result from using the SDR, even when such credit consists of transfers of funds which have been duly earned to borrowers who have not earned them. In the United States at the moment there are apparently hundreds, perhaps even thousands, of savings and loan associations which are bankrupt. It is estimated that it will cost the Federal institutions concerned $90 000 million to bail them out. No one for that reason blames the ballooning quantities of credit based on the savings of depositors who have earned them. The real culprits, much more than imprudent loan officers, are the distortions between long-term interest rates and rates on sight deposits, and those distortions are due to the chronic instability of money.

The most serious fault in the SDR system is not the SDR itself but its vehicle, the dollar. The term 'liquidity' contains the idea of fluidity, which is fruitful provided that it is not sidetracked. In the case of the international dollar it is sidetracked from its rightful purpose and has been used to allow the United States, for the last 30 years, to finance its trade and budget deficits with the assets of the rest of the world.

It is not by abolishing the SDR, or by developing its use, that a monetary system which has without question been deflected from its real purpose can be brought back on to the correct path. The only way to do it is to abolish the use of a national currency for international functions and replace it by a currency that is really neutral, belongs to no single state and has stable value.

COMMENTS

Comment on page 190. Once the quantitative factor has been determined, there is still the velocity of circulation, which is just as important. The higher rates of return possible at present on liquid assets have had the effect of reducing the velocity of money. This is an unhoped-for benefit for the monetary authorities, whose failure to hit their targets is thereby compensated for. But once the floor is reached the circulation will start to increase and will accelerate once again, especially if there is a threat of higher inflation. This is a 'vicious' characteristic that is typical of national or foreign financial instruments but which would not affect instruments denominated in a neutral, stable, extranational currency unit.

Comment on page 192. The preponderant role assigned to 'final consumption' should not lead the reader to overlook the other transactions, which are more numerous by far but which have no effect on existing goods or on services, which are carried forward. The frequency of final consumption transactions (that is, transactions involving the destruction rather than the processing of production) is in the region of five per year. That is the income velocity, or the ratio of production to the mass of means of payment in circulation. The frequency of transactions is the rate at which a sum of money moves from one account to another, and depends on the categories. It may be taken to be 50 in the case of the financial operations that interest us (the transaction velocity).

The essential aspect of money is the phenomenon of transaction. Its dynamic nature is indicated by the velocity of circulation. That is what distinguishes what is payment money (with the power to carry out transactions) from what is not. The feature of velocity is what helps to dissipate the confusion in which intermediate states of money, such as near-money, are enveloped.

A term deposit, which would normally be classed as payment money (because it could be used to make a payment without having to go through a current account first) should all the same be classified as non-money because of its infinitely small income velocity.

Comment on page 198. Some days after the break with gold, I wrote an article entitled 'Thank you Mr Nixon' which was published in the *Revue Politique et Parlementaire*. Raymond Aron took it up in *Le Figaro* in order to lambast me and others like me as 'unconscious demolishers'. My argument was that the state of advanced collapse in which the Bretton Woods monetary system found itself at that time made its replacement a question of necessity. I was right to argue that the system was in a state of advanced collapse, but I was wrong to suppose that it would be replaced by anything better. And yet the inconsistency of the system was flagrant: the dollar's conversion rate into gold had remained unchanged since 1934, whereas its purchasing power had fallen by much more than two-thirds. At the same time, American residents had been subjected to a prohibition, also since 1934, regarding the holding of gold! So the convertibility of the US dollar into gold was limited in practice. The Bretton Woods agreements had put the United States under an obligation to guarantee convertibility in theory whilst at the same time restricting it in practice to those central banks abroad which cared to ask for their dollar holdings to be converted into gold (which the Bank of France did on many occasions, to its considerable profit). The whole system was upside down.

After 1972 floating exchange rates took over and for a time there was a monetary free-for-all, financed by bank credit, until barriers were erected to contain the ever-expanding money supply, followed by a period of disinflation through unprecedentedly high interest rates.

16 In Order to Explain the ES: Some Thoughts on Bank Money

The project that has been expounded in these pages boils down to organising the gradual creation by a group of Eurobanks (the consortium) of a mass of means of payment which is extranational (that is, reserved for use in international trade) and denominated in a new monetary unit that is equipped with an exceptional property.

The mechanism for doing this is itself based on a central money which is reserved for the exclusive use of the consortium and is issued in the form of claims on itself by a central institution which will be private, or rather Community-controlled.

A NECESSARY EXPLANATION WHICH CONTRADICTS THE ORTHODOX DOCTRINE

The traditional conception of money is as 'representative of something', and the traditional conception of bank money is as an emanation of central bank money through the mechanism of a 'multiplier'. In the ES mechanism proposed here there is no 'thing' which the central bank money of the system could represent and there is no 'multiplier' behind the creation of bank ES.

This may seem disturbing, which is why it will probably be useful if some further explanations are supplied here for the benefit of those curious spirits who would like to know more. The concept of being representative of something (whether a commodity or asset) that is attributed to central bank money is nothing more than the transformation into a revealed truth of something that is merely a means of meeting the need for security. There is no point in looking for this security in something that the money is supposed to represent: it makes more sense to look for it in the quality of the issuer of the money and in the degree of stability of value of the monetary unit in which the claim on that issuer is denominated. What the issuing bank enters in its balance sheet as the 'counterpart' of the money that it has created certainly constitutes a form of security, but it is a global form of security and, conceptually, it has no connection with the money that has been created any more than the lock on a safe is related by nature to what is inside the safe.

Like all concepts, even mistaken ones, that are used to found a doctrine, this one had beneficial effects (such as the creation of the gold standard in the nineteenth century). But it also had bad ones: it opened the door to the excesses of John Law's banking system at the beginning of the eighteenth century (when the currency was backed by the *Ferme des Tabacs* and the Mississippi) and paved the way for the inflationary *assignats* of the revolutionary era (when it was backed by the confiscated property of the Church and the *émigrés*). It was also partly responsible for the paralysis of mind which prevented steps being taken in time to rescue the world from the great deflation of the 1930s and, several decades later, to prevent the great inflation of the 1970s (bank money, representing a claim on a borrower, was in inadequate supply during the 1930s because people were not borrowing enough, whereas in the 1970s there was far too much of it because people were borrowing too much).

As for the 'multiplier', which is supposed to inflate the balloon of bank money, on the basis of central bank money, to a precise and controllable extent (and to the great satisfaction of monetary regulators), it does not exist. It is the result of mistaken reasoning.

The traditional demonstration of how the multiplier works goes as follows. Suppose that Bank A has 100 in central bank money. It puts 25 aside as a reserve and lends 75 to borrower (1), whose account it credits. (1) pays (2) by cheque, and the cheque is credited to (2)'s account at bank B. A transfers 75 in central bank money to B, which repeats the operation of putting a quantity (20) into its reserves, and lends the balance (55) to (3).

These operations are repeated. Bank D receives 40 in central bank money and creates a deposit of 10; at this stage, therefore, there is a total of demand deposits created equal to 75 + 55 + 40 + 30 = 200, and a continuing process of multiplication.

	A		B		C		D	
Reserves	25	100	20	15 (2)	15	55 (4)	10	40
	+ 75		+ 55		+ 40		+ 30	
Claims	75	75	55	55 (3)	40	40	30	30

This is the mechanism by which, according to the standard textbooks, bank money is created. It multiplies central bank money by a coefficient which is a function of the reserve requirement.

This explanation of how bank money is created is not in agreement with the mechanism proposed for the ES, but that is because it is wrong. In order to see why, all we have to do is look at B's balance sheet after (3) has transferred 55 to (4)'s account.

B

Reserves 20	75 [(2)'s deposit]
Claim on borrower 55	

(2)'s deposit is stymied by the claim of 55 which B still has on the assets side of its balance sheet. It is not fully available for the purpose of making a payment. Only that fraction equal to the free reserve, over and above the legal reserve, is still available. Even if there were no legal reserve, the amount of disposable assets available to fund a drawing by (2) on his deposit would still be only 20, and that in turn would be further reduced after any further loan had been made.

The multiplier presented here leads to a process of extinction which even includes the 100 of central bank money from which everything else in the example springs. In fact, though, it is not like that. Another mechanism comes into play, and that mechanism is the bankers' clearing. The mistake made in explaining the creation of money by a multiplier consists, in the example quoted above, of not carrying the investigation further, to the point where (2) draws a cheque to pay a creditor.

The role of bank money in the economy is so important that it is vital that the mechanism by which it is created should be understood as it actually is. It is the very condition for effective monetary regulation. It is also an imperative necessity if a new payment money is to be rationally conceived. These are the reasons for the amount of space devoted in this book to the clearing mechanism.

CLEARING: THE MECHANISM BY WHICH BANK MONEY IS GENERATED

The spectacular development of bank money and the fact that it has almost completely replaced central bank money (to the extent of 90 per cent) are based on a mechanism – namely, interbank clearing of mutual claims – which is virtually ignored by traditional teaching in this field.

It is the clearing mechanism that makes it possible for money issued by the banks in the form of claims on themselves to effect 'transactions': that is, to set off the process of transfer of claims which is fundamental for the economy since it is what makes trade possible and, even more importantly, to promote the conversion of final production into consumption (whether immediate or deferred).

The essence of the clearing process for the banks that take part in it is the opportunity it provides for condensing into one operation, in a matter of minutes, the collection of what is owed to them (in the form of cheques paid in) and the settlement of what they owe (in the form of cheques drawn on them) without having to go through the strict sequence of successive operations which paying each debt with the proceeds of a claim implies.

Each clearing bank directly offsets the total of its debts against the total of what is owed to it, no matter how many and how diverse the creditor and debtor banks, and without there being, usually, any direct creditor–debtor relationship between them. In the simplest form of clearing, involving three banks, B's claim on A is not balanced by any claim by A on B. A third bank, C, however, has a claim on B and a debt with regard to A. The clearing then takes place between these three components: A owes something to B, B owes something to C and C owes something to A. These cases are elementary forms of clearing and their possible permutations are limited. When there are 40 or 50 banks, or even more, clearing in tiers, the possibilities increase exponentially.

Table 16.1 brings out this factor. The sums owed by each bank to each other bank (in the form of cheques or transfer orders) are entered in the boxes. The balance for each bank – that is, the total amount that it owes (cheques drawn on it and deposited at other banks) less the total amount owed to it (cheques drawn on other banks and deposited with it) – represents the sum that it will have to transfer (negative balance) or which it will receive (positive balance) in central bank money at the end of the clearing session.

By way of example, Table 16.1 shows clearing between five banks, A, B, C, D and E. Each box shows the total value of the cheques drawn on one bank and deposited with another (for example, a total of 60 has been drawn on B and deposited with D). Cheques drawn on B and deposited with A, B, C, D and E amount to 280, whereas cheques drawn on A, B, C, D and E and deposited with B amount to 345. B will therefore receive the difference (that is, $345 - 280 = 65$) in central bank money. Each day the final balances are settled in central bank money shortly after the close of the clearing session, by crediting or debiting each bank's account at the central bank. The sum of these transfers and, therefore, the total volume of transactions, is 1535. Out of this total, the total amount of transactions executed in the form of claims on the central bank is 270. The amount executed in the form of claims on commercial banks is therefore $1535 - 270 = 1265 \times 2 = 2530$.

Table 16.1 shows how this clearing mechanism makes it possible for the banking system to go a long way towards replacing central bank money entirely by its own money (in the form of claims on the member commercial banks), using this central bank money as a kind of catalyst.

Table 16.1 can be completed by entering in the places marked x the amount of internal clearing in each bank, between its own customers and its correspondents (irrespective of whether the bank is a big one, the sums concerned can be large: in times gone by it made the fortune of several big British banks, even before the Bankers' Clearing House had been invented).

Within a particular country, clearing is carried out in a series of 'tiers'. This could be represented by putting several tables end to end. The final balance of each one would then become one of the starting data for the next one, until the last tier was reached. Similarly, 'leaks' out of the system (that is, withdrawals by the public in central bank money) would also need to be included to give the complete picture for a national system.

The way 'leaks' are dealt with in a national system gives the monetary authorities one of its means of monetary regulation. In order to obtain the bank notes that it needs to cope with withdrawals in cash a bank has to sell one of its assets to the central bank or borrow from it. This is the mechanism that the central bank uses to regulate interest rates, since the bank, if it is obliged to borrow, will pass on (plus an extra margin) the interest rate it pays to the central bank to its own borrowers. A banking system with no 'leaks' would deprive the monetary authorities of one of their regulatory levers.

The banks themselves should always be able to find the central bank money they need to settle their negative final balances on the money market, since the total of the positive balances is equal to the total of the negative balances: debtor banks can thus borrow what

Table 16.1 The clearing mechanism

Owed to by	A	B	C	D	E	Total Owed by	Receiv- able	Balance −	+
A	X	80	100	15	60	255	355		100
B	100	X	110	60	10	280	345		65
C	80	110	X	100	15	305	410		105
D	105	65	120	X	55	345	285	60	
E	70	90	80	110	X	350	140	210	
Total re- ceivable	355	345	410	285	140	1 535	1 535	270	270

they need from creditor banks. Theoretically, therefore, the system could operate like a closed circuit, without any need of new central bank money, which is why the 'working capital' in central bank money needed for the clearing process to work (the amount of the banks' reserves at the central bank) is equal to only 1 or 2 per cent of the total of bank money used to make payments.

In the ES system there will not be any 'leaks' because there will not be any central ES in circulation. This could result, in the ES system envisaged here, in an uncontrolled proliferation of bank ES. That is why the central institution will constantly calculate each member bank's balance in central ES as it results from the bank-to-bank transfers, which must pass through its books. In this way it will be in a position to impose a measure of discipline (if necessary by imposing a ceiling on the volume of ES loans by the banks or, more usually, by establishing maximum and minimum base rates for loans and deposits) so as to keep the growth of bank ES within specific limits.

IN ADDITION TO THE NATIONAL 'M'S: A EUROSTABLE 'M'

The power to create payment money that results from the practice of interbank clearing of claims is put to good advantage by national banking systems, and it would be used in exactly the same way by an ES system. Thanks to the clearing system, governments share with commercial banks a privilege which was formerly their exclusive prerogative within their national territories (but which they have never had in the extraterritorial space outside their frontiers).

In the case of the ES there is no such need to worry about any 'transfer of responsibility' of this kind in the issue of money, whereas it must be admitted that within the territory of states the gradual replacement of state-issued money by bank money as the main medium of payments has profoundly altered the banking mechanisms (this is something that was not realised soon enough).

By relinquishing its privilege of minting money, the state has made possible the beneficial growth of bank credit; at the same time it has imposed upon itself the redoubtable task of controlling the growth of the payment money that results from this credit and from conversions of foreign currencies.

This is the thought with which we shall conclude our theorising and demonstrations before summing up, with an image which will live longer in people's memories, what constitutes the very essence of claim money and the opportunities that it offers the ES.

A VEHICLE AND ITS LOAD OF 'RIGHTS TO SOMETHING'

After this concession to the requirements of statistics with which this sector is already familiar (I have taken advantage of this opportunity to introduce the ES M amongst the main ones), there is a need, before concluding, to hark back to the essence of the argument that has been expounded here: it is much less concerned with statistical measurements of the volume of money than with the uses to which it is put and its movements and value.

A unit of money consisting of a claim on a bank can be looked on as a vehicle which moves from account to account, from the payer's to the payee's, causing a contrary movement, from the payee to the payer, of goods and services.

The 'rights' that are 'loaded' on to the vehicle are given tangible form in the shape of units of money. As they move from one account or pocket to another, these units of money exercise rights and carry out transactions, such as the payment of supplies, exchanges, loans, reimbursements, and so on. The units are created by the sender (the issuer) and transferred from the payer to the payee, after which the payee, becoming in turn a payer, transfers them to his creditors and so on, until they are finally destroyed (by repayment of the original loan that created them).

Within a national territory, the vehicle, given official identity by the state, includes certain units with a special function in its load.

That function is to effect transactions for the immediate or deferred consumption of production (amortisation). In the load, these units are present in proportion to their income velocity compared with the transaction velocity (see p. 200). The process of absorption (destruction) of production which they set off makes the load vulnerable and impairs its effectiveness. There is spillage (loss of purchasing power) from one stage to the next until the end of their life cycle.

Within the extranational sphere there are also vehicles that circulate loaded with rights to things (the ES). The units of money that give official form to these rights are created in the same way by the sender (bank loans); like them, they are transferred from payer to payee, then from the payee, who has become a debtor, to his creditors in order to pay for supplies or reimburse loans, and so on. There is, however, one difference: the load, unlike similar loads transported within national territories, is not subject to the risks of inclement weather conditions and it does not include those units with the special function of promoting the conversion of production into consumption. It arrives in the hands of the final sender to be destroyed, still with the same value that it had at the outset.

By now we are far from the world of theory; too far, perhaps, for some people's taste. But these examples do provide a means of overcoming an obstacle, namely the doubt felt when confronted by something that one has never seen before. Once it is thus freed of the various concepts that give rise to controversy, money can be seen more clearly than usually for what it is: that is, a means of conveying 'rights (or claims) to something' which have been created *ex nihilo*, even if for reasons of accounting convenience – and peace of mind – they are balanced by 'counterparts' (usually other claims).

Within the confines of a state, this vehicle sheds part of its load; within the extranational space th⁻' lies outside states' frontiers the load arrives at its destination *in to* . This is the property that the ES exploits.

FROM AN IMAGE TO A CONCLUSION

In connection with the theoretical foundations for the ES, we have already had occasion (see p. 193) to make use of this image of a vehicle loaded with 'rights to something'. It is a faithful reflection of what happens in reality. Any reader who is by now tired of abstractions (rebarbative but necessary, unfortunately) should refer back to this passage. It will help all such readers to follow my concluding thoughts, which are meant for theoreticians of money, financiers and 'Europeans'.

First, the theoreticians: a more searching investigation than usual shows that the process by which the value of a unit of payment is created excludes the possibility of endowing the national currency of a given state with constant purchasing power by, as it were, 'building it in'. The value of a currency can only be maintained by measures of financial, economic and social discipline which, as is well known, involve risks and uncertainties because they are dependent on a multitude of other factors, some of which cannot be brought under control.

In the case of an extranational currency which would be kept for use in the virtual or actual space that lies between the frontiers of states (the 'high seas' of finance), the process of consumption of production, which is what decides the value of a monetary unit, does not exist. It is possible in such circumstances to create a currency defined in such a way that it does not lose any purchasing power because its value does not depend on the relative forces of demand for it and the quantity available and, having created it, make it available for the exclusive use of this extranational territory. Supply and demand only affect it to the extent of determining the level of interest rates on loans in this currency: its actual value, defined as what it will buy, remains immutable.

Next, the financiers: never before have circumstances been more favourable for the creation of an extranational currency equipped with this special property of constant value. The creation of such a currency would open up a promising and enticing market for its potential customers (guaranteed constant value) as well as in terms of volume (creation of a mass of means of payment) and profit margins (seigniorage).

When a Eurodollar bank (a bank domiciled outside the United States which operates in dollars) makes a loan, it only retains the portion of the interest paid to it by the borrower corresponding to the credit distribution margin, or spread, which is often very small. Part of the rest, which is the seigniorage, ultimately stays with the American banking system, which created the dollars that the Eurodollar bank borrows, lends and uses in its business. In the case of the ES, the medium of the loans would be created by the banks making them, so they would receive both the spread *and* the seigniorage.

The extranational territory for which the ES is intended is unrestricted and wide open to private initiative: it is also immense. It includes the Euromarket, the pools of foreign exchange, assets of non-residents and central banks' reserves. The Euromarket alone exceeds a total dollar value of $2000 thousand million. The currency in use in this immense territory is the national currency of a state, one that is being increasingly questioned and which is in any case subject to the uncertainty of value that affects all national currencies.

There is a role, alongside the Eurodollar, for an extranational currency which will be desirable and desired because it will have been rendered immune to this uncertainty of value. If the option is available, it is preferable to produce something of higher quality oneself, rather than borrow something inferior from one's competitors and pay them for it into the bargain. An unprecedented opportunity exists to launch an enterprise which will confer prestige and profit on those who take the initiative.

Finally, the Europeans: the lessons learnt and the experience acquired with this experiment will make it possible for the European Community, when the time is ripe, to equip itself with a currency of its own with constant real value. This property, which no other currency has ever had, would constitute a prestigious symbol of European unity and would at the same time be an effective instrument of stabilisation and management.

This is the supposedly Utopian project which this book has claimed to be entirely feasible, whilst indicating the means available for carrying it out.

COMMENTS

Comment on page 208. From time to time, an article in a newspaper or magazine which is deliberately attempting to be sensational announces the 'death of monetarism' or, more simply, asks: 'What is left of monetary policy?' This latter sort of approach is less brutal and less definite but just as negative. In support of such arguments or interpretations there is a facile thesis: the inaccuracies and indecision which inevitably arise when an aggregate has to be chosen to act as the payment money indicator. This aggregate is indeed the pivotal feature of any monetary policy based on control of the money supply.

In France, this kind of approach, which was introduced in 1977 at the initiative of the then Prime Minister, Raymond Barre, marked a tardy admission of the importance of bank money as a component of the total mass of means of payment, as well as being the practical application of a precept of monetary management which requires the supply of payment money to be kept at the right level. This is the target that must be hit in order to regulate the growth of the stock of transaction money.

This precept of management calls for some clarification and requires some choices to be made. This is where opinions start to diverge and scepticism and opposition are stiffened. The supply of means of payment cannot in fact be accurately defined, especially as payments for final consumption only, which represent a tiny fraction of total transactions, are involved. This leads to the need to have recourse to an aggregate by relying on a mere correlation (verified *a posteriori*) with the stock of transaction money as measured by statistics.

These are the 'Ms' with which the public has begun to familiarise itself. There is indeed a wide range to choose from, going from MO to M7 (in the United States). MO is the simplest: it consists of central bank money, notes in circulation and banks' reserves at the central bank only. M3 consist of all that plus various components which cannot be used in any situation as payment money but which, experience shows, have a reliable correlation to payment money.

None of these 'M's is really satisfactory; hence the periodic amendments to the definitions and choices by the monetary authorities. For a long time the Bundesbank preferred MO whilst the Bank of England preferred a particularly all-inclusive form of M3. Quite recently, the Bundesbank has abandoned MO in favour of a form of M3, whilst the Bank of England has jettisoned M3 and gone back to MO!

From all of the above, we can conclude that it is no easy matter to measure the money supply but that it is nevertheless essential to keep it under control. Monetary mistakes before the war (shortage of means of payment) and after it (excess of means of payment) are enough to justify the efforts that are being made by the monetary authorities today, even if their measuring instruments are far from perfect.

This new type of M, made up of the ES, is not subject to the hesitations and uncertainties that affect the national 'Ms', particularly as additions of new money to the money in circulation and its velocity are without any effect on it. But it is possible to define an ES M which would be added to the others, in a sector which is not privileged in this respect: namely, the international sector. The volume of ES held as assets or owed as debts would constitute an indicator of international trade imbalances, and would thus provide a warning light for the TCRs (indicating the need for an exchange rate realignment).

Epilogue: A Letter to a European

AN EXAMINATION OF THE POLICY OF 'ALL OR NOTHING' AS FAR AS EUROPE IS CONCERNED, AND ITS CONSEQUENCES

The thesis that you have set out regarding the creation of a stable European currency is interesting. But it can only apply to an extranational currency, one that is used in international transactions only, whereas what we are seeking to create is a single currency for the whole territory of the European Community. The inconveniences that you mention in connection with the use of the ECU ought to disappear during the last stage of the process of movement towards monetary union in the Community, when the ECU will become the genuine single European currency.

This extract is from a letter sent to me by Mrs Edith Cresson in response to my sending her a copy of my latest book, *Monnaie Européenne: de l'Utopique au Réalisable*. In this letter Mrs Cresson states the position of the French government, in terms of laudable clarity, in order to refute my proposal for the completion of the formula by which the payment ECU is defined so as to give it that indispensable property (stable purchasing power) which is necessary if it is to succeed in establishing itself as an international means of payment in competition with the dollar, the Deutschemark and the other main world currencies.

Mrs Cresson is a former Minister of Foreign Trade. She is, as such, familiar with extranational currencies, which are the instruments of trade with foreign countries, and the very *raison d'être* of the private ECU. This policy of 'all or nothing' which she sets out follows hard on the project for economic and monetary union (EMU) in Europe which was prepared by the Delors Committee and adopted, at the European Council meeting in Madrid last June, by the Community member state governments.

Of all the decisions and choices that must be made if Europe is ever to achieve the goal of union, none are more important than those concerning money. It was mistaken decisions in the monetary field which, at the beginning of the 1930s, turned what should have been nothing more than a passing stock market crisis into a deep and lasting depression which plunged the world first into poverty and then into war. During the 1970s better monetary management would have prevented the great inflation that characterised those years. These reflections on recent and not so recent past events in the monetary field justify some questions on certain decisions that have been taken in the monetary sphere. They concern the future of each one of us.

Irrespective of the fundamental question of the merits and demerits of the ultimate goal of EMU, one problem of monetary tactics cannot be avoided. It may be summed up in three points: (a) the period of time that must be allowed for the goal to be achieved; (b) the consequences of the monetary vacuum that will obtain in the interval; and (c) in the event that these consequences should be unfavourable, what steps should be taken to counter them.

The answer to the first question is quite unambiguous: the goal of complete EMU will not be achieved in the near future and may not be achieved at all. Delors himself points out, in his Committee's report, that it took more than 15 years to reach the stage where an architect who had qualified in one member state was allowed to practise in all the other member states of the Community. The need to harmonise conditions, as a prelude to EMU, in the economic, financial, political, fiscal and even social and cultural fields is ineluctable. The most committed of the European 'unionists' themselves admit as much. And then there is the open opposition of the British government. The French press is mistaken in not attempting to take the passion out of the debate and explain Mrs Thatcher's hostility to EMU in terms other than the British people's 'traditional insularity', or 'obstinate conservatism'. The fact is that Mrs Thatcher's arguments are well thought out: if they were freely and faithfully set out in the pages of a French newspaper they would find an echo.

Of course, sometimes our neighbours give way to irritation, in itself a sign of what British resistance to the project is likely to be. This was the case in particular when the then Chancellor of the Exchequer, Nigel Lawson, made the following statement, at a conference organised on 25 January 1989 by the Royal Institution for International Affairs:

It is difficult to escape the conclusion that this divisive and intensely difficult new issue has been propelled into the forefront of European debate at this time either out of culpable carelessness, or as a smokescreen to obscure a lack of sufficient progress towards the Single Market – or, worse, as a means of running away from taking the practical but difficult steps the Single Market requires, running away from the challenge of freedom.

This passage has been quoted here not because of the validity of the arguments but as proof of a particular state of mind. Let no one think that the Labour Party's position, if it were in power, would be any different. The subject on which it attacks Mrs Thatcher is British membership of the EMS, a relatively minor matter that has nothing like the importance of EMU.

The underlying arguments advanced by Mr Lawson are more solid. They are based on the fact that a European Central Bank and a single European currency imply the existence of some institution to which the managers of that currency would be accountable, one to which they would be subordinated and to which they would be required to report. Such an institution could only be some kind of pan-European government, and that is something we are still a long way away from: 'The concept could only properly make sense in a truly federal Europe . . . But that is simply not on the current or foreseeable agenda.'

Without, let us hope, risking being taxed with having 'deserted' Europe, we must ask whether the present French enthusiasm for EMU will go the way of its similar enthusiasm for the Werner Plan in 1972. At that time the talk was all of an 'irreversible commitment', and President Pompidou himself appeared on television to make a solemn announcement to the effect that there would be a single currency in Europe by 31 December 1980.

However, there is not even any need to refer to past events in order to admit that achievement of the EMU project in its present form is in any case a distant prospect. That being so, the question cannot fail to arise: what may be the consequence of an absence of any interim solution, of the 'monetary vacuum' which that implies over years and perhaps even decades? The answer is that the vacuum will be filled by the German currency: the Deutschemark will be the European currency and the Bundesbank will become the Community's *de facto*, if not *de jure*, Central Bank.

The French government is undoubtedly aware of this. It thinks that it can counter this trend by pressing for a speeding-up of progress towards the creation of a European Central Bank and a single currency, in the hope that the weight of Germany in this new

Community institution will be counterbalanced by those of the other 11 members. Such a hope would be understandable – and it would even be possible to share it – if the chances of the project being realised were not so uncertain and, in any case, distant. What is impossible to understand, however, is the refusal to make any attempt to fill a monetary vacuum of indefinite duration by something else that will help to curb the rise of the Deutschemark. Such an attempt would be all the more justified as the ECU is in existence and a grouping of 83 big banks has been set up in order to promote the ECU from the stage of being a unit of account, which is what it is at present, to being a genuine currency unit for use in payments.

The ECU, whether private or not, is not to the taste of the Germans, however. It is not difficult to see why. Here is what Otto Poehl, Governor of the Bundesbank, has had to say on the matter:

In practice, the ECU has played only a negligible role in the EMS, if indeed it has played one at all. The hope that this unit of account would become something like a European currency has been disappointed. It is the Mark which has taken on this role, *de facto* . . . Even the Delors report relegates the question of the ECU to the sidelines and shows very little enthusiasm for it. The concept of a parallel currency has been settled in a few lines and, I hope, postponed to the Greek Calends. (From a speech delivered to the Institute of Directors in London, 15 June 1989)

One might imagine that the French government would reply to that by defending what was until recently its policy: not at all. Instead it has taken refuge in the vague hope of a monetary paradise where amends will be made. It is easy to understand Dr Poehl's 'joy and satisfaction' (his own words) at being able to announce that 'at present the utility of establishing the stability of the Mark as the norm was expressly acknowledged by all the heads of central banks in the Delors Report'.

It is not possible to overlook the risks for the stability of Europe that are implicit in a monetary vacuum which is likely to continue for an as yet indefinite period and which Dr Poehl tells us can only conclude in the very distant future:

Neither a single currency nor a European Central Bank are indispensable prerequisites for economic and monetary union . . . Once parities are irrevocably fixed, the various currencies will be fully interchangeable, one for another; it will then be possible to give these currencies some common appellation, that is, replace them by a single currency; all the same, that is a development that is still a very long way off.

The only chance the French government has of seeing a European Central Bank and a single currency one day is to do something in the meantime. It has the means; even better, it has prepared them. How can one then explain its sudden decision not to make use of them except in terms of a refusal to accept monetary reality for what it is (something of which history offers all too many examples)?

The 170 states of this planet need a common monetary medium which they can use in their financial and commercial dealings and which will act as a standard of reference, a reserve instrument and means of exchange. At present the only common monetary medium in use is the US dollar, but the Deutschemark and the yen are coming up close behind. Once it has established itself and become the Community's common means of exchange, the Deutschemark will stay there, kept in place by the sheer fact of its existence, of the role it is playing and the force of habit. Even now, in the language of foreign exchange dealers, the area of the Community is known as the Deutschemark zone. Ultimately, the road to that single currency which Edith Cresson says the ECU will become will be blocked by the Deutschemark. All one needs to do to be convinced of that is to consider the staying power of the dollar in its role as international currency in spite of the fact that the forces which originally propelled it up to that eminent position have either weakened or have moved in the opposite direction (stability of value becoming instability).

The Deutschemark as the common European currency will confer unparalleled advantages on the Germany: advantages of prestige initially, and then of political weight. In addition, there will also be financial, industrial and trade benefits. In order to evaluate them, one only needs to consider what the dollar has represented – and still represents – for the United States. Financially, it will confer the benefit of seigniorage, accruing to Germany in all the financial centres of the world; commercially, it will open the way for German industry to spill over into the markets of the world, after inundating the Community's own internal market. There are many Germans who, aware of the past history of their country and concerned for its future, are starting to worry about this and understand the point of view expressed by Mr Michel Debré, in a recent article published in *Le Monde* on 5 July 1989 under the title '*L'Europe du renoncement*':

Money is a matter of sovereignty and whoever obtains responsibility for it becomes political leader. Under present conditions European monetary union would lead to the pre-eminence of the German Mark. I leave to the historians the task of judging the behaviour of those ideologues who are preparing, on a technical pretext, to give the Germans the power which they recently failed to obtain by other means.

It is only a matter of the merest pragmatism to try to ensure that the vacuum that will persist until full EMU is achieved is not filled by the Deutschemark, merely by virtue of the force of circumstances, and notwithstanding that the German monetary authorities may try to oppose such a move. To do that, the fact that the payment ECU is an exclusively external currency circulating in its own space in parallel with several other world currencies needs to be turned to account. Because it circulates only externally, it has the advantage of certain special characteristics which favour the objective that is to be achieved. But a policy of this sort is only conceivable provided proper cognisance is taken of the fundamental difference between an exclusively external currency and one that is used both internally and externally. The Delors project does not make this vital distinction; it confuses the two things.

Each of the members of the Delors Committee will have some undoubtedly sensible ideas on this matter. But it is well known that the innovatory capacities of a committee are in inverse proportion to the number of its members (17 in this case). And we can already see the material representation of such an extranational *numéraire* before our very eyes, each and every day: each of the world's big banks constitutes a pool of a number of major currencies into which it pays the counterparts of the amounts of national currency that it receives and which it draws upon in order to obtain the funds it needs to deal with requests for conversion of national currencies. This medium of exchange, or third currency, which constitutes the pool has quite naturally graduated from the role of intermediary to that of a fully-fledged instrument for direct trade relations: an importer in France, for example, pays for a cargo of oil bought from an Arab exporter in dollars; the Arab exporter's bank then lends these dollars to a Brazilian importer, and so on. This is how the Euromarket grew up, starting from pools of bank liquidity, to which capitalised reserves in major currencies were then added.

The great innovation of the post-war years as regards forms of monetary organisation has been the emergence of a brand-new extranational space – what might be called the 'high seas' of finance – which is situated virtually or actually outside the frontiers of states. This area, or rather this neutral monetary territory, is that of the Euromarket and it has appropriated for this specifically external use one or two world currencies, starting with the US dollar. These currencies are national currencies by origin, issued by the relevant national banking systems. Once they penetrate the territory of the Euromarket these currencies lose their nationality and, whilst retaining their value in terms of the purchasing power that they had in their countries of issue, they acquire or lose certain characteristics.

The commercial or private ECU, the only payment ECU at present in use, does not circulate within the frontiers of any states, only between them. It is the very epitome of the kind of currency unit that the Euromarket exists to give a home to. As such, it benefits from that special property that is peculiar to exclusively external currencies: namely, the capacity to be defined in such a way that it retains its purchasing power. This property is not available to any currency that circulates as a payment medium both outside and inside a national territory.

The project expounded in the Delors Committee report does not explicitly distinguish between internal and external currencies. What needs to be remembered is that a currency is an internal-use currency when it is used in dealings between two residents, whereas it is an external-use currency when it is used in dealings between a resident and a non-resident or between two non-residents. Though not explicitly stated, this distinction is implied in the sense that the report comes out against the parallel circulation of the ECU and the national currencies of the Community countries, on the grounds that it would lead to disruption of the monetary systems (which is true, but only within a national territory, not outside it). At the same time, it recommends that there should be no discrimination against the private use of the ECU and that administrative obstacles should be removed. The only interpretation that reconciles these two recommendations is to argue that the use of the private ECU should be limited to the extranational space and the ECU itself excluded from circulating in parallel with national currencies. This is a vital distinction, potentially extremely fruitful since it would make it possible to give the ECU the property of stability in real terms which has for so long been desired but has never so far been achieved with any payment currency.

Outside national frontiers, in the external markets, no payment *numéraire* can be rendered obligatory. It is all a question of market-

ing, and it is one with which the 83 member banks of the ECU
Banking Association (EBA), and their clearing house, Clearing-
ECU, will have to grapple. This is what the Governor of the Bank of
England, Robin Leigh-Pemberton, had to say on this matter when he
addressed the EBA on 6 December 1989:

> 'the private ECU will stand or fall on its commercial attractions.
> Let us by all means look to the future – but with the vision of
> level-headed practicioners . . . Its development should surely re-
> main in the hands of the private sector. Its growth should be a
> pragmatic, self-generating process that needs encouragement,
> without intrusion, from official quarters'.

The present ECU is being eaten away by inflation at a faster rate
than many of its component currencies. Paradoxically, it is also
unsuitable for use as an intervention medium on the exchange markets (a role which continues to be assigned to other currencies)
because of the mathematical incongruence of its formula.

The transmutation of the ECU from unit of account, which is what
it is at present, into a genuine circulating payment currency depends
on the EBA, and on the EBA alone. This enterprise is of vital
importance for the monetary future of Europe, and it will be a
difficult one. The private ECU which the EBA issues in the form of
loans or deposits will be converted into national currencies after one
or two transfer movements, and sometimes before, because of the
greater convenience of using national currencies and the insufficient
'commercial attractiveness' of the ECU. Under present circumstances the EBA will not succeed in keeping the ECU in circulation
as a transaction currency in competition with the world's major
currencies. That would be an unjust fate for a noble enterprise and
for those who have striven to realise it.

The ECU could, however, be turned into the best currency in the
world by taking advantage of its composite nature, its neutrality and
the fact that it is disconnected from the official ECU. All that would
be needed would be for the private ECU to be equipped with the
exceptional property mentioned earlier (namely, stability of value)
by making appropriate adjustments to its composition formula.

By rejecting (rightly) the idea that the ECU might circulate in
parallel with the national currencies, the Delors Report, when re-
commending the development of the private ECU, proposes what
amounts to a 'dual system', using national currencies internally and

an extranational currency externally; this system is in line with market practice and satisfies a need. If such a system is to function and flourish, all it needs is the 'encouragement' of one or more governments.

If the matter is looked at from this point of view, it is impossible to see in what sense a currency of this kind would be likely to harm the grand design of a single currency for Europe, as Mrs Cresson maintains. On the contrary, it would serve to protect the road that must be taken to reach that goal.

The British, who are openly hostile to a European Central Bank and a single currency, have an interest in seeing an alternative solution adopted. The Germans have no such interest, and yet it is they whom France has chosen as her allies in a game of monetary 'all or nothing' which will result in a prolonged vacuum. That vacuum will be filled by the Deutschemark thus jeopardising that great enterprise that is the process of European unification. The achievement of that ideal cannot be taken for granted. Valéry Giscard d'Estaing, asked to estimate the chances of success, replied 'two in three, no more'. There are some decisions where mistakes cannot be allowed, and monetary decisions are among them.

Anyone who believes in Europe ought to conceive of it as a new, independent political entity, something distinct from the old countries that compose it. This political entity must have a currency of its own, one that is reserved for trade between the Community member states and between them and non-Community countries, without competing with Community state national currencies within their borders. A currency of this kind would be able to benefit from the prestigious property of having 'organic' stability of value in real terms.

Without requiring prior harmonisations and consensus, without setting one government against another, without affecting the aim of ultimate EMU, a currency of this kind would help to affirm Europe's collective identity and would constitute a factor for economic and political progress.

Index

223